*Affirmative Action's Testament of Hope*

**Mildred García**

# *Affirmative Action's Testament of Hope*

*Strategies for a New Era in Higher Education*

STATE UNIVERSITY OF NEW YORK PRESS

Production by Ruth Fisher
Marketing by Hannah J. Hazen

Published by
State University of New York Press, Albany

© 1997 State University of New York

All rights reserved

Printed in the United States of America

No part of this book may be used or reproduced in any manner whatsoever without written permission. No part of this book may be stored in a retrieval system or transmitted in any form or by any means including electronic, electrostatic, magnetic tape, mechanical, photocopying, recording, or otherwise without the prior permission in writing of the publisher.

For information, address the State University of New York Press, State University Plaza, Albany, NY 12246

**Library of Congress Cataloging-in-Publication Data**

Affirmative action's testament of hope: strategies for a new era in
  higher education / edited by Mildred Garcia.
     p.  cm.
    Includes bibliographical references and index.
    ISBN 0-7914-3413-3 (hc : alk. paper). — ISBN 0-7914-3414-1 (pbk. : alk. paper)
    1. Discrimination in higher education—United States—Prevention. 2. Affirmative action programs—United States. 3. Universities and colleges—United States—Admission. 4. College teachers—Selection and appointment—United States. 5. Minorities—Education (Higher)—United States. I. Garcia, Mildred.
LC212.42.A39   1997
379.2'6—dc21                                             97-12988
                                                                                     CIP

10 9 8 7 6 5 4 3 2 1

# *Contents*

| | |
|---|---|
| Acknowledgments | vii |
| 1. The State of Affirmative Action at the Threshold of a New Millennium • *Mildred García* | 1 |
| 2. Affirmative Action in Historical Perspective • *John R. Howard* | 19 |
| 3. There is Much More To Do • *Robert W. Ethridge* | 47 |
| 4. Affirmative Action: A Path Towards Enlightenment • *Linda Flores and Alfred A. Slocum* | 75 |
| 5. Reconciling College Access and the Affirmative Action Debate • *Sylvia Hurtado and Christine Navia* | 105 |
| 6. Faculty Diversity and Affirmative Action • *Caroline Sotello Viernes Turner and Samuel L. Myers, Jr.* | 131 |
| 7. Affirmative Action and Beyond: The Woman's Perspective • *Bonnie E. Busenberg and Daryl G. Smith* | 149 |

8. Toward a More Inclusive Vision of Affirmative
      Action: Improving Campus Environments
      for Lesbian, Gay, and Bisexual People •
      *Robert A. Rhoads*                                           181

9. Strict Scrutiny: The Law and Its Special
      Favorites • *Alfred A. Slocum*                               205

10. The Hopwood Case: What It Says and What It
      Doesn't • *Albert H. Kauffman and
      Roger Gonzalez*                                              227

Conclusions: Strategies for a New Era • *Mildred García*           249
List of Contributors                                               263
Index                                                              267

# Acknowledgments

This book could not have been possible without the advice, support and guidance of countless colleagues and friends. I want to take this opportunity to thank them publicly. I am grateful to William Tierney, who initially encouraged me to take on this task. Many thanks to Estela Bensimon, Michael Olivas, Laura Rendón, and Daryl Smith for their scholarly advice. My heartfelt thanks also goes to Lois Patton, Nancy Ellegate, Ruth Fisher, and Ann Fenech Vitarella of SUNY Press for their constant help and insight while producing this volume and for their direction in requiring chapters of high quality. Special thanks to my assistant, Marie Sparks, whose assistance has been invaluable and Mary Cólon, Mayra Yrizarry and Barbara Shore for their tremendous assistance in preparing this manuscript. To my friend, David Gómez, I offer my eternal appreciation for always pushing me to strive.

Finally, I dedicate this book to my parents, Leopold and Lucy García, and my sisters and brothers, Alicia, Sally, Louie, Lucy, and Leo, for instilling in me the belief that we must always strive to ensure equal opportunity and educational equity for all.

Mildred García

# 1
## *The State of Affirmative Action at the Threshold of a New Millennium*

From admitting students to hiring faculty, administrators and staff to making tenure decisions, affirmative action has made an indelible imprint on the university environment. Over 30 years has passed since the implementation of Title VII in 1965 and questions, issues and challenges continue to be brought to the forefront. In an effort to respond to the most important questions, confront the most pressing issues and identify the most serious challenges, this book reviews the impact of affirmative action in higher education. This introductory chapter starts with a look at the origins of affirmative action. The following sections establish the context, reframe the arguments and highlight the myths. Finally, there is a brief overview of the subsequent chapters.

### Setting the Scene

> Our job is to turn the American vision of a society in which no one has to suffer discrimination based on race into a living reality everywhere in our land. And that means we must secure to every American equal access to all parts of our public life—to the voting booth, to the schoolroom, to jobs, to housing, to all public facilities including lunch counters.
>
> John F. Kennedy, July 10, 1960
> NAACP Rally, Los Angeles, California

That was 1960, the start of a decade that will be forever marked in history as the era of social conscience in America. Change seemed to be the hallmark of the 1960s and affected almost every facet of American life. A powerful feminist movement arose which challenged male domination. Women's political organizations gained force, insisting on equal pay for equal work and demanding an end to sex discrimination. The era also saw the birth of the environmental movement, which brought the issues of pollution and waste control to the American consciousness. The American public also began challenging the power of the seller and the consumerism movement launched efforts to secure truthful and clear disclosures about both products and services. At the same time, the civil rights movement was strongly beginning to confront the unjust treatment of blacks. The summers of 1963 and 1964 brought to the headlines the urban riots of our cities and the nation tuned in to the Los Angeles district of Watts, where the largest urban riot in America was reported.

In his collection of speeches and writings by John F. Kennedy, Theodore Sorenson (1988) notes that Kennedy "was shocked by the brutality endured by civil rights protesters across the nation and determined to enforce judicial orders admitting blacks to state institutions of higher learning. . . [and] launched in mid-1963 an unprecedented and comprehensive, regulatory, and educational drive to fundamentally change this country's course in black-white relations." Later that year, Kennedy was assassinated and the torch was passed to Lyndon Johnson, whose administration ushered in sweeping social change. Among the most notable was Title VII, which prohibits employment discrimination on the basis of race, color, religion, sex, or national origin. Affirmative action was born with the implementation of Title VII and then shaped by the passage of Executive Order 11246 (pertaining to discrimination by contractors), Executive Order 11375 (which included sex as a protected class), judicial decisions, and the passage of state laws.

On college campuses across the nation, the debate over affirmative action policies began with the implementation of Title VII. For some, the implementation of affirmative action programs was viewed as a catalyst which would play a significant role in diversifying our institutions of higher learning. At the same time, opponents of affirmative action created illusions and misconceptions that something was occurring on college campuses that warranted organized resistance (Gittel, 1975).

Today, affirmative action is no less controversial. In fact, the fire has been fanned by fierce political grandstanding, setting the stage for increasingly intense debate in the years to come. But regardless of where individuals or institutions stand with regard to affirmative action, colleges and universities are legally bound to the specifications of Title VII and are required to ensure that their employment practices expand opportunities for people of color and women. In practice, institutions of higher learning have been at the forefront of expanding opportunities to minorities and women. Based on a recognition that educational excellence and diversity are mutually intertwined, many colleges and universities have voluntarily engaged in expanding equal opportunity admissions for students who historically have been excluded.

Numerous research studies have demonstrated that education continues to be the most powerful vehicle for achievement. As one public policy researcher stated, "Increasingly the dividing line between those who are moving ahead and those who are moving behind is the educational link. Those who get it have a chance. And those who don't get it don't have a chance" ("Redeeming the American Promise," 1995).

Our colleges and universities are at the heart of the social conscience of this nation—places where artificial barriers of race, religion, class, sex, sexual orientation, and language can be transcended and where we can inspire and develop leaders who will marshal a just society. Affirmative action provides the vehicle to create campuses which transcend past and present injustices. Clearly, those involved in higher education must do a better job of educating both the public and policymakers about the importance of an inclusive society, not only for the benefit of people of color, but for us all. Common sense tells us and research confirms that the economic and competitive edge of the nation depends on the availability of educational opportunities and gainful employment for every American.

## Defining Affirmative Action: Then and Now

While President Kennedy was the first to use the term "affirmative action," it was President Roosevelt in 1941 who issued an executive order barring defense contractors from discriminating against minorities. After the passage of Title VII, President Johnson issued Executive Order 11246 in 1965 which prohibits contractors from discriminating against any employee or applicant for employment and requires that contractors take affirmative action to ensure that applicants are employed and treated during their employment without regard to race, color, religion, or national origin. Two years later in 1967, President Johnson signed Executive Order 11375, which included sex as a protected class. The intent was—and still is—to boost the number of minority and women employees in employment settings that receive federal funding.

On a broader level, however, affirmative action describes those practices that attempt to correct past or present discrimination and prevent future occurrences of discrimination (Report of the Citizens' Commission on Civil Rights, June 1984). Other definitions—variations on the theme—abound. In a 1960 speech, John F. Kennedy noted that affirmative action programs recognize that we are "one nation and we are all great people. Our origins may be different but our destiny is the same, our aspirations identical. There can be no artificial distinctions, no arbitrary barriers" (Sorenson, 1988). More recently, the Rev. Jesse Jackson referred to affirmative action as "a conservative remedy to generations of unfair practices that favored white men" (New York Times, June 4, 1995). Several weeks later, President Clinton spoke to the purpose and meaning of affirmative action in his response to Republican opponents:

> Our search to find ways to move more quickly to equal opportunity led to the development of what we now call affirmative action. The purpose of affirmative action is to give our nation a way to finally address the systemic exclusion of individuals of talent, on the basis of their gender or race, from opportunities to develop, perform, achieve, and contribute. Affirmative Action is an effort to develop a systematic approach to open the doors of education, employment,

and business development opportunities to qualified individuals who happen to be members of groups that have experienced long-standing and persistent discrimination..." (New York Times, July 20, 1995).

There are those who view affirmative action as America's response to a past which includes slavery, racism, and sexism. Others emphasize a future orientation, defining affirmative action as programs designed to ensure full participation by those who have been historically excluded from colleges, universities, and the work force (Wilson, 1995). Clearly, all of these definitions are more similar than different. And just as clearly, all leave substantial room for interpretation, debate, and political maneuvering.

## Reframing the Questions

As the arguments about affirmative action continue to escalate and passions run high, it is imperative to step back, review the fundamental issues, and take a hard look at the questions that underlie the current debate. In part, this involves challenging common assumptions about issues such as qualifications, admissions standards, and equal opportunity. And in part, reframing the questions requires stepping into the political arena to examine the nature of the misconceptions and fabrications which have begun to make inroads into the American consciousness.

For example, what does it mean to be qualified for employment or college admission? It is proposed by those seeking to eliminate affirmative action, i.e., Ward Connerly, University of California Regent, that we need a merit-based system of hiring, that we need to hire those who are qualified, and that everyone must compete equally. Clearly, qualifications for employment and even admissions are based on a set of standards. Who sets those standards and on what basis? Guinier (1995) notes that, in the United States, there is a universal fixed standard—a one-size-fits-all criterion that applicants for a position or for higher education admission must meet.

To illustrate her point, Guinier cites the victorious lawsuit brought by women against the New York City Police Department which challenged the requirement that police officers be at least six feet tall. By winning the lawsuit, the doors to the police force were not only opened to women, but to Latino men, Asian-American men and even short white men. More importantly, it highlighted the arbitrary nature of a universal fixed standard. And did the removal of this standard affect the performance of the police department? According to Guinier, performance was enhanced as a result of the change. For example, female police officers were found to be outstanding in domestic violence and other family-related cases.

What about admissions standards? If admissions decisions were based exclusively on specific standardized exams such as the Scholastic Assessment Test (SAT) or the Law School Admissions Test (LSAT), would all applicants be on equal footing? Studies show that the SAT alone does not accurately predict success in college. The SAT has a range of error of at least 40 points, which means that someone who scored 900 one day could retake the test the following day and score anywhere from 860 to 940. If standardized test scores alone were the determining factor in admissions decisions, many students would be barred from their institutions of choice because they were nervous about taking the test, simply had an "off" day, or any of a number of human possibilities. Even more important is the fact that standardized test scores do not accurately measure how one will actually perform during the college years since they do not take into account such factors as motivation and ambition (Holmes, 1995).

A study at Harvard University demonstrates this last point (Guinier, 1995). Three graduating classes were asked to identify the qualities of a student who succeeds. Their definition of success was defined by income, professional satisfaction, and community involvement. The findings indicated that there was a high correlation between success and two criteria: low SAT scores and students who come from blue-collar backgrounds. The implications are clear: Those who are given an opportunity and who are "hungry" to succeed will do better in life than those who take higher education for granted.

Similarly, Guinier's LSAT study (1995) found that the test is both arbitrary and exclusionary. It is arbitrary because it does not correlate very well with performance in law school and exclusionary because LSAT scores correlate with parents' income. In other words, applicants from middle-class backgrounds who can afford to go to the best public and private schools and who have access to preparatory exam classes are better prepared to excel on standardized exams like the SAT and LSAT, and are therefore more likely to be admitted.

In *Savage Inequalities: Children in America's Schools*, Jonathan Kozol noted that urban schools throughout the United States are typically unhappy places where segregation thrives and where filth and despair are evident and pervasive. He asked a simple and profound question: How can we allow so many of our children to attend educational institutions where no politician, board president, or businessperson would dream of working? How can standardized exams be objective when some schools offer preparatory courses and others lack basic texts and supportive learning environments? And what happens to the generations of students who attend the schools that Kozol described? Are they simply to be dismissed and discarded until the system is restructured to ensure equal opportunity?

Further, what does it mean to be equal? The debate over affirmative action speaks to the necessity of giving everyone an equal start and truly equal opportunity. Given the history of this country, have we even begun to do this? Has affirmative action rectified our inequalities? The founding fathers of this nation were men who believed in patriarchy and assumed privilege—privilege that assigned women the role of second–class citizens. And while African Americans have been in this country for 376 years, slavery—or something very close to it—existed for 246 of those years and cultural and constitutional subordination existed for another 100 of those years. It was not until 1965 that the voting rights and civil rights acts were implemented.

To adequately and accurately assess the impact of affirmative action over its brief 30-year history, it is essential to consider the facts. For example, while the median family incomes for African Americans and Latinos in 1993 were $21,542 and $23,654 respectively, white families averaged $39,000. Moreover, African Americans experienced a slower median-income growth rate than whites from 1973 to 1989, and the median family income for Latinos actually declined between 1979 and 1989. The 1995 report of the Glass Ceiling Commission found that although white males make up 43 percent of the work force, they hold 95 percent of the nation's senior-management positions (defined as vice president or above) (Harris and Merida, 1995; Phillip, 1995). In higher education, people of color represent 23 percent of the student enrollment and 12 percent of faculties (Carter and Wilson, 1995).

If affirmative action had been successful, wouldn't the numbers be higher? Wouldn't admissions and hiring patterns show marked improvement? To gain some perspective on the numbers, we need only to return to the schools that Kozol described in *Savage Inequalities*. As he went from one urban school to another—most of which were 95 to 99 percent non-white—he was surprised and dismayed to see that segregation had actually intensified and concluded that segregation was not a past injustice, but an ever-present state of affairs. Kozol's reaction to his school visits deserves note:

> What seems unmistakable, but, oddly enough, is rarely said in public settings nowadays, is that the nation, for all practice and intent, has turned its back upon the moral implications, if not yet the legal implications, of the Brown decision. The struggle being waged today, where there is any struggle being waged at all, is closer to the one that was addressed in 1896 in *Plessy v. Ferguson*, in which the court accepted segregated institutions for black people, stipulating only that they must be equal to those open to white people. The dual society, at least in public education, seems in general to be unquestioned. (p. 4)

Kozol's observations are central to the current debate over affirmative action and illustrate how desperately this nation needs a systematic approach for producing real integration and inclusion in our classrooms, board rooms, newsrooms, and on our faculties. For this nation to be competitive and economically sound in the next century, we must bridge the gaps between Americans and learn to embrace those who think differently and whose experiences are profoundly different from our own. We will need to take advantage of all Americans and use their talents to rethink the ways we as a nation function.

Americans are concerned for their livelihoods. Some of those concerns are fueled by changing demographics. For example, it has been predicted that by the year 2010, one of every three Americans will be a person of color. Women and people of color are entering the work force in larger numbers than ever before and, for the first time, many white men are feeling the competition and fear associated with loss of privilege and power. Reasons had to be found to explain these phenomena and a scapegoat was identified: Affirmative action has become the target of attack, the object to blame. This process has created untruths and misconceptions which political leaders have used to capture the public's attention and galvanize support to enhance their own careers. To better understand this process—and its consequences—it is essential to explore some of the most common myths which continue to enter and influence public discourse about affirmative action.

## Debunking the Myths

### Affirmative action requires the establishment of quotas for hiring minorities and women.

This belief misconstrues the law. The intent of affirmative action in employment and admissions has always been to establish hiring and admissions goals for underrepresented groups. *Bakke v. Regents of the University of California* (1978) outlawed the use of quotas, but the court also established the need for colleges and universities to consider race as one factor that can be used to help achieve diversity in a student body.

### In higher education, affirmative action requires the admission of minorities and women at the expense of white males.

This statement implies that the sole criterion for admission is a standardized test score. However, as was mentioned earlier, standardized tests alone are not adequate predictors of academic success. Further, no institution of higher education selects entering students solely on the basis of merit as defined by grades and test scores (Lennin, 1995). American colleges and universities seek to bring together a diverse group of people who can learn from each other, creating a microcosm of the world they will enter as productive leaders and citizens (Burd, 1995). And in reviewing applicants for eligibility, admissions officers consider not only test scores, but past performance, leadership potential, activities, recommendations, and the outcome of interviews. As one admissions officer stated, "To say one person is more qualified for admission than another is tough to do" (Burd, 1995). So the question remains: What are the standards for determining who is qualified, and who sets those standards?

## Affirmative action has produced reverse discrimination against white males.

The facts simply do not support this statement. A draft study conducted for the United States Department of Labor that analyzed discrimination cases handled by both district and appellate courts indicated that a high proportion of so-called reverse-discrimination cases are simply without merit. Moreover, the Equal Employment Opportunity Commission's reports indicate that out of the 91,183 discrimination complaints filed for fiscal year 1994, only 1.5 percent alleged that white men had been discriminated against because of their race (Harris and Merida, 1995). At a time when the American public is uncertain about employment and concerned because of corporate restructuring and the threat of massive layoffs, affirmative action has become a convenient object of contempt and a target of opportunity for conservative politicians seeking to dilute or dismantle many of the social programs ushered in during the 1960s.

## Title VII alone is sufficient to address discrimination.

Diversity is essential to every facet of American society. Even the opponents of affirmative action would agree that hiring people with diverse experiences, outlooks, and opinions is important. But for many Americans, diversity is no more than an admirable concept, a politically correct term that can be applied in myriad ways. There may be a lot of talk about multiculturalism and diversity, but the fact remains that employers still tend to hire—and promote—people who are like themselves. The fact that the senior management of Fortune 100 firms is 95 percent white illustrates, among many other things, corporate America's discomfort with the realities of diversity. Clearly, race still matters in employment. In their study of nearly 2,000 able-bodied men from several ethnic groups in Los Angeles, Johnson and Farrell (1995) found that those men with darker skin tones were more likely to be unemployed. As evidenced by the verdict in the O.J. Simpson case and the October 1995 Million Man March, the black-white gulf in America is widening and those in positions of power and privilege will be less likely to go out of their way to hire people of color unless they are required to do so (Lehman, 1995). Regrettably, what W.E.B. Du Bois stated in 1903 is still the case today: "The problem of the Twentieth Century is the problem of the color line" (DuBois, 1903).

## Merit is the measure we should use for employment and admissions.

With respect to employment, the Glass Ceiling Commission found that the most significant barriers to the progress of women and minorities are the entrenched stereotypes and prejudices of white men. The report also pointed out that white men have insulated themselves within their own culture and continue to hire individuals who most closely fit their own personalities. One manager stated that, "What's most important is comfort, chemistry, relationships and collaborations" (Kilborn, 1995). If this is the case, where does merit come in?

As for admissions, when opponents of affirmative action speak to merit, they are speaking only of standardized tests. In addition to the arguments presented earlier, it must be noted that admissions decisions based purely on this definition of merit make determinations about students before they have had the opportunity to prove themselves. They are being judged on a measure that depends heavily on who their parents are, how much they earn and what kind of environment, both academic and personal, they come from (Lehman, 1995). Is this the definition of merit that proponents of this myth such as Steele, Dole, and Connerly seek?

Unqualified individuals are being hired and promoted for the sake of diversity and affirmative action.

Many business leaders recognize that a diverse work force gives them a competitive edge in the global marketplace. Increasingly, they also recognize that it is necessary to encourage people with diverse viewpoints to contribute innovative ideas and to contribute to solving the world's new challenges (Kilborn, 1995). A prime example of a company that acknowledges the power of diversity for corporate success is U.S. West Inc. This is a telecommunications company which was formed as a result of the breakup of A T & T in 1984 and employs thousands of employees. They have recognized that a diverse work force is crucial to the success of the company (Kilborn, 1985). As the chairman and CEO of U.S. West, Richard D. McCormick stated, "Diversity gives us strategic advantage" (Kilborn, 1985). At the same time, the leadership of U.S. West acknowledge that, if affirmative action were not in effect, the gains the company had made would not be as evident.

Employers under Title VII can use two permissible bases for the use of affirmative action in hiring. The first is to remedy a clear and convincing history of past discrimination by the employer and/or the union. The second is to cure a manifest imbalance in the employer's work force. Those who believe that affirmative action is used to hire unqualified individuals do not know the definition or comprehend the intent of affirmative action. They also don't comprehend the legal interpretations accepted by the courts. Neither anecdotal nor isolated incidents should be used to make blanket statements that affirmative action supports the hiring of those who do not meet the job specifications. If abuses or misinterpretation of affirmative action are in use by some, then these companies or individuals need to be educated as to the purpose and meaning of affirmative action rather than calling for the elimination of it (American Association of University Women, April 1995).

Affirmative action has hindered the progress of women and people of color.

Steele (1990) states that affirmative action programs actually hinder people of color and women by creating a sense that they were hired not based on their strengths, but due to their gender or racial/ethnic background. The assumption is that if affirmative action programs were eliminated, the stigma would disappear. But that is clearly not the case. As Kweisi Mfume stated in *Black Issues in Higher Education*, "Any stigmas and negative stereotypes associated with race in this country existed long before affirmative action was ever thought of. They don't exist because of it, they exist in spite of it" (Mfume, 1995).

To illustrate Mfume's assertion it is important to review the studies by The Glass Ceiling Commission. They found in its studies that significant barriers exist for women and minorities in the work force. These barriers include, among others, entrenched stereotypes. Many of these white men who are in positions of authority and thus are able to hire for employment believe that black men are undisciplined and always late, women are not tough enough and are unwilling or unable to relocate, and Latino workers are foreign born, lazy, heavy drinkers, drug users, and don't want to work. White males cited in this report also believe that neither women nor minorities play golf. Furthermore, the report found that women and minority groups are not receiving the support or mentoring that majority men automatically receive from other majority men (Kilborn, 1995). It is clear that the elimination of affirmative action would not wipe out these stereotypes. In order to abolish these ingrained views this country needs to do a better job of educating for diversity. This report highlights that we are still confronting racist and sexist views among those in positions of power and, therefore, we are not yet prepared to eliminate affirmative action. What is hindering the progress of women and people of color are the beliefs found in this report by those in authority and not an action plan like affirmative action which was created to confront these views.

The *American Heritage Dictionary* offers as one of its defintions for the word *myth*, "A notion based more on tradition or convenience than on fact." The myths on affirmative action have been created because an explanation needs to be fabricated to explain the loss of power among white males. As Kilborn states (1995), "some white men are frightened and angry that people unlike them are vying for their jobs" (p. A14). The Glass Ceiling Report further goes on to cite that barriers exist "because of the perception of many white males that as a group they are losing—losing the corporate game, losing control and losing opportunity" (Kilborn 1995, p. A22).

Secretary of Labor Robert Reich summarizes why these myths have emerged. "Angry white males are venting their frustrations at minorities and women when the real problem they face (along with everyone else) is an increasingly competitive global economy that has produced massive changes in the domestic economy and drastically altered the nature and demands of the job market" (Wilson, May 1995).

Educators, politicians and leaders need to present the facts and realities in order to eliminate these myths so that this nation can embrace a true democratic diverse society.

## *The Case for Affirmative Action*

This volume is a collaborative effort among colleagues trained in several disciplines to analyze the impact of affirmative action in higher education. The contributors present more detailed analyses of this complex dilemma from the perspective of their particular fields.

John Howard offers a historical perspective on affirmative action. He examines affirmative action in the larger context of the long struggle of people of color for equal rights. Robert Ethridge reviews the progress that has been made nationally and differentiates between federal and state-supported programs. Linda Flores and Alfred Slocum examine the most recent legal cases and their implications in this new political environment. Using applicable law, research, and observation, they document how these decisions are reactions to the loss of white male privilege. The impact on admissions is discussed by Sylvia Hurtado and Christine Navia. They address in depth the concerns raised about entrance requirements. Caroline Turner and Samuel L. Myers' chapter on faculty underscores the slow progress which has been made in the hiring of faculty of color even with the implementation of affirmative action programs. Bonnie Busenberg and Daryl Smith highlight the need for women to continue to support affirmative action. They explore the current status of women in academia and emphasize why women need to continue to join in the battle with people of color to uphold affirmative action. Robert Rhoads addresses discrimination against gays and lesbians on college campuses and suggests ways that institutions can create a more inclusive vision of affirmative action. Chapter Nine by Alfred Slocum addresses how white men have benefited from affirmative action. Citing legal cases and affirmative action programs, the authors document how many of those in the majority who are calling for the demise of affirmative action have actually been the beneficiaries of such programs. Finally, Albert Kauffman and Roger Gonzalez analyze the impact of the fifth circuit court's controversial Hopwood decision on higher education. They list the issues on appeal to the U.S. Supreme Court and outline the implications of the decision for colleges and universities.

There is no doubt that affirmative action has faced serious challenges in the last three decades. The Reagan and Bush administrations worked hard to shift the views of the courts on affirmative action and mounted an offensive campaign to abolish it as it was conceptualized (Winter, 1992). But there is also no doubt that diversity is here to stay, bringing with it continuing challenges to discrimination and demands from oppressed groups not covered under Title VII to be granted protected-class status. It is an opportune time to rethink and reevaluate affirmative action by faculty and practitioners in the field of higher education and to explore multiple answers to a single question: How can affirmative action be constructed for the 21st century to protect those individuals who have been discriminated against and excluded from our colleges and universities? The following chapters begin that process.

## REFERENCES

American Association of University Women, "Affirmative Action: Myth vs. Reality," Program and Policy Statement, April 1995.

Bergheim, Kim, "White Males Fight Back," *The Hispanic Outlook in Higher Education*," July 1, 1995, 6–7.

Chafe, William H., "Providing Guarantees of Equal Opportunity," *The Chronicle of Higher Education*," June 30, 1995, B1–2.

Cross, Theodore, and Slater, Robert Bruce. "Alumni Children Admissions Preferences at Risk: The Strange Irony of How the Academic Achievements of Asians May Rescue Affirmative Action for

Blacks." *The Journal of Blacks in Higher Education*, Winter 1994/1995, 87–90.

DuBois, W.E.B. (1903), *The Souls of Black Folk*, New York: Penguin Books.

Gittell, Marilyn. "The Illusion of Affirmative Action," *Change*, October 1975, 39–43.

Guinier, Lani. Unpublished Luncheon Keynote Address at Educating One-Third of a Nation Conference, Kansas City, Missouri, October 22, 1995.

Harris, John F., and Merida, Kevin. "Affirmative Action Under Fire," *The Washington Post National Weekly Edition*, April 24–30, 1995, 6–7.

Holmes, Steven A. "Programs Based on Sex and Race are Challenged," *New York Times*, March 16, 1995, A1.

Holmes, Steven A. "A Rage for Merit Whatever That Is," *New York Times*, July 30, 1995, E6.

Kilborn, Peter T. "Women and Minorities Still Face 'Glass Ceiling,'" *New York Times*, March 16, 1995, pg. A22.

Kilborn, Peter T. "White Males and the Manager Class," *The New York Times*, March 17, 1995, pg. A14.

Kilborn, Peter T. "A Leg Up on Ladder, but Still Far From Top," *New York Times*, June 16, 1995, pgs. A1, A22.

Kozol Jonathan. *Savage Inequalities*. New York: Harper Perennial, 1992.

Lemann, Nicholas. "What Happened to the Case for Affirmative Action?" *New York Times Magazine*, June 11, 1995, 36–43, 52–54, 66–68.

Mfume, Kweisi. "Mfume Criticizes Attacks on Affirmative Action," *Black Issues in Higher Education*, June 29, 1995, 4.

*New York Times*, "Excerpts from Clinton Talk on Affirmative Action," July 20, 1995, pg. A10.

*New York Times*, Editorial, "Affirmative Action Affirmed," June 4, 1995, pg. 14E.

Philip, Mary-Christine. "Antidote to an 'Epidemic of Rage'," *Black Issues in Higher Education*, May 18, 1995, 12-19.

Purdum, Todd S. "President Gives Fervent Support to Fighting Bias," *New York Times*, July 20, 1995, pgs. A1, A10.

Sorensen, Theodore. *"Let the Word Go Forth." The Speeches, Statements, and Writings of John F. Kennedy 1947 to 1963*. New York: Delacourte Press, 1988.

Southern Education Foundation, Panel Report, *Redeeming the American Promise*, Atlanta, 1995.

Steele, Shelby. *The Content of Our Character*, New York: St. Martin's Press, 1990.

Wilkins, Roger. "Affirming Affirmative Action," Unpublished Opening Keynote Address, at Educating One-Third of a Nation Conference, Kansas City, Missouri, October 19, 1995.

Wilson, Reginald. "Affirmative Action: Yesterday, Today, and Beyond," American Council on Education, May 1995.

Wilson, Reginald. "Affirmative Action Policies Have Helped Minorities, Women Progress," *Higher Education & National Affairs*, American Council on Education, September 25, 1994.

John R. Howard

# 2
# Affirmative Action in Historical Perspective

In December 1964, the *Reporter* magazine carried an article entitled "Preferential Treatment for Negroes." Coming just months after the passage of the Civil Rights act of 1964, the article addressed a new and potentially divisive issue posed by the relative success of the movement's long struggle to end legal discrimination. The essential moral claim of the movement had been that blacks and whites should be treated alike; there should be no distinctions in law based on color with regard to the rights enjoyed by citizens. Decades of struggle had been devoted to advancing the claim to equal treatment in a society in which both the law and popular sentiment supported unequal treatment and entrenched forms of racial subordination.

The *Reporter* article argued the case for transforming the agenda of the civil rights movement. A society which had consistently underinvested in black students ought to now adopt race-based policies aimed at helping young blacks overcome the deficits yielded by segregation. It was not sufficient to adopt a "color blind" stance. The legacy of decades of systematic deprivation could be overcome only by color-conscious policies directed at the victims of that deprivation ("Preferential Treatment for Negroes," 1995).

The controversy engendered by the article foreshadowed the debate which eventually pushed all other policy issues involving race and rights to the side. By the end of the Twentieth Century the outcome of the affirmative action debate seemed to portend the direction race relations would take in the United States well into the Twenty-first Century.

Opponents of affirmative action have sought to seize the moral high ground, arguing that such policies betray the central ethical claim which drove the civil rights movement in its long struggle against segregation. People ought to be accorded equal treatment without regard to race, gender, or other extraneous characteristics. Proponents of affirmative action policies have not been able to articulate as clear or compelling a defense. Indeed, former beneficiaries of such policies have questioned their continued existence.

The issues posed by affirmative action in the post-civil rights era are nuanced and subtle. Ultimately however, affirmative action policy is driven by the same legal and moral premises as the historic civil rights movement. The contradiction between the legal and moral claims made by the movement throughout its long struggle against segregation and those made in the post civil rights affirmative action era are more apparent than real.

This chapter examines affirmative action in the larger context of the century-long black struggle for equal rights. The objective is to facilitate a better understanding of affirmative action policy by placing it in the context of the circumstances which produced it. The discussion is organized into three parts. The first section focuses on the origins of legal segregation and on the evolution of the civil rights movement's legal and moral challenges to segregation, culminating with the enactment of the Civil Rights Act of 1964. That historic piece of legislation codified many of the instrumental and moral objectives of the movement.

The second part of this chapter focuses on a set of conditions and practices, long in existence, but whose meaning did not become manifest until after the passage of the 1964 Civil Rights Act. These were conditions and practices which could not have assumed primacy in terms of the formulation of remedial policy until legal segregation and lawful race and gender discrimination in employment had been confronted and statutorily prohibited.

Part three of the chapter focuses on the multiple legal challenges to affirmative action under a claim of "reverse discrimination" and on the Supreme Court's responses to those challenges, particularly with regard to higher education. Insofar as the fate of affirmative action rests ultimately with the Supreme Court, considerable attention is given to the evolution of the Court's holdings on the matter.

The chapter's conclusion sets forth a position with regard to affirmative action in higher education, taking into account its legal status, moral implications, and historical evolution. The burden of the argument is that the proponents of affirmative action have failed miserably to make a persuasive case despite the fact such a case can be made. There is no contradiction between the ethical premises of the historic civil rights movement and the moral premises underlying affirmative action; rather, there is continuity both with regard to moral premise and legal argument. It is argued, in addition, that affirmative action policies, properly understood and implemented, offer a more rational way for institutions to make decisions with regard to the allocation of access than the models in use prior to affirmative action.

## The Origins of the Civil Rights Movement

The 10-year period following the end of the Civil War saw a remarkable set of laws put in place intended to ensure equal rights for blacks. The Fourteenth and Fifteenth Amendments were added to the Constitution, and a series of so-called "enforcement acts" were put on the books conferring authority on the federal government to prosecute night riders given the indifference or complicity of local law enforcement. The decade culminated in the passage of the Civil Rights Act of 1875, which barred discrimination in public accommodations.

The year 1876 became pivotal in the history of race and rights in the United States. The presidential election ended in a virtual deadlock, leading the Republicans to negotiate acquisition of the White House in return for removing the last remaining federal troops from the states of the defeated confederacy, thereby turning the fate of southern blacks over to their former masters.

Another key turning point came seven years later. In what are known as *The Civil Rights Cases of 1883*, the Supreme Court declared the public accommodations provisions of the Civil Rights Act of 1875 unconstitutional on the grounds that Congress lacked the authority to curb private acts of racial discrimination. The Equal Protection clause of the Fourteenth Amendment curbed state action, but left private parties free to discriminate (*The Civil Rights Cases, 1883*). Bitterly decried by Frederick Douglass and other black leaders, the effect of the holding was to read blacks out of civil society.

The Court was also beginning to address the issue which would be crucial to the legal debate involving affirmative action a century later: Can government make racial distinctions in law without violating the Equal Protection clause of the Fourteenth Amendment? The pivotal case with regard to that question, *Plessy v. Ferguson*, decided in 1896, had been preceded by other cases in which the Court spoke to the matter of racial distinctions in law. In *Pace v. Alabama* it had upheld the constitutionality of a law punishing adultery between a black and white couple more severely than adultery between two whites or two blacks on the grounds that no distinction was really made (*Pace v. Alabama*, 1882).

The distinctive feature of *Plessy* and the reason for its historic importance was that it advanced a framework reconciling race-based state laws with the language of the Equal Protection clause. The separation of the races promoted peace and harmony between them, therefore a state might mandate such separation provided the services afforded blacks were equal to those afforded whites.

*Plessy* represented the culmination of a struggle over race and rights which had begun at the end of the Civil War. The efforts of the defeated southern states to reduce newly freed blacks to a form of serfdom via generously interpreted vagrancy laws and onerous "labor contracts" generated a movement in Congress for the passage of laws intended to bar state action directed at racial subordination or abuse.

From the Northern perspective the War had been fought for two purposes: to preserve the union and end slavery. Preservation of the union had been the initial driving force but the abolition of slavery came, eventually, to be a key motivating element in the battle to defeat the Confederacy. With the war barely over and with union dead still being returned from the battle fields, the South appeared to be using state law to preserve a system it had been unable to sustain on the battle field. Congress responded with the first civil rights law in the nation's history, the Civil Rights Act of 1866, and with a proposed constitutional amendment putting a limit on state action.

Spearheading the Congressional effort, Thaddeus Stevens and Wendall Phillips offered an amendment explicitly barring the states from making *any* distinctions in law based on race ("The 14th Amendment That Wasn't," 1993). Had such language been incorporated into the proposed Fourteenth Amendment, the Jim Crow laws enacted by the southern states in subsequent decades would have been explicitly unconstitutional, but so also would the state-sponsored affirmative action programs formulated a century later to redress racial deprivation.

An explicit constitutional bar on any racial distinctions in law was rejected in favor of more general language offered by Ohio Congressman John Bingham holding a state to a constitutional mandate of "equal protection" for all its citizens. The language as it was finally drafted for the Fourteenth Amendment read "no state shall deny to its citizens the equal protection of the laws".

Southern resistance to the reform laws and Amendments of the post-Civil War era was aided in no small part by a series of Supreme Court decisions limiting their scope and meaning. The 31-year period between the end of the Civil War and *Plessy* had proven to be an interim in which the nation moved from slavery as the legal framework within which relations between most whites and most blacks was structured to segregation as its alternative. And just as slavery was accorded legal legitimacy and substantial moral affirmation throughout most of its history, so segregation also enjoyed constitutional legitimacy and substantial moral support throughout most of its history.

The *Plessy* decision did not create a stir at the time it was handed down. Whereas *Brown* made headlines across the nation *Plessy* received only brief notice in the *New York Times* several days later. And indeed for many years it was not even regarded as a landmark case. At the time and for many years after, the decision was seen as relatively uncontroversial. The long struggle of the civil rights movement was begun in an era in which black subordination was assumed to be part of the natural order of things. The Supreme Court allowed the states to condition the enjoyment of rights on group membership—and that stance was regarded as both legally sound and morally impeccable. The movement as it took shape in the years after *Plessy* was directed at changing the law and at transforming the moral consciousness of the majority white population.

## The Civil Rights Struggle in the Segregation Era

Given the constitutional legitimacy accorded race-based laws by the Supreme Court, the civil rights struggle initially focused on the failure by state governments and entities under their authority to honor the "equal" dimension of the separate but equal equation. In *Cummings v. Richmond County*, decided three years after *Plessy*, the Supreme Court rejected the argument that a failure to provide a high school for blacks while providing one for whites violated *Plessy's* separate but equal mandate. The states were not constitutionally obliged to provide education for anyone, hence the *Plessy* doctrine held for only those services the state was obligated to provide (*Cummings v. Board, 1899*). Decided on the eve of the Twentieth Century, *Cummings* sanctioned evasion of any obligation to leaven separate with the provision of equal.

The post-*Plessy* legal struggle for equal rights was begun in an inhospitable, judicial atmosphere. Ironically, the legal reasoning, arguments and language used to eventually overcome segregation came to be turned against the proponents of race-conscious meliorative policy in the affirmative action era. An examination of the evolution of those arguments in the context of the civil rights struggle serves to yield a better understanding of the affirmative action debate and helps to establish the continuity of the legal and moral argument for reform in both the civil rights and the affirmative action eras.

By the time the *McCabe* (1915) case came before the Supreme Court on the eve of World War I, the Court had tacitly sanctioned a number of state excuses for failing to provide equal service. Many of these excuses were based on an implicit theory of "group rights." If the black demand for first-class accommodations on the railroad was small, the states argued that there was no obligation to require the provision of a first class car for blacks. Similarly, if the number of blacks pursuing medical or legal training was small there was no need to provide in-state black professional schools. The Constitution as interpreted by the Supreme Court allowed the states to separate the races by law and required only that they provide equal services. But in given circumstances, even that modest demand could be evaded or ignored. The state was not obliged to provide services in a given area in any event and if they chose to provide them for one sector of the population but not another they were merely exercising their rights under federalist principles to determine how tax money would be spent. The black demand for a service was small, making it economically foolish to provide a black-only medical school or law school, and considerations of racial harmony dictated barring them from white institutions.

The Supreme Court-sanctioned segregationist position rested on a theory of group rights. The individual black enjoyed rights of access to a scarce but desired state resource only insofar as his group enjoyed that right. Thus, if the group did not enjoy access, the individual member of the group did not enjoy access. Central to the legal and philosophical challenge of the civil rights movement to segregation was the contention that rights under the Constitution were meant to be held by individuals rather than groups. The individual's enjoyment of rights could not be conditioned on racial affiliation. It is interesting to note that, opponents of affirmative action policies in the post-civil rights era have argued that they derive from a theory of group rights and are, therefore, as reprehensible as the old, historically discredited policy of racial segregation.

The formulation of an accurate and useful language with which to discuss and debate affirmative action policy requires a clear understanding of the historical context within which the civil rights argument evolved. A grasp of historical context establishes the simplistic and inaccurate nature of an argument of moral or legal equivalence of the premises of segregation and affirmative action.

*McCabe* involved a black plaintiff excluded from first-class railroad accommodations. Justice Charles Evans Hughes, writing for a Court majority, offered a doctrine which was both progressive by the standards of the time and which eventually became crucial to both the legal and moral claims of the civil rights movement in the fight to end segregation. Rights belong to an individual not to the racial group. *Plessy* did not provide a rationale for blanket evasion of the "equal" obligation on the grounds that there were few blacks seeking a particular service. Nor, by implication, did it confer a superior claim to any individual because of his membership in a particular group. *Plessy* did not mean that, as a matter of constitutional doctrine, a white had a *right* to expect more from the state because he was white (*McCabe v. Atcheson*, 1915).

Hughes left the Court in 1916 to run for president but returned in 1931 as Chief Justice to preside over the first of a series of cases which led eventually to a repudiation of *Plessy*. The doctrine he had articulated in *McCabe* remained in abeyance through the 1920s, a period which might be termed "the golden age of segregation." The system enjoyed near unquestioned legal and moral legitimacy and faced comparatively few legal challenges.

Hughes' return to the Court coincided with a number of events which undermined the national consensus on a variety of key issues. The collapse of the economy in 1929 and the formulation of New Deal policy following the election of Franklin Roosevelt led to a rethinking of federalism. The role of the federal government in managing the economy expanded as did its role in state affairs. The rise of Nazism in Europe highlighted the horrors attending a national obsession with racial superiority. And, under the leadership of Charles Houston, Dean of the Law School at Howard University, the legal struggle against segregation assumed a new and sharper thrust.

The strategy built on Hughes' early doctrine came to be employed in a set of cases which crystallized the legal and moral argument against racial discrimination. Writing for a Supreme Court majority in *Gaines* in 1938, Hughes supported the National Association for the Advancement of Colored People argument advanced by Thurgood Marshall. The state of Missouri had to admit Lloyd Gaines to its law school given that it had failed to create a law school for blacks. Gaines enjoyed his right to a law school education as an individual and not as a member of a group. The obligation of the state to refrain from denying him equal protection of the law was not conditioned on his group affiliation (*Gaines v. Canada*, 1938).

In the segregated America of the 1930s, the Hughes' argument was regarded as progressive and indeed the case came to be viewed as a landmark in advancing the cause of racial justice. Blacks should be judged as individuals and not be denied rights because of group affiliation. A similar argument would be offered half a century later in the context of the affirmative action debate.

Echoes of *Gaines* and its progeny are heard in the contention that affirmative action conditions privilege on group affiliation whereas the Constitution confers rights on individuals without regard to group affiliation.

The immediate consequence of the Houston and Hughes approach was a series of cases which questioned whether the Equal Protection clause of the Fourteenth Amendment could accommodate *any* racial distinctions. In the 1950 *Sweatt* case, the Court held that it was not possible for Texas to create a law school for blacks which would be the equal of the existing whites-only law school given that such intangibles as historic reputation would be impossible to confer on or duplicate in a newly created blacks-only institution (*Sweatt v. Painter*, 1950). And in *Brown*, the Court held that racial distinctions embodied in segregationist education laws violated the Equal Protection clause in so far as they implicitly presupposed black inferiority and had an indelible destructive impact on black children. State-mandated separate could not be equal.

## From Brown to the Civil Rights Act of 1964

The *Brown* holding contributed to the erosion of the moral legitimacy accorded segregation. *Plessy's* lone dissenter, Justice John Marshall Harlan, had stated that the Constitution is "color blind" and those words had armed the civil rights movement with a moral and a legal claim in the ongoing struggle against segregation and discrimination. Racial classifications were *per se* invidious (*Brown v. Board of Education*, 1954). If the United States stood for anything, it was the proposition that individuals were judged on their own, not by their group affiliation. There could be no such thing as a benign racial classification in law.

Following *Brown*, the struggle to end segregation took on even greater urgency. The legal and moral thrust of the civil rights argument was that race should not be the basis for making legal distinctions or arranging the social order. Violent segregationist responses to peaceful protest lent a new moral authority to the civil rights movement. In 1957, blacks led by the young Martin Luther King,

Jr., boycotted segregated buses in Montgomery, Alabama. In 1960, black students "sat-in" at department store lunch counters calling for an end to the denial of service on racial grounds. In 1961, black and white "freedom riders" committed acts of civil disobedience in defying segregationist laws in interstate travel. And finally, in 1964, in part in tribute to the recently murdered President, John Kennedy, a sweeping civil rights act was passed.

In its particulars, the Civil Rights Act of 1964 was more sweeping than any law or Amendment enacted during Reconstruction. Title II reversed the *Civil Rights Cases of 1883* by prohibiting racial discrimination in public accommodations. Title VI, which later became one of the grounds for Alan Bakke's suit against the University of California at Davis' affirmative action program, barred discrimination by educational institutions receiving federal monies. And Title VII provided a federal "cause of action" for plaintiffs alleging discrimination in employment. The Equal Employment Opportunity Commission was created to administer Title VII.

The underlying values of the Civil Rights Act of 1964 reflected the ethical premises of the civil rights movement. Race was repudiated as a basis for making legal distinctions. But even as it was being bitterly fought on the floor of Congress by segregationists and by state's rights advocates such as Arizona Senator and Republican presidential candidate Barry Goldwater, the issues later crystallized in the affirmative action debate.

Advocates of tough sanctions against employers who discriminated on racial, gender, or ethnic lines were accused of covertly seeking quota hiring for minorities and women. The bill's supporters countered with explicit denials of the supposed dangers. Hubert Humphrey, long-time civil rights advocate and floor manager of the bill in the Senate, declared that the proposed Act "does not require an employer to achieve any kind of racial balance in his work force by giving any kind of preferential treatment to any individual or group" (*Legislative History of Titles VII and Title IX of the Civil Rights Act of 1964*). His ally in the fight for passage of the new act, Senator Joseph Clark of Pennsylvania, also asserted that the purported danger was illusory, "Quotas are themselves discriminatory" (*Legislative History*).

Passage of the Civil Rights Act of 1964 represented a signal event in the history of the Republic, a victory for racial justice achieved after decades of struggle and at enormous cost against powerful and tenacious foes. Almost immediately it served to reduce the day-to-day indignities blacks encountered in simply going about their business. It held organizations to a standard of racial and gender fairness hitherto not expected of them.

Almost immediately, however, events conspired to expose its limitations, creating the need to rethink the civil rights agenda in terms of a new set of policies which soon came to be grouped under the rubric "affirmative action." The phrase communicated the need to vigorously pursue an end to discrimination and had been used in a racial context from time to time since 1960 or 1961 by President John Kennedy and Vice President Lyndon Johnson in terms of the traditional civil rights agenda.

A series of social cataclysms in the four-year period following the passage of the Civil Rights Act of 1964 combined with a set of new perceptions and analytic approaches generated by the Act itself served to transform the vague term "affirmative action" into a set of federal and state policies addressing new racial, ethnic, and gender realities.

## The Coming of Affirmative Action

In August 1965, a bloody race riot erupted in the Watts section of Los Angeles. Although triggered by a police-civilian encounter, it highlighted ongoing problems of economic marginalization and political exclusion. In 1967, a series of race riots swept the country, putting the problems of the inner city on the national agenda for the first time. In April 1968, Martin Luther King, Jr., was assassinated, again triggering massive rioting and evoking a new sense nationally that something had to be done to cope with the ongoing problem of racial discrimination.

Concurrent with these social catastrophes was the emergence of a new way of looking at race and exclusion generated in part by the attempt by the newly created Equal Employment Opportunity Commission to implement the Civil Rights Act and, in part, by scholars and activists addressing issues of race. The new law conceptualized discrimination as a malevolent act directed at an individual. Indeed, its proponents had stated that it was directed only at intentional acts of racial discrimination. As cases of alleged job discrimination came before the EEOC, however, it became increasingly clear that black and female exclusion might, in given instances, be as much a function of the way in which an employer traditionally did business as of an intent to discriminate. The networks ordinarily tapped, the tests ordinarily used might generate exclusion as effectively as intentional discrimination. Nondiscrimination was not enough. Nondiscrimination by an employer or by a college might still leave many blacks and minorities marginalized, outside the mainstream, and embittered candidates collectively for riots, or individually, for criminal acts.

The new social and intellectual realities crystallized in three propositions which came to serve as the basis for new social policy:

1. Blacks were excluded from full participation in the society by intentional discrimination and by what came to be termed "institutional racism." The latter involved seemingly neutral policies which had the consequence, nevertheless, of generating racial exclusion. In the legal context, institutional racism relative to employment was called "disparate impact" discrimination and involved racial, ethnic, or gender exclusion generated by hiring criteria having a disparate and negative impact on a "protected class" without being job-related in the sense of predicting successful or unsuccessful job performance.

2. Bringing minorities and women into the mainstream required going beyond the mere forbidding of discrimination. It was necessary also to take affirmative steps to break down subtle institutional and cultural barriers to full and equal participation in the society.

3. Breaking down institutional barriers entailed reexamining some of the criteria conventionally used to mediate access to schools, colleges, universities, and the work place.

These propositions departed from the century-long moral claim of the black struggle regarding the need to repudiate race as an element in public decision-making. Over time they were codified in a series of affirmative action policies at the federal and state levels.

Although political parlance tends to cite something called "affirmative action," in reality, a number of different programs and policies came into existence which had somewhat different purposes and consequences and were supported by different legal and sociological theories.

At the federal, state, and municipal levels, so-called "set-aside" programs were put together. Typically, such programs sought to direct a percentage of public spending to minority or female vendors either directly or by requiring primary contractors to allocate a certain percentage of a proposed job to such vendors. As policy, "set asides" evolved in response to evidence of discrimination in the allocation of public contracts and in recognition of the fact that the legacy of discrimination left many minority and female vendors genuinely unable to show the kind of track record or bonding capacity necessary to be viable competitors for state contracts under the traditional rules.

At the state level, a number of programs evolved in the area of higher education intended to increase minority presence on campus. In February 1967, representatives of the New York Board of Education, the Manhattan and Brooklyn Archdioceses, and 39 metropolitan-area colleges and universities met to plan a program, partially supported by foundation money, to help needy black and Puerto Rican students gain access to college by providing individualized instruction, small classes, and a guarantee of college admission with adequate performance (*New York Times*, February 5, February 14, 1967). A program was also inaugurated in the City University of New York with the intention of facilitating access for "disadvantaged" students. At the State University of New York level, an Equal Opportunity Program came into existence directed at the economically and educationally disadvantaged students, but widely understood to be a mechanism for increasing black and Latino presence on campus.

Other states and other institutions developed similar programs, some having an explicit racial or ethnic focus. Mary Washington College instituted a minority scholarship fund. Florida State University funded programs to recruit and retain minority students. California moved to take race and ethnicity into account, along with other factors, in the allocation of places in its undergraduate and professionals schools.

Although initially propelled by the imperative bringing blacks and other minorities into the mainstream, affirmative action programs in higher education also came to be championed on the grounds that diversity itself was a legitimate and valued objective. Since students will live their adult lives in a more racially and ethnically diverse society, schools could properly adopt diversity in the student body as part of their mission.

## The Opposition to Affirmative Action

The crystallizing of affirmative action as policy generated enormous controversy. Former segregationists adopted the language of the civil rights movement with regard to the Constitution being color blind. Other opponents were moved by philosophical considerations. The Washington Legal Foundation became a major player in the legal battle against affirmative action in higher education, seeking out cases allowing them to "assert the principle that racial classifications are wrong" (*Black Issues in Higher Education*, 1994).

As the struggle over affirmative action developed, it fell to the United States Supreme Court to define racial justice and the meaning of the Constitution in the post-Civil Rights era. Through its holdings, the Supreme Court has the capacity to confer moral as well as legal legitimacy on particular policy approaches. An adverse or ambiguous holding may compromise the legal status of a policy and also rob it of moral legitimacy. While the function of the Supreme Court is to interpret the Constitution, its holdings have the consequence of conferring the mantel of "fairness" on a contested public policy or of damning it as "unfair." Without intending to do so, the Court can also give impetus to or stall the momentum of a social movement by affirming or discrediting the constitutionality of a movement's objectives or methods. The checkered history of affirmative action as a political issue has been very much influenced by the Court's shifting stance with regard to its constitutional legitimacy.

The fundamental question posed in the key cases coming before the Court challenging affirmative action policy has always related to the constitutionality of racial distinctions in law. Is it not the case that the "equal protection" language of the Fourteenth Amendment denies to the states and their constituent agencies the right to allocate opportunities, goods, and services on the basis of race? Was this issue not settled by *Brown* and the line of cases leading up to it?

## The Supreme Court Confronts Affirmative Action

The Constitution as interpreted by the Supreme Court allows state law to classify and sort people with regard to such matters as minimum age for drinking, driving, or getting married. But the Court has also stated that classifications involving race pose a special concern. In *Korematsu v. United States* (1944), the Court addressed the constitutionality of the statutes under which Japanese citizens in designated areas on the West Coast were required to report to "assembly points" for relocation. Writing for the Court majority, Hugo Black upheld the legality of the relocation provisions but also stated that statutes making distinctions among citizens based on race should be subject to particularly close examination. Given that law had been a key instrument in promoting and sustaining racial oppression, there should be a particularly heavy burden on the state to justify such distinctions. Traditionally, states had made distinctions among citizens on the basis of race for the purpose of denying some the rights and benefits enjoyed by others. The Court should not assume, therefore, that such distinctions were either neutral or benevolent. American history taught that they were devised for no good purpose and hence ought to be examined with particular care and concern.

By the time the first challenges to affirmative action policy came before the Court, a so-called "strict scrutiny" test had come to be applied to matters involving race. Racial classifications in law were inherently suspect and hence the state bore a heavy burden of justification. A law survived only if the state could establish that the distinction served a compelling and legitimate state interest. Most of the cases coming before the court dealt either with employment or with so-called "set asides" but generated principles which guided the decisions of lower courts in cases involving challenge to affirmative action in higher education.

The evolution of the constitutional status of affirmative action is very complex and multifaceted. For purposes of this discussion, that complex history will be summarized and traced out through five cases: *North Carolina State Board of Education v. Swann* (1971), *Weber v. Steelworkers* (1979), *Bakke v. Regents* (1978), *Croson v. Richmond* (1989), and *Podberesky v. Kirwin* (1995).

*North Carolina v. Swann* and *Weber v. Steelworkers* addressed the issue of whether the use of racial classification for benign rather than malevolent purposes was consistent with the mandate of the Constitution. In a more subtle sense, *Swann* addressed the issue of whether a law prohibiting the use of race in favor of a "color-blind" approach can have malevolent purposes or deleterious consequences. In effect, the *Swann* question is posed. May a "color-blind" policy be inconsistent with government responsibility to promote fair and reasonable access to public goods and opportunities?

The *Swann* decision occurred in the midst of a storm of ongoing litigation involving efforts to implement *Brown* by dismantling North Carolina's racially segregated school system. Fifteen years after *Brown*, many schools in the state remained segregated in fact, although not by law. Resistant to court efforts to desegregate the system via mandated busing, the North Carolina legislature passed a law forbidding the use of race as a criterion in assigning students to schools for any purpose, including the establishment of a "racial balance." In effect, North Carolina was arguing that the lower courts were ordering local school officials to act in defiance of the Constitution by making decisions based on race rather than neutral criteria.

Implicit in the Supreme Court's rejection of North Carolina's argument was a recognition of the fact that the Fourteenth Amendment does not prohibit government from making *any* decisions based on race. A consideration of race is proper where necessary to overcome the effects of past discrimination. This proposition is one of the key elements examined by courts in cases challenging the constitutionality of specific affirmative action programs in higher education and elsewhere. To what extent is a program remedial in the sense of redressing the effects of past discrimination? The eradication of racial discrimination is a "compelling state interest," allowing policies which might otherwise violate the equal protection clause of the Fourteenth Amendment to survive "strict scrutiny."

Although *Swann* and a host of other cases made it clear that racial distinctions could be made in law where necessary to overcome the effects of past discrimination, they did not address the issue of whether such distinctions could be made in a context in which there had been neither a judicial finding of past discrimination nor an admission of discrimination by an employer or a school seeking to defend an affirmative action program. In other words, to what extent could voluntary affirmative action programs be accommodated by the law and the Constitution? This issue was first posed in *DeFunis v. Odegaard* (1974).

Marco deFunis had applied to the University of Washington Law school in 1971, one of more than 1,600 applicants competing for 150 openings. Using a formula based on LSAT scores and grades in the last two years of college, the admissions committee sorted the applicants into numerically defined categories ranging from very good to reject. Black, Chicano, American Indian, and Filipino applicants were compared only with each other, however. DeFunis was denied admission and sought redress in federal court, claiming a violation of his rights under the Equal Protection clause. A trial court agreed with him and ordered his admission to the law school only to be reversed by the Washington Supreme Court. By the time DeFunis' appeal from the Washington decision reached the United States Supreme Court, he was in his last year in law school.

A divided court evaded the question of the constitutionality of voluntary affirmative action programs on the grounds that the case was moot given that DeFunis was about to graduate. Four dissenters correctly predicted that the issue was sure to come before the Court again and ought therefore to have been squarely faced. The dissenters also previewed some of the arguments raised when the issue did reappear. William O. Douglas, otherwise known as a Court liberal, contended that "If discrimination based on race is constitutionally permissible when those who hold the reins can come up with compelling reasons to justify it, then constitutional guarantees acquire an accordion-like quality... so far as race is concerned any state-sponsored preference to one race over another... is in my view 'invidious' and violative of the Equal Protection Clause." Ironically, in later years judicial conservatives were to take up the Douglas line. Justices Brennan, Marshall, and White also argued in dissent that the case should have been heard. A few years later they gained an opportunity to address the issue of voluntary affirmative action plans in *Bakke v. Regents*.

The facts in *Bakke* were similar to those of *DeFunis*. Alan Bakke had applied to the Medical School at the University of California at Davis and had twice been denied entrance. In seeking redress in the courts, he argued that the University had set aside 16 of the 100 spots in the first-year class for minority applicants. He argued also that he was better qualified according to traditional criteria than many of the minorities admitted under the special program and that he therefore had been rejected solely because he was white in violation of his rights under Title VI of the Civil Rights Act of 1964, and of his right to the equal protection of the laws. The California Supreme Court ordered Bakke's admission to the medical school and prohibited the University from using race as a factor in the admissions process.

At stake in the case was the fate of voluntary affirmative action programs. The Supreme Court had allowed government and its agents to take race into account in a remedial context, but otherwise, considerations of race in the allocation of public goods was at all times suspect given the nation's history of racial abuse, sanctioned by law. The University of California Medical School had never discriminated against minorities in the admissions process nor had it been charged with doing so. The use of race as a factor in the allocation of a scarce but desired good could not be justified therefore in remedial terms.

The holding as it emerged in June 1978 revealed a Court deeply divided on the issue of voluntary affirmative action. Irrespective of the divisions, the Court's holdings constitute the rules of the game. They indicate what can be done constitutionally and what is beyond the bounds. Four such rules emerged from *Bakke*:

1. The California court's decision holding the special admissions program unlawful was affirmed. Programs which set hard and fast numbers are not likely to survive challenge insofar as fixed numbers, of necessity, generate decisions based solely on race.

2. On the other hand, the lower court's decision that race could not be taken into account at all was incorrect. There

are conditions under which considerations of race may be proper other than in the context of being a remedy for prior acts of discrimination.

3. The pursuit of diversity may be a legitimate institutional objective. However, if that objective is pursued by segregating one group of applicants on racial or ethnic grounds and rating them only against each other, there may be a problem even in the absence of fixed numbers. The institution is probably making decisions based solely on constitutionally suspect criteria.

4. The proper context for bringing race into the equation is one factor among many in evaluating an applicant against all other applicants on academically relevant criteria.

*Bakke* was a watershed in terms of affirmative action regarding admissions in higher education. Most programs were voluntary and most were subject to restructuring in the light of the decision. At UC-Davis, the uncertainty and tension created by the case as it wound its way through the courts led to a drop in minority enrollment. Many years later, Trevor Chandler, Assistant Vice Chancellor for Academic affairs, referred to this as a "Bakke blip." Decisions such as *Bakke* compromise the commitment and efforts of admissions people generating the need on the part of other committed parties to refocus policy and regenerate enthusiasm for minority recruitment. Additionally, many schools probably continued to sustain, or gradually moved back to sustaining, programs which arguably were in conflict with *Bakke's* somewhat murky mandate, opening the door to further legal challenge.

Many schools have also sought to increase minority representation in the ranks of the faculty. Some institutions created incentives of various sorts to encourage minority recruitment and appointment. Shortly after *Bakke*, the Supreme Court spoke to the issue of voluntary affirmative action in an employment context.

Prodded by the civil rights community, Kaiser Aluminum and the Steelworkers Union entered into an agreement under which, without admitting fault or prior discrimination, they established a series of training programs intended to increase the number of black workers at skilled and craft levels. Pursuant to this agreement, the Kaiser plant in Gramercy, Louisiana, established a program open to both black and white workers selected on the basis of seniority from separate lists, one black and one white. Brian Weber applied for the program in his plant but was rejected although he had more seniority than some of the blacks who had been selected for participation.

In seeking redress, he claimed a violation of Title VII's prohibition against racial discrimination in hiring, promotion, training, and other employer directed activities. In popular parlance, Weber was claiming "reverse discrimination." Neither Kaiser nor the union had been found to have discriminated on the basis of race, and neither was admitting discrimination. The selection of workers for participation in the training program could not be justified as a remedial measure intended to redress prior bad acts.

The narrow issue before the Supreme Court was whether racial selection for the program violated the plain language which seemed to bar employers from making any decisions based on race. The larger issue had implications far beyond the fate of Brian Weber. Could private employers, public universities, or any other institution initiate voluntary affirmative action programs relative to minority job recruitment and appointment without admitting past fault? An admission of prior discrimination brought with it the risk of suits for damages and back pay by punitive victims. On the other hand, were Weber to win, the initiation of affirmative action job recruitment programs without admitting fault would raise the specter of being sued by white or male workers for "reverse discrimination."

Again, a divided Court addressed the question using sharp and bitter words. The issue was one of statutory interpretation. Did the literal language of Title VII indicate that Congress intended to prohibit voluntary affirmative action programs? In a vitriolic dissent, William Rehnquist accused the majority of an Orwellian approach to the law, contending that the plain language of Title VII prohibited the use of race as a factor in employment decisions and that Brian Weber's rights had been shamelessly violated.

The majority countered by going to the minutes of the Congressional committee meetings and conferences from which the Title VII had emerged. The intention of the people who had drafted the law had been to bring blacks into the economic mainstream, according to the Court majority. It would be ironic indeed if an employer were now to be barred from voluntarily pursuing the law's objective via programs which were temporary, narrowly tailored to reach proximate goals, and which did not injure white workers in the sense of denying them a benefit to which they would otherwise have had a claim.

*Weber* provided constitutional support for voluntary affirmative action programs in an employment context provided certain rules were followed. Programs which were temporary, narrowly tailored, and which did not injure white workers in terms of any proprietary interest such as loss of job or loss of legitimate seniority rights would survive challenge.

One year after *Weber*, Ronald Reagan was elected president. Philosophically closer to Barry Goldwater than to Richard Nixon, Reagan like Nixon had pledged to nominate justices committed to a more limited reading of the Fourteenth Amendment and less inclined to adapt its language to an expanded and evolving conception of civil rights. By the time the *Croson* case reached the Supreme Court, its composition had changed significantly. William Rehnquist had become Chief Justice and Reagan nominees Sandra Day O'Connor, Anthony Kennedy, and Antonin Scalia had joined the Court. Of the four, O'Connor was the most difficult to fathom. She had graduated from Stanford Law School near the top of her class but had been unable to find a job in the then male-dominated world of law. By contrast, her fellow Stanford alum, William Rehnquist, had been offered an opportunity to clerk for a Supreme Court justice. Whereas neither Rehnquist nor Anthony Kennedy had personal experience of discrimination and therefore had little impetus based on their personal biographies to question the precepts underlying their judicial philosophy, O'Connor had been the victim of discrimination. She shared the perspective of her more conservative colleagues, however, and thus took the lead in writing the holding of *Croson*, a case which was later cited as precedent for overturning Maryland's Banneker Scholarship program directed at black students.

At one level, *Croson v. Richmond* involved municipal set asides. At another level, it redefined the terms by which government had to justify race-based programs involving the allocation of opportunities or services. The facts were uncomplicated. The Richmond city counsil voted to allocate 35 percent of municipal spending to minority vendors, citing Richmond's history as capital of the confederacy and long history as a bastion of segregation and discrimination as justification for now seeking to use government as an instrument for redressing economic exclusion rather than as a means for promoting it.

In practice, the set aside program required primary contractors, almost invariably white, to seek out minority sub-contractors. Claiming to be unable to include minority subcontractors in cost-effective terms relative to bidding on work on a new jail, the J.B. Bonn company sought a waiver and when the waiver was not forthcoming went to court claiming that the set aside law violated the Equal Protection clause of the Fourteenth Amendment.

In writing for the Court majority, Justice O'Connor allowed that the state might make decisions based on race in a context of a remedy. It was necessary, however, to present clear, substantial, and convincing evidence that there had been prior discrimination and any remedial program had to limit redress only to the identifiable victims of that discrimination.

It was an extremely difficult test to meet. It did not allow for a circumstance in which discrimination had been so longstanding and pervasive that potential victims had ceased even to come forth and seek the job, bid on the contract, or apply to the school, or had been rendered genuinely subject to disqualification on objective grounds as a consequence of generations of exclusion. Its consequence with regard to education did not become clear until the *Banneker* case.

In 1989, Daniel Podberesky, of Hispanic-Jewish descent, sought admission to the University of Maryland. Having scored 1360 on the SAT and having a high school grade point average of 4.0, he applied for an academic scholarship. The University maintained more than 50 scholarship programs, including one directed at black students. The Banneker program had evolved over a number of years, partially in response to the efforts of the Federal Office of Civil Rights to force the state to undo its segregated system of higher education.

For many years the state had limited blacks to attending one of four "black" schools in the State: Bowie State, Coppin State, Morgan State, and the University of Maryland—Eastern Shore. The Banneker scholarship program originated as part of a remedial effort to overcome the legacy of a history of discrimination. When challenged in Court by Podberesky, Judge Frederick Motz had affirmed the constitutionality of the program, citing the state's long record of racial discrimination and the need to overcome its consequences. In reversing the District Court, the Fourth Circuit Court of Appeals cited *Croson*. Whatever the state's sorry history, it had not been established that this race-based program could be justified as a remedy for the immediate victims of the state's bad acts. The race-based program was held to violate the law.

*Banneker* narrowed the grounds on which affirmative action programs in higher education can be legally justified, but by no means determined the fate of affirmative action policies. The decision is part of an ongoing reexamination of opportunity and justice in the post-civil rights era. As was indicated at the beginning of this chapter, opponents of affirmative action have sought and seized the moral high ground by taking a stance in favor of "color blind" decision making. Indeed, some have claimed the mantle of the civil rights movement and accused affirmative action advocates of a betrayal. The courts, ever influenced by the public debate, have tended increasingly to read the Equal Protection clause as if it really did bar any consideration of race in law.

At present, three key questions dominate the ongoing public discourse on affirmative action: To what extent do the rhetorical and legal assaults on affirmative action in the context of higher education reflect a lack of understanding of how colleges and universities actually function? To what extent do affirmative action policies simply reflect a more rational way of making decisions with regard to access to higher education, apart from any consideration of race, ethnicity, or gender? To what extent is the claimed moral inconsistency between affirming civil rights in the classical sense and supporting affirmative action in the post-civil rights era, more illusory than real?

## Conclusion

Historically, academics have had a voice in the legal struggle attending race and rights. The *Brown* decision was influenced by the research and testimony of Kenneth and Mamie Clark regarding the psychological impact of segregation on black children. Other psychologists and sociologists played a role in the cases which laid a foundation for *Brown*. As the future of affirmative action begins to unfold there is yet an important role for academics to play. The basic legal issue posed by affirmative action is whether government can make racial distinctions in law without violating the Equal Protection clause of the Fourteenth Amendment. An intelligent address to that question in a higher education context requires an understanding of how decisions are made in such institutions.

Most *Bakke*-type law suits involve a claim by white plaintiffs that minorities have been admitted who scored on the average 10 points less on the LSAT, or 35 points less on the SAT, or the like. Implicit in that kind of legal claim is the proposition that justice would require the admission of students in a linear fashion based solely on test score. If that is not the implicit claim, it is a most peculiar argument in fixing on race as the basis for challenge. The argument would seem to be saying that the University of California at Berkeley Law School, for example, might admit a white candidate from Nebraska who scored 10 points lower on the LSAT than the plaintiff without justice being offended. But if a black who scores five points lower is admitted, damage has been done to the Constitution.

As the law is presently written, there is no basis for claiming "geographical discrimination," but the logic of the anti-affirmative action position pushes, nevertheless, toward a claim that quantitative measures are the only basis for making admission decisions. Remarkably, the academic community has not challenged the underlying premise of the typical "reverse discrimination" suit.

As discussed by Hurtado and Navia in Chapter 5, admissions criteria have always been multifaceted. No school admits students in a linear fashion based solely on quantitative measures. Unless desperate for students, schools establish a pool of applicants who are qualified to do the work according to objective measures. A variety of factors then come into play in selecting applicants from the pool. Age and geographical diversity may be sought. Students who are qualified academically but also show diverse interests may be looked upon favorably. Veterans may receive special consideration. The student with the highest SAT score or highest high school GPA may comfortably find a place in the pool, but even a pool comprised wholly of white candidates would not yield assurance of being admitted. In the context of how admissions decisions are actually made, it is not immediately obvious why a policy of racial diversity in terms of a pool of otherwise qualified candidates is more problematic legally than age or geographical diversity.

There is, of course, the claim that the minorities are not "otherwise qualified," that elite schools admit blacks who cannot do the work, and who drop out in high numbers, their dreams and egos shattered by the well-intentioned but misguided policies of do-gooders. This assertion might have legal weight were there any data to support it. In fact, however, blacks at Yale, Harvard, Wesleyan, and Dartmouth graduate at rates of 90 percent or higher, and close to that at other elite institutions ("The Myth That Preferential College Admissions Create High Black Student Dropout Rates," 1993).

There are implicit fallacies in many of the legal challenges to affirmative action. Those familiar with the way in which institutions actually work and the bases on which decisions are made are in a position to move the national debate away from rhetorical fictions and closer to substantive realities. Additionally, affirmative action policies, properly structured, may offer a more rational basis for decision-making than any alternative.

The conservative critique of affirmative action would base selection solely on quantitative measures, admitting students in a linear manner based on test score. This approach fails to take into account that these measures are, at best, a partial predictor of student performance during the first year. They do not predict four year graduation rates, nor ultimate career success. To the extent that affirmative action policies allow for additional factors related to background, character, and ultimate contribution to society to come into play in a broadened pool, they facilitate a more rational response to institutional interests and societal needs. To the extent that they encourage seeking out and supporting candidates who might not ordinarily be in a pool, they enable the nation to more fully use its human resources.

In a vastly more complicated and competitive world, human capital is a nation's most valuable resource. Affirmative action policies have allowed the United States to capitalize more fully on its human resources. There are many more minorities and women of talent in positions of responsibility than would have been the case had bias, traditional practices, and measures of only modest predictive value continued to impose irrational barriers. To that extent, apart from questions of equity, such policies have had beneficial consequences for the nation.

Finally, although it might appear that the defense of affirmative action betrays the historic objectives of the civil rights movement with regard to achieving a color-blind society, such is not the case. A brief comment on the career of Thurgood Marshall establishes the continuity of the civil rights argument. Marshall argued many of the classic civil rights cases outlined earlier in this chapter. He made the case again and again for an end to segregation. During the last 25 years of his career, he was an associate justice of the Supreme Court, sitting in judgment on cases challenging affirmative action policy.

Marshall saw no contradiction between his challenge to segregation and his support for affirmative action. The cases he had argued stood for the proposition that race should never be the *sole* factor excluding the individual from a public good. It did not follow that it could not be one factor among many relative to a goal of inclusion. By implication in Marshall's various holdings, if race, ethnicity, or gender were the sole factor yielding access to a scarce but desired public good, an equal protection problem would be presented. In other words, any affirmative action program having a fixed number or percentage for inclusion, other than as a remedy for prior discrimination, would raise a red flag.

Marshall's ultimate goal, and that of the civil rights movement, was inclusion on a basis of fairness. Both Marshall and the movement recognized in the *Swann* case that the "color blind" argument could be used to perpetuate segregation's irrational and unfair exclusion. Race or ethnicity as one factor among many promoting legitimate objectives such as a more rational selection of candidates for admission to a program, or of candidates more likely to serve social needs such as working with under served populations, is not equivalent to the categorical exclusion of segregation.

Race has been the source of much pain in American history. The paradox in these complicated times may be that societal interests are better served if it continues to be a limited factor in the formulation of public policy.

## REFERENCES

*Bakke v. Board of Regents*, 438 *U.S.* 265 (1978).
*Brown v. Board of Education*, 347 *U.S.* 483 (1954).
*The Civil Rights Cases of 1883*, 109 *U.S.* 3 (1883).
*Croson v. Richmond*, 57 *L.W.* 4135 (1989).
Cross, Theodore L. "The Myth That Preferential College Admissions Create High Black Student Dropout Rates," *The Journal of Blacks in Higher Education*, no. 1, Autumn 1993, 73.
*Cummings v. Board*, 175 *U.S.* 528 (1899).
*DeFunis v. Odegardd*, 416 *U.S.* 312 (1974).
*Gaines v. Canada*, 305 *U.S.* 337 (1938).
Hechinger, Fred. "Preferential Treatment for Negroes," *The Reporter*, December 3, 1964.
*Korematsu v. U.S.*, 323 *U.S.* 214 (1944).
Kull, Andrew. "The 14th Amendment That Wasn't," *Constitution*, Winter 1993.
*McCabe v. Atcheson*, 235 *U.S.* 151 (1915).
*New York Times*, February 5, 1967, 1:1, February 14, 42:6.
*North Carolina State Board of Education v. Swann*, 402 *U.S.* 43 (1971).
*Pace v. Alabama*, 106 *U.S.* 583 (1882).
*Podberesky v. Kirwan*, 956 F2d 52, 1995.
Shabazz, Malik. "Providing the Punch for the Right's Rhetoric," *Black Issues in Higher Education*, November 17, 1994.
*Steelworkers v. Weber*, 99 S.Ct, 2721 (1979).
*Sweatt v. Painter*, 339 *U.S.* 629 (1950).
"U.S. Educational Opportunity Commission," *Legislative History of Titles VII and IX of the Civil Rights Act of 1964*, Washington, D.C.: *U.S.* Government Printing Office, n.d., p. 3005.

Robert W. Ethridge

# 3
## *There Is Much More To Do*

Affirmative action has had a major impact on the way colleges and universities have endeavored to increase the diversity of the faculty, staff, and student body since Executive Order 11246 was signed by President Lyndon B. Johnson in 1965, and subsequently amended by Executive Order 11375 in 1967 and Title IX of the Education Amendments of 1972. Employment policies and procedures have changed to enable a broader spectrum of individuals to apply for positions while, concurrently, special admissions programs have been developed to increase the representation of minorities in the student body at the undergraduate, graduate, and professional levels in state-supported and private higher education institutions. Although the efforts to diversify the racial and gender composition of college and university communities are laudable, the journey has not been made without several challenges along the way.

The following chapter reviews the progress which has been made nationally, a few of the major impediments, and several of the reasons affirmative action efforts need to be enhanced if additional progress is to be made. The differences between federally supported and state supported programs will be emphasized. Selected court cases will be referenced to indicate their impact on state supported and private higher education institutions, as will statistics, to support the thesis that while affirmative action has resulted in progress in higher education, much more needs to be done.

## Background

American University Distinguished Professor of Economics Barbara Bergmann indicates in her yet-to-be published book that affirmative action and quotas are the only effective devices for reducing racial disparities in the labor market (Myers, 1995). Mitch Pearlstein, white male president of the Center of the American Experiment, argues that he was unsuccessful in his bid for an administrative position in higher education only because of affirmative action. He believes that affirmative action is bad for race relations because it produces tensions and conflicts among different races in society (Myers, 1995). Pearlstein's comments reflect the feelings of many white males who are angry because they believe their opportunities for advancement have been limited because of affirmative action programs. Those same white males assert that women and people of color have been granted jobs and higher salaries because of race or gender. Pearlstein further comments that positions are advertised in *The Chronicle of Higher Education, Black Issues in Higher Education,* and other publications encouraging women and minorities to apply. According to Pearlstein, a job announcement encouraging white males to apply would be construed as discriminatory by women and people of color; therefore, announcements encouraging women and minorities to apply conveys the message that "white males need not apply." In spite of such encouraging language in job announcements, the number of women and minorities in higher-level positions in higher education has not increased materially. Women and minorities argue that, although they are encouraged to apply, preferences for directly related experience or working knowledge of the specific policies and procedures of the institution or system prevent women and minorities from being selected. Because there are few minorities and women in the pipeline as department chairs or deans, the likelihood of any change is remote. A survey conducted by Caroline Sotello Viernes Turner of the member institutions of the Midwestern Higher Education Commission "found that 325 institutions with less than 5,000 students did not, on average, have even one minority department chair. The average number of minority department chairs at 39 institutions with more than 10,000 students was three" (Myers, 1995).

Although Executive Order 11246 was signed in 1965, the effects of the legislation were not evident until 1970, when the Labor Department issued Order No. 4, requiring government contractors with 50 employees or more and government contracts of $50,000 or more to prepare a written affirmative action program with goals and timetables. Revised Order No. 4 was issued in 1971 and applied to non-construction contractors. The order specified that goals and timetables for women and racial/ethnic minority groups must be included in a properly constructed affirmative action plan.

Early studies compared the employment statistics of government contractors to those of noncontractors. Between 1974 and 1980, employment participation of black males and females, other minority males, and white females increased significantly faster in contractor establishments than in noncontractor establishments. According to Jonathan Leonard, for example, the annual growth rate for black male employment was 0.62 percent greater in the sector covered by affirmative action than in the noncontractor sector. At the same time, the annual growth rate for white males was 0.2 percent slower among contractors than noncontractors. Thus, affirmative action shifted the demand for black males relative to white males by nearly 1 percent (0.82) per year. The annual demand shifts relative to white males for other groups in the late 1970s were higher for nonblack minority males (1.48 percent) and black females (2.15 percent), and lower but positive for white females (0.66 percent) (Leonard, 1990). These percentages indicate that contractors showed greater affirmative action progress than noncontractors.

Colleges and universities, as government contractors, attempt to employ more minority faculty and staff. According to Calvert (1979), "In the large University of California system, the percent of minority faculty members was 13 percent in 1975 (up from 11.8 per cent two years earlier) and 29 percent among career (nonteaching) staff (up from 27.6 percent years earlier). In 1976, Black and Hispanic teachers held 4.1 percent of the faculty jobs at the State University of New York." The small representation of minorities was evident in the administrative ranks as it was in the faculty ranks. In a 1975–1976 study conducted by the College and University Personnel Association, it was reported that minority males and females represented 5 percent and 2 percent, respectively, of college administrators. White males held 79 percent of the positions. Chicanos were less well represented in that, according to a 1975 study conducted by Casso and Roman, they held less than one-half of 1 percent of administrative positions (Calvert, 1979).

## The Decade of the 1970s: a Period of Change

The impact of affirmative action policies and procedures was more evident during the 1970s resulting in an increase in the representation of women and minorities on the faculties and staffs of many colleges and universities. The new concept of trying to ensure all individuals equal opportunity through affirmative action functioned effectively for a short period of time during the 1970s when it received strong support from the U.S. Supreme Court. A landmark decision was rendered in *Griggs v. Duke Power Company*, 401 U.S. 424 (1971). In that case, the Duke Power Company was administering an intelligence test to all of its applicants for employment. The test had absolutely nothing to do with the requirements of the jobs, but it did serve as a mechanism to screen out applicants. Even though the test was not a predictor of success on the job, it caused minority applicants to be screened out in disproportionately large numbers. One such applicant, Mr. Griggs, filed a complaint of race discrimination against the company because of the testing. The lower court determined that the employer had to prove that the employment practice, which was having a negative impact on minorities, was justified on the basis of "business necessity." The employer was not able to do so and lost the case. The company subsequently appealed the decision to the U.S. Supreme Court, which ruled in favor of the plaintiff and required the employer to discontinue the illegal practice and make restitution to all of its victims. This decision set the standard against which future cases would be judged.

A second landmark decision which shook the foundation of affirmative action was rendered in the case of *The Regents of the University of California v. Bakke*, 438 (1978). In that case, the university had conducted a study of the healthcare needs of the poor and minority communities locally and nationally. Based on the study, it was clear that there was an underrepresentation of minority physicians and a tremendous need for their services; therefore, the school decided to implement a special minority recruitment program to increase the number of minority doctors. The method they selected was to set aside 16 seats for minorities in each entering class. They also used different lists from which they drew the minority students to eliminate the requirement that they compete directly with white applicants. The U.S. Supreme Court determined that the university had established a quota system by setting aside a specific number of seats for minorities and by establishing different admissions criteria. Because the quota was not imposed by a court after a finding of discrimination, it was declared illegal and the practice had to cease. Although the decision did not sound the death knell for affirmative action, it weakened the program, caused many organizations to proceed much more cautiously, and increased the use of the term "reverse discrimination."

However, one year later, the Court strengthened affirmative action programs by deciding that numerical goals and timetables were legal ingredients in a voluntary affirmative action program. In the case of *United Steel Workers v. Weber*, 443 U.S. 193 (1979), the Kaiser Aluminum and Chemical Corporation and the United Steel Workers of America agreed to a plan which sought to reserve 50 percent of the slots in an in-house craft training program for black employees until the percentage of skilled crafts workers approximated their percentage in the local labor market. At the time the agreement was entered into, blacks held less than two percent of the skilled crafts positions even though they represented 39 percent of the local labor market. Under the plan, separate seniority lists were established for blacks and whites. Brian Weber, a white Kaiser employee, was not selected even though he had greater seniority than several of the black employees who were selected. He filed suit under Title VII of the Civil Rights Act of 1964. The lower courts found against him and he appealed to the United States Supreme Court. In a five to two vote, the Court decided that the plan was permissible because it was a temporary plan to eliminate a "manifest racial imbalance in traditionally segregated job categories." The Court further supported the plan because it was temporary and did not "unnecessarily trammel the interests of white employees." The decision had significant impact on higher education because it made it possible for colleges and universities to establish hiring goals based on race and/or gender to eliminate the under-representation of women and minorities in faculty and staff positions.

The decisions regarding affirmative action became less clear when the U.S. Supreme Court decided *Firefighters Local Union No. 1784 v. Stotts* (1984). The Court determined that it was legal to have an affirmative action plan but, in the event of a layoff or reduction in force, it was legal to lay off or fire the last-hired first. Such a decision was devastating because a major layoff at a company or at an institution of higher education could cause the release of many of the women and minority employees who had recently been hired through an affirmative action program. Two years later, in *Wygant v. Jackson Board of Education* 476 U. S. 267 (1986), the Court used the precedent established in *Stotts* to decide that the seniority provisions in most union contracts which require that layoffs and recalls be done on the basis of seniority could not be bargained away to preserve the gains made by the implementation of an affirmative action program. The decision was hailed by opponents of affirmative action as the end of so-called preferential programs. On the other hand, proponents of affirmative action found solace in the fact that race could be considered as one of the factors in hiring decisions. Nonetheless, the different interpretations of the decision made it more difficult to determine the outcome of other cases which were pending.

## The Decade of the '80s: A Period of Retrenchment

The 1980s proved to be even more challenging to affirmative action programs due to a series of Supreme Court decisions. In anticipation of the decisions the Supreme Court would render during the summer of 1986, the American Association for Affirmative Action, a not-for-profit association of more than 1200 professionals in the field of equal opportunity and affirmative action, conducted a roundtable discussion on the campus of Emory University in Atlanta, Georgia, in March 1986 to discuss all aspects of affirmative action, including the difference between goals and quotas. Participants included

William Bradford Reynolds, Assistant Secretary for Civil Rights; Clarence Pendleton, Chair of the U.S. Commission on Civil Rights; Leonard Biermann, Deputy Director of the Office of Federal Contract Compliance Programs; Robert Ethridge, President of the American Association for Affirmative Action; Betty Newcomb, Co-Chair of the Roundtable; Everett Winters of Southern Methodist University; Beth Wilson of the University of Oklahoma; Gazella Summitt of Vincennes University; and other selected members of the association. The discussion was lively, but Reynolds and Pendleton insisted that goals were actually quotas and were therefore illegal. They expressed confidence that the Supreme Court would decide the cases before that summer on that basis. Biermann and the members of the association expressed confidence that if the Court found that goals were flexible targets and an employer demonstrated a "good faith effort" toward achieving them, the decisions would not be detrimental to affirmative action.

The Court heard and decided the cases before it in June 1986. The first decision was in the case of *Local 28, Sheet Metal Workers v. EEOC*, 478 U.S. 421 (1986). By a four to five vote, the Court upheld the Federal District Court order reinstating a voluntary nonwhite hiring goal of 29 percent for a union that had continuously refused to admit blacks. Its opinion stated that, "A plurality of Justices held that in cases of 'persistent' or 'egregious' discrimination, Title VII does not preclude race-conscious affirmative action remedies that benefit individuals who are not themselves identified victims of discrimination" (CRS p. 13). The plurality opinion carefully noted the temporary and flexible nature of the membership goal which was to be used as a benchmark rather than a strict quota against which to measure the union's efforts. (A quota is a remedy which can be imposed by a court after a finding of discrimination.)

A second and equally important decision was rendered in *Local 93, International Association of Firefighters v. City of Cleveland* (1986). The Court decided that federal courts may approve consent decrees in which employers agree to preferential hiring of minority group members to eliminate their underutilization in specific job areas. In *Wygant v. Jackson Board of Education*, 476 U.S. 267 (1986), the Court determined that under an affirmative action plan, race could be one of the factors in an employment decision. However, the use of race or national origin classifications must be based on a compelling governmental interest and must be narrowly tailored to serve that interest. The school board and the teacher's union met the test of a narrowly tailored program for employment purposes, but both the school board and the union went too far when the agreement included provisions that protected employees from lay-off on the basis of their race (Id., p. 276, 277). The decision answered the question of whether colleges and universities could legally maintain their affirmative action gains in the event of a lay-off. The answer which was provided in the *Stotts* decision in 1984 and reaffirmed in *Wygant* in 1986 was that the last hired must be the first fired when seniority is involved.

The Court revisited the permissibility of affirmative action plans adopted under Title VII in *Johnson v. Transportation Agency of Santa Clara County, California*, 480 U.S. 616 (1987). In *Johnson*, the Court reviewed a voluntary program under which a public agency had promoted a qualified woman to road dispatcher over a somewhat-better-qualified male applicant. The agency's affirmative action plan permitted the consideration of race or gender as a factor in the promotion process, provided that there was proof of under-representation in a traditionally segregated job category. In the skilled-craft-worker category at issue in the case, women did not hold any of the 238 positions. The plan was flexible and did not include numerical quotas. The unsuccessful male applicant challenged the plan as a violation of Title VII. By a vote of six to three, the Justices ruled that the plan did not violate Title VII. Applying the Weber standard of "manifest imbalance," the Court concluded that the county agency's consideration of gender in the promotion process was a permissible way of addressing female underrepresentation. The Court also noted that the measure did not unnecessarily trample the rights of male employees nor bar their advancement (Id. 14).

Although the 1986 decisions previously referred to supported affirmative action, such was not the case in 1989. The tide changed dramatically when the Court, in *Martin v. Wilkes*, permitted firefighters in Alabama to challenge the race-conscious promotions which were being made under a bona fide consent decree. Many individuals and groups in the civil rights and affirmative action arenas were concerned that such a decision would "open the flood gates" and lead to wholesale challenges to consent decrees. That did not happen, but two decisions rendered that year caused additional challenges to affirmative action. In *Wards Cove Packing Co. v. Antonio* (1989), the Court approved using a lower standard to enable an employer to disprove an allegation of discrimination. According to the decision, all an employer had to do to defend itself against a charge of illegal discrimination was to demonstrate a business necessity for the practice which the employee deemed to be discriminatory. Unlike previous decisions, the burden of proof now shifted from the respondent to the complainant. The decision made it more difficult for an individual to prove discrimination, thereby resulting in fewer charges of discrimination.

A second decision which was harmful to affirmative action related to a minority set aside program. In the *City of Richmond v. J. A. Croson* (1989), the Court ruled that any minority set aside program must pass the close-scrutiny test to ensure that the program consisted of narrowly tailored remedies to correct identifiable past discrimination. The city council passed an ordinance requiring prime contractors doing business with the city to subcontract 30 percent of the dollar amount of each contract to minority-owned or minority-controlled businesses. The Court struck down the program on the basis that the city council had not made a strong enough case of racial discrimination in the construction industry in Richmond. Because the decision referred to affirmative action and quotas, there was a tendency on the part of opponents of affirmative action to use the decision to sound the deathknell for affirmative action. Such was not the case because the decision reemphasized the requirement that a voluntary affirmative action program must be narrowly tailored, specific, and based on identifiable past discrimination. In *Croson*, the 30 percent goal was illegal because it was higher than the availability of minority-controlled contractors in the Richmond construction industry.

Although affirmative action programs and the basic premise for affirmative action were shaken by these attacks, two new laws were passed in the 1990s which supported the rights of protected-class members. "Protected class" members include persons who are protected from discrimination on the basis of race, sex, age, color, national origin, religion, or disability. The first such law was the Americans with Disabilities Act (1990). Despite its categorization as an affirmative action law, it moved through the legislative process with great ease. One could speculate as to why Congress and the President approved the legislation so rapidly. Perhaps it was because no legislation had been passed to protect the rights of people with disabilities since the Rehabilitation Act of 1973. Perhaps it was because the legislation required taking positive action to meet the needs of people with disabilities, not "traditional" minorities or other protected classes. Or it could be that goals and timetables were not included, thereby eliminating the primary area of contention in previous affirmative action legislation. Although there may be several reasons for the introduction and subsequent passage of the legislation, the fact remains that the Americans with Disabilities Act was very broad in scope because it included public accommodations, employment, transportation, the provision of services, and a general category for miscellaneous issues not covered under the other three titles.

The second piece of civil rights legislation that was introduced in 1990 was the Civil Rights Restoration Act. The Act moved through the legislative process successfully, but was vetoed by the President. The bill was then returned to Congress for a possible override of the President's veto. Although the bill previously received a majority vote in both the House and the Senate, the override attempt failed by one vote. The bill came up again for consideration in 1991; this time, however, it included limits to the amount of punitive and compensatory damages. As a result of this change and others, the bill was passed by Congress and signed into law by the President. The effect of the new Civil Rights Act was to amend *Wards Cove* (1989) by shifting the burden of proof of discrimination back to the respondent. It also amended *Martin v. Wilkes* (1989) to prevent whites from challenging affirmative action policies to which they previously agreed. The new bill seemed to signal a legislative shift in favor of civil rights and affirmative action.

## The Decade of the 1990s: Further Retrenchment

Although affirmative action programs survived the assaults of the 1980s, they were attacked again in the 1990s. Michael Williams, Assistant Secretary of Education, issued a December 18, 1990 letter for example to the Fiesta Bowl stating that if it awarded the anticipated $100,000 Martin Luther King Scholarship to the universities of Alabama and Louisville and the universities received and administered those funds, they would be in violation of Title VI of the Civil Rights Act of 1964 which bars discrimination on the basis of race, color, or national origin. He said they would risk losing all of their federal financial aid because the scholarships were race exclusive in that they were intended for black students attending those institutions. Five years later, the Supreme Court had *Adarand Constructors v. Pena* 115 S. Ct. 2097 (1995) and *Podberesky v. Kirwan* 38 F.3d 147 (4th Cir. 1994), *cert. den.*, 115 S. Ct. 2001 (1995) on the docket. In *Adarand*, the federal government awarded a contract to construct guard rails along a stretch of highway in Denver, Colorado. Adarand, a white contractor, submitted the lowest bid, but the contract was awarded to a minority contractor, Pena. Adarand sued on the basis of race discrimination. Using the Croson decision as the precedent, the Supreme Court decided that racial classifications established by Congress must meet the same close-scrutiny standard that applies to racial classifications established by local and state governments (*Winston*, p. 2). Just as in 1989, many opponents of affirmative action declared that this was the end of the road. And their sentiments were reinforced when a second major case was placed on the U.S. Supreme Court docket in 1995. However, the Court decided not to hear the University of Maryland's appeal of the case of *Podberesky v. Kirwan*, 38 F.3d 147 (4th Cir. 1994), *cert. den.*, 115 S. Ct. 2001 (1995).

In this case, Podberesky, an Hispanic student, applied for one of the university-sponsored Benjamin Banneker scholarships. The scholarships were established specifically to increase the enrollment of outstanding black students on campus. The university also believed that the black students who were recruited through the

Banneker Scholarship program would serve as role models for other black students on campus. Additionally, as outstanding students, they would dispel the negative stereotypes many whites had about blacks. Further, the addition of the Banneker scholars would improve the climate on campus. In spite of the articulated goals of the scholarships, the specific race orientation of the program made it illegal according to the decision which was rendered by the Fourth Circuit Court of Appeals. On review, the U.S. Supreme Court let stand the decision of the Fourth Circuit by refusing to hear the case. Many interpreted the action to mean that all minority-oriented scholarships were illegal and must be discontinued. Those individuals could have based their opinion on the position on race-exclusive scholarships that was taken in December 1990 in the Fiesta Bowl incident. They might have interpreted the decision in *Adarand* to mean that race-targeted scholarships authorized by Congress were illegal. In fact, such is not the case. The Department of Education promulgated final policy guidelines in the February 23, 1994 issue of the *Federal Register* aimed at assisting colleges and universities in understanding the applicability of the statute's nondiscrimination provision to financial aid programs that are based in part on the basis of race or national origin. The following principles apply to such scholarships:

Principle 1: Financial Aid for Disadvantaged Students

"A college or university may make awards to disadvantaged students even if the awards go disproportionately to minority students"(p.8758).

Principle 2: Financial Aid Authorized by Congress

"A college may award financial aid on the basis of race or national origin if the aid is awarded under a Federal statute that authorizes the use of race or national origin"(p.8758).

Principle 3: Financial Aid to Remedy Past Discrimination

"A college may award financial aid on the basis of race or national origin if the aid is necessary to overcome the effects of past discrimination"(p. 8758).

Principle 4: Financial Aid to Create Diversity

"A college should have substantial discretion to weigh many factors—including race and national origin—in its efforts to attract and retain a student population of many different experiences, opinions, backgrounds, and cultures—provided that the use of race or national origin is consistent with the constitutional standards reflected in Title VI, i.e., that it is a narrowly tailored means to achieve the goal of a diverse student body"(p. 8758).

Principle 5: Private Gifts Restricted by Race or National Origin

"Title VI does not prohibit an individual or an organization that is not a recipient of Federal financial assistance from directly giving scholarships or other forms of financial aid to students on the basis of their race or national origin. Title VI simply does not apply"(p. 8758).

Principle 2 which states that race–targeted financial aid authorized by Congress would not violate Title VI of the Civil Rights Act of 1964, has not changed as a result of the *Adarand* decision. The decision made it clear that even racially based financial aid programs authorized by Congress must pass the close-scrutiny test when the program is reviewed by a federal court as the result of a constitutional challenge. According to *Winston* (1995), *Adarand* reaffirmed the use of race–based measures to remedy the present effects of past discrimination as a compelling governmental interest. However, the race–based measures must be narrowly tailored. *Winston* (1995) further indicates that race or national origin may be used to promote diversity in higher education (Id., p.2). Although the speculative comments about the meaning of the *Banneker* decision led many individuals in colleges and universities to believe they had to dismantle their race–based scholarship programs, the principles that were promulgated by the Department of Education provide the guidance to enable these important recruiting and retention tools to remain intact.

## The National Climate

In spite of the damaging blows affirmative action has received, it has survived as the one approach that has had a demonstrable effect on the employment status of minorities and women. One year after the implementation of the Executive Order 11246, a 1966 Bureau of Labor Statistics report indicated that women constituted 35 percent of the total labor force and blacks made up 6.5 percent. In 1980, the figures for women increased to 42 percent, blacks made up 9.4 percent, Hispanics 5.6 percent and Asians accounted for 1 percent of the labor force. By 1990, the figures for women, blacks, Hispanics and Asians had increased to 45 percent, 10 percent, 7.5 percent, and 2.6 percent respectively. The increased participation rates of these "protected classes" could have supported the argument that affirmative action had leveled the playing field and was no longer necessary.

Two additional reasons for eliminating affirmative action were cited in the May 4, 1995 issue of *Black Issues in Higher Education*. First, affirmative action benefits only middle class blacks and those prepared to become middle class, not poor blacks; and second, affirmative action is really "reverse discrimination" (*Thompson*, p. 32). A third reason which appeared in the January 17, 1995 *Congressional Research Service Report for Congress*, indicates that affirmative action's perceived preferential treatment is more important than ability (p. 25). Meritocracy, part of the foundation on which the United States of America was founded, was playing second fiddle to group racial or gender identity. A fourth reason could be that substantial increases in the number of women and minorities who will enter the work force by the year 2000 will mitigate past problems of under-representation of women and minorities in the work force. This argument suggests that if white males are to become the minority by the year 2000, they, rather than women and minorities, will need affirmative action programs to assist them in finding and retaining employment.

In the 1980s, polarization continued because conservative elements on college and university campuses complained about policies which were designed to ease racial tensions. The term "political correctness" was coined to be a pejorative term, linking it to the so-called "thought police," whose job it was to keep members of the university community from discussing controversial issues. As if these issues were not enough, David Duke, former Grand Dragon of the Ku Klux Klan, ran for governor of the State of Louisiana in 1990. He lost the election, but the fact that he received a substantial number of votes was indicative of the deplorable state of race relations at that time.

The narrow interpretations of the law by the U.S. Supreme Court during the Reagan and Bush administrations, and more recently with the *Adarand* and *Banneker* decisions, have created an anti-affirmative action tone. All of the Republicans who have announced their intention to seek the 1996 presidential nomination have taken strong stands against affirmative action. Governor Pete Wilson of California has "outlawed" affirmative action in the state government. He also chaired a meeting of the Board of Regents of the University of California system at which the board voted to eliminate affirmative action considerations in all admissions and financial aid decisions. However, the Board did interject the caveat that they would not violate any federal laws. Also, the California Civil Rights Initiative has been introduced and will be on the ballot in 1996 to eliminate affirmative action programs statewide. Today, the prevailing philosophy is one of rugged individualism or, "pulling yourself up by your bootstraps." There is a cry for all so-called "preferential programs" to end because the playing field is now level and any programs which are designed to assist women and minorities to secure better-paying jobs or move into decision-making positions are construed as nothing more than reverse discrimination. If discrimination were as rampant as some individuals allege, many more minorities and women would occupy top-level positions in companies, corporations, and universities. In fact, the converse was true. Minorities and women seemed to reach a plateau beyond which they could not rise. Because women and minorities complained about reaching a dead end in promotions, the director of the Office of Federal Contract Compliance Programs stated that she was going to study "A Report on the Glass Ceiling Initiative" to ascertain how women and minorities can break through the "glass ceiling" many of them encounter in companies and corporations.

## Diversity: Is It the Answer?

The U.S. Department of Labor has issued reports which project major demographic shifts in the work force by the year 2000. One of the most striking projections is that women will comprise 47 percent of the paid work force. In addition, approximately 450,000 legal immigrants are expected to enter this country, adding almost six million immigrants. If illegal immigrants are counted, the estimated 450,000 immigrants will increase to 750,000. According to "Work Force 2000," the majority of the new entrants into the labor force will be from groups that have been underutilized and have had labor force problems. Those new entrants, women and minorities in particular, will account for 80 percent of the net additions to the work force by the year 2000 (Department of Labor, 1985).

In addition, the average age of the labor force is expected to increase from 35 to 39 years of age. The increase in the age level is attributable to the aging of the "Baby Boomers." It is also predicted that illiteracy will continue to be a problem and that existing as well as future jobs will require higher-level analytical and quantitative skills. Increased demand for highly skilled employees will make it increasingly difficult for minimally or unskilled individuals to find employment and increased competition for business in the global marketplace will require that the nation utilize all of our human capital (Department of Labor, 1985). Excluding anyone for non-job-related reasons will prove to be more detrimental and have more economic consequences.

According to Thomas of the American Institute for Managing Diversity, the goal of managing diversity is "to get from a heterogeneous work force the same productivity, commitment, quality, and profit that we got from the old homogeneous work force" (Thomas, 1990, p. 191). Such a statement assumes that the homogeneous work force of the past was highly productive. If such had been the case, the "sudden" interest in competing in the global marketplace in order to maintain an appropriate share would not be receiving its current attention. Additionally, the idea of managing diversity without first understanding and valuing it misplaces the emphasis. Individuals who place significant interest in managing diversity may view the diversity movement as a means of eliminating affirmative action. According to some individuals, a program that depends on the good will of all parties to interact and increase the representation of "protected-class" members may be more palatable than a program that requires the use of goals and timetables to measure progress. Eliminating goals, timetables, and government enforcement virtually ensures slow or no progress in the future and signals a return to the 1980s, when enforcement by government agencies ceased.

## The Impact of Affirmative Action

Advocates state that affirmative action has opened employment opportunities for protected-class professional and blue-collar workers. Critics counter that affirmative action policies should be discontinued because they have done little to improve the economic status of those most in need and have taken attention away from their most pressing needs. Several studies have been conducted over the years to determine the impact of affirmative action.

Leonard (1990) concluded that the "impact of affirmative action on nonblack minorities and on white females has been mixed and is sensitive to the specification of the statistical test"(p. 385). He also studied the impact of the contract-compliance program on employment changes by testing across occupations. He concluded that for black males who made the greatest overall gains, there was a pro skill bias:

> The contract compliance program has not reduced the demand for black males in low-skilled occupations. It has raised the demand for black males in the highly skilled professional and technical occupations and in white-collar clerical jobs than in the blue-collar operative and laborer occupations (p.131–132).

Leonard's findings indicate that black males benefited at all levels, but the highly skilled individuals benefited the most. He also found increased demand for black women across white-collar and blue-collar occupations and in training programs and increased demand for Hispanic, Asian and Native American males in white-collar occupations and training programs. For reasons which Leonard has not been able to explain, white women did not share in the employment gains. Moreover, he had no information on the gains of non black minority women because they were not included in the study. In spite of the study's limitations, Leonard did conclude that "with the puzzling exception of white females, affirmative action appears to have contributed to the occupational advance of members of protected groups" (p. 135).

Four authors of earlier studies analyzed Equal Employment Opportunity (EEO) data from 1966-1973 and found a significant positive relationship between contractor status and black male employment. While this finding was similar to Leonard's, these studies did not support Leonard's statistics with respect to the employment status of black women. They also found no evidence that any group made significant advances under the contract-compliance program. Only one study found compliance reviews to be helpful in advancing any group covered by the contract-compliance program. Leonard explained the differences by indicating that the studies were conducted prior to the time of vigorous contract-compliance reviews:

> These past studies are all based on data for a period that largely predates the beginning of substantial enforcement of regulations barring sex discrimination, the start of aggressive enforcement in the mid seventies, and the major reorganization of the contract compliance agencies into the OFCCP in 1978 (p. 264).

James P. Smith and Finis Welch conducted a study of employment effects over the 14-year period from 1966–1980 using EEO reports and data from the Current Population Survey. They concluded that an affirmative action program which is effective and adequately enforced should increase the representation of minorities more at organizations that report to the Equal Employment Opportunity Commission (EEOC) than at those that do not. Furthermore, they expected the gains at organizations that are government contractors and therefore required to report on the EEO form to be more substantial than those that do not have to report because they have more to lose as government contractors (Smith and Welch, 1984). In the "Officials and Managers" category, Smith and Welch found that over the 14-year period, the percentage of black employees, males in particular, increased more at EEOC-covered institutions than at non-EEOC-covered institutions. The gains for black women during that same time frame at EEOC-covered institutions were greater than for black males. Smith and Welch also found that the greatest increase in black employment occurred between 1966 and 1970, although the growth from 1970 through 1974 slowed somewhat. These results were surprising because EEOC and the Office for Federal Contract Compliance Programs (OFCCP) had limited resources and enforcement authority (Smith and Welch, 1984).

In view of the progress that was made at a time when the two main enforcement agencies had minimal authority and resources, it can be assumed that the positive climate which led to the passage of the Civil Rights Act of 1964 also caused employers to move vigorously toward implementing affirmative action programs. By the end of the 1970s, organizations covered by affirmative action increased the representation of minority employees by 20 percent, approximately twice the increase of nongovernment contractors. Women also fared well during the 1970s. Their employment increased by 15 percent among government contractors as compared to approximately 2 percent for noncontractors. There were large increases in the employment of women and minority fire fighters, and sheet metal and electrical workers (*Washington Post*, June 20, 1983, p. A3). Both middle-class and working class women, and minority group members benefited from affirmative action during this decade.

Whereas the decade of the 1970s saw progress in the increase in employment of women and minorities, the decade of the 1980s can be viewed as a period of major retrenchment. The Reagan and Bush administrations took a "hands-off" approach to affirmative action and virtually eliminated any sanctions to government contractors that did not meet their affirmative action requirements. Both Presidents Reagan and Bush demonstrated how the lack of presidential leadership can render an effective program ineffective. It was common knowledge in many circles that President Reagan had a new executive order on his desk that would modify Executive Order 11246, as amended, so extensively that it would be ineffective. The possibility of such action on the part of the

President confirmed his intent to eliminate affirmative action. Civil rights and affirmative action advocacy groups launched a letter-writing campaign to convince the President and Congress that Executive Order 11246, as amended, should not be replaced by the order that the President contemplated signing. The large volume of letters the President and Congress received convinced President Reagan that he should not risk his political career by signing the proposed executive order which would repeal the existing executive order. The campaign was successful.

Executive Order 11246, as amended, provided the framework for affirmative action. However, Order No. 4 and Revised Order No. 4, promulgated in 1970 and 1971 respectively by the Department of Labor, provided the specifics of implementation. One aspect of implementation, the use of compliance reviews, increased during the 1980s. However, other sanctions such as debarment, back-pay awards, affected class findings and administrative complaint filings were not often used in the 1980s. During the Carter presidency, debarment—declaring a contractor ineligible for government funds—was used 13 times. During the Reagan and Bush administrations, debarment was used only four times by each. As for using back-pay awards as an additional device to cause contractors to comply, "The Reagan administration's opposition to back-pay awards resulted in a decline in such awards from $9.2 million in FY 1980 to $1.9 million in FY 1986" (OFCCP Quarterly Review and Analysis Reports, 1994, p. 2). Not only was the enforcement authority of the Office of Federal Contract Compliance Programs diminished, but the agency's budget was reduced. A report of the U.S. Commission on Civil Rights reported that "measured in 1980 dollars, the OFCCP's budget appropriation fell from $53 million in FY 1980 to $33 million in FY 1986, and its authorized full-time employment fell from 1,454 to 906" (from U.S. Civil Rights Commission, Federal Enforcement of Equal Employment Requirements, July 1987).

During the Reagan-Bush assault on affirmative action, college-educated black males lost ground with respect to salaries. In 1967, the median salary for college-educated black males working full-time was 67 percent of that of their white male counterparts. In 1979, the median salary had increased to 81 percent of that of their white male counterparts. However, in 1992, the median salary had dropped to 74 percent, due in great measure to the assault on affirmative action

(U.S. Bureau of the Census, 1992, p. 60). According to Newsnotes of the National Committee on Pay Equity, college-educated black and Hispanic males earn $7,324 and $10,430 less per year respectively than their white-male counterparts. Black and Hispanic women fare no better, earning $12,873 and $15,984 less respectively than their white-male counterparts. Even white males with no college education earn $2,717 more than college-educated women. College-educated white men earn $11,667 more than college-educated women (Winter 1994). According to the Bureau of Labor statistics for 1993, female managers earned 33 percent less than male managers, female college professors earned 23 percent less than male professors, female information clerks earned 15 percent less than male information clerks, and female elementary school teachers earned 22 percent less than male elementary school teachers (Newsnotes/Winter 1994, p. 6). Additional information about the status of women and minorities as compared to that of white men is available in Newsnotes/ Winter 1994 by the National Committee on Pay Equity. The information in the publication makes it very clear that women and minority-group members do not enjoy the same employment status and wages as their white-male counterparts.

As previously indicated, white males, regardless of level of education, fared better with respect to employment and wages than did women or members of minority groups. A comparison of the race/ethnicity and gender of the faculty at institutions of higher education in 1981 and 1991 is most revealing. Such a comparison is included in the *Thirteenth Annual Status Report of Minorities in Higher Education*, by Carter and Wilson. In 1981, men constituted 73.2 percent of the faculty and women constituted 26.8 percent. Ten years later, representation of men changed to 68.2 percent and that of women changed to 31.8 percent. A closer look at the details of the figures for men and women shows that white men (non-Hispanic) constituted 90.7 percent of the males in 1981 and 87.7 percent in 1991. White women constituted 88.4 percent of the women faculty in 1981 and 86.5 percent in 1991. The change for men and women from 1981 to 1991 was 3.8 percent and 32.2 percent, respectively. The percentage of change for all faculty was 11.4 percent for the same 10-year period.

In 1981, the representation of minority faculty was 9.3 percent. In 1991, it increased to 12.3 percent. The increase during the decade represented a 48.6-percent change. Minority men experienced a 46.3-percent change from 8.4 to 11.8 percent. Minority women experienced a 53.0-percent change, from 11.6 to 13.5 percent. The representation of African American faculty showed an increase of 25.1 percent, from 4.2 to 4.7 percent. Of the remaining minority groups, Asian Americans showed the largest increase of 78.3 percent, from 3.2 percent in 1981 to 4.7 percent in 1991. Hispanics showed the next largest increase of 57.6 percent, from 1.6 percent in 1981 to 2.2 percent in 1991. Native Americans showed the smallest percentage increase of 15.7 percent, but their representation on the faculty was 0.3 percent in 1981 and in 1991 (Carter and Wilson, 1994, p. 88).

In higher education, scholarship assistance has made it possible for individuals with insufficient funds to attend colleges or universities. Scholarships traditionally have been awarded based on financial need. Financial need, however, was not the only reason higher educational institutions granted scholarships. Other scholarship programs were designed to increase the diversity of the student body and to redress discrimination based on racial and gender biases. Richard F. Rosser, President of the National Association of Independent Colleges and Universities, addressed the importance of minority-oriented scholarships in a news release which responded to the December 1990 letter from Michael Williams, Assistant Secretary of Education, prohibiting minority-oriented scholarships. In his news release, Rosser spoke against such a prohibition because the new regulations Williams proposed would effectively dismantle most of the effective affirmative-action programs used by 90 percent of private colleges and universities to create diversity on campuses. He went on to state that, "Private colleges and universities each year award 16,000 minority scholarships, generally based on financial need or merit. These scholarships constitute less than 3 percent of the $4 billion of aid given by private colleges and universities to students each year, but are extremely important in encouraging minorities to attend college and graduate school" (p. 2).

Because many institutions award scholarships after students have been admitted, special admissions programs were developed to attract women and minority students to undergraduate, graduate, and professional schools. One such program was developed at

Rutgers following the race riots of the 1960s in Newark. The Rutgers Law School Minority Student Program includes a special admissions process, orientation program, and support services. This one program has changed the face of the New Jersey bar (National Women's Law Center, 1995, p. 2). Programs like the Banneker Scholarship program at the University of Maryland have increased black enrollment and improved the racial climate on campus. The black students who are recruited by such programs serve as positive role models for black and white students alike. They also debunk the stereotypes others have of blacks. The race-neutral and need-based scholarships offered by the university have not been successful in achieving such ends (ibid., p. 2). Blacks are not the only individuals for whom special scholarships have been established. Numerous scholarships have been established to attract women to male-dominated fields such as science, biological and biomedical science, engineering, math, and computer science. Gender-based scholarships and other support programs have increased the representation of women in many typically male-dominated fields. Need-based scholarships alone could not have been successful in achieving such ends (ibid., p. 2). According to Rosser (1991), "The symbolic importance of the scholarships and the financial aid itself have helped private four-year colleges and universities enroll a slightly higher percentage of minorities (18.2 percent) than similar public institutions (17.8 percent)" (p. 2). Minority and women-oriented admissions and financial-aid programs are particularly important because a large number of scholarships are awarded to children of major donors, alumni, or other friends of the institution. Women and minorities typically are excluded from such a list of eligibility. Unless the need-based criteria are changed to ensure the inclusion of women and minorities, and the special category for children of alumni and benefactors is eliminated, special programs such as the ones previously indicated will be necessary. Eliminating the programs now will cause the enrollment of women and minorities to decrease below their present levels. Such decreases would make it very difficult for colleges and universities to actualize their commitment to achieving a diverse student body which, in turn, will result in a diverse faculty.

## Equity in the Future: Summary and Conclusions

If the past can be used to predict the future, issues of equity for women and minority group members will not disappear. The probability is that the changing demographics that are predicted for the year 2000 will exacerbate the problems referred to earlier in this chapter. If future efforts in this country are directed toward having the same homogeneous work force that purportedly was so productive in the past, significant numbers of women, minority-group members and individuals with disabilities will be denied the opportunity to be employed to their capacity. Failing to systematically include them will impede the nation's ability to successfully compete in the global marketplace.

The failure to address issues of equality will have a devastating effect on women who will continue to be discriminated against in terms of both wages and level of positions. The studies referenced earlier in this chapter seem to indicate that the white male power structure thwarts women's efforts to rise to decision-making levels. The "glass ceiling" is a fact for women, verified by many studies. If equity is to be achieved, intervention through legal means seems to be the most effective method. The legal means is already in place in the form of affirmative action policies and procedures. When enforced properly in the past by federal agencies, the representation of women and minorities increased. Conversely, gains decreased or stopped totally when the vigorous enforcement, or threat of enforcement, stopped during the 1980s.

Study after study shows that affirmative action programs, when properly conceived and implemented, have been effective in increasing the representation of women and minorities and those increases have been made without causing undue personal or financial hardship to white males. In fact, there are very few bona fide cases of so-called "reverse discrimination." Further, the assertions that affirmative action has benefited only middle-class blacks distort the purpose of affirmative action: open doors for qualified or qualifiable minorities, women, and other protected class members to positions which previously were denied to them. It follows that college-educated minorities and women, sometimes referred to as middle class, would be the most immediate beneficiaries of such a program because their qualifications enabled them to participate successfully in such a program. If training programs were implemented through an affirmative action program to prepare unqualified individuals for employment opportunities, the entire debate about who benefits would be moot. Rather than engaging in debates about who has benefited most or least from affirmative action, the program needs to be expanded to include more protected-class members who could benefit from a job or enhanced skills that allow them to move into higher-level positions.

Several organizations around the country have developed programs for individuals who are unlikely to benefit from traditional affirmative action programs, but lack of funds continually limits their efforts. One such agency is Community Friendship, Inc. (CFI). CFI in Atlanta assists homeless individuals with mental problems through the Work Opportunity Program. Upon completion of the program, Work Opportunity clients are hired by CFI or other employers who support the program. The clients typically assume entry-level positions, but more than one has expressed an interest in moving into a more responsible position. And those clients have indeed earned promotions.

Unless and until more is done to educate the general public about what affirmative action is and is not, unscrupulous politicians and others will continue to misrepresent the facts. Rather than engaging in substantive activities to broaden the scope of affirmative action programs, we will find ourselves 30 years hence defending the program. Until female and minority representation increases in the student bodies of our colleges and universities, as well as at all levels of the faculty and administration, the need for affirmative action will continue. As long as the "good-old-boy network" continues to grant preference to other "good old boys," affirmative action programs will be necessary to counteract its effect. If preferences were actually being granted to women, people of color and individuals with disabilities, as the opponents of affirmative action claim, there would be many more women and people of color on boards of directors, teaching on college and university faculties at the senior levels, serving as presidents of colleges and universities, running major companies and corporations, and holding decision-making positions in more of our major income-generating enterprises. The current wage gaps based on race and gender would not exist. The gains that have been made by women and minorities through vigorous enforcement of affirmative action legislation will stop or decrease just as they did in the 1980s if affirmative action is "retired." Now that the gains from affirmative action are becoming more obvious, it would be ill-advised to discontinue the program—especially when no viable alternative has been offered.

Affirmative action—management by objectives if you will—must be permitted to move into the next phase, which is called upward mobility. Monitoring promotional decisions to ensure that subjectivity does not result in discrimination against individuals or classes of people because of race, gender, or disability will be even more important in the future than it was in the past. In spite of 30 years of affirmative action, equity has not been achieved in this country because the playing field is still not level. A fine-tuning of affirmative action may be necessary, but that is precisely what the American Association for Affirmative Action is doing as it conducts a series of training programs for new and experienced affirmative action officers. The training enables the officers to develop greater expertise in interpreting the applicable laws and statutes and then applying them in their everyday work. The time is not right to give affirmative action a "gold watch" to signal the end of its usefulness after 30 years. Clearly, there is much more to do.

## REFERENCES

*Adarand Constructors Inc. v. Pena*, U.S. Sup Ct., No. 93–1841, LW 1185, June 13, 1995.
Bruno, A. (1995). Affirmative action in employment. Congressional Research Service.
Calvert, R., Jr. (1979). *Affirmative action: A comprehensive recruitment manual*. Garrett Park Press, Garrett Park, MD.
Casso, H. J., and Gilbert, D. (1975). *Chicanos in higher education*. University of New Mexico Press.
*City of Richmond, VA v. J.A. Croson Co.*, 488 U.S. 109 Ct. 706 (1989).
*Firefighters Local Union No. 1784 v. Stotts* (1984).

Glasser, I. (1988). Affirmative action and the legacy of racial injustice. In Katz, P. A., and Taylor, D. A. (Eds.) *Eliminating Racism*. New York. Plenum Press.

*Griggs v. Duke Power Company*, 401 U.S. 424 (1971).

Institute for Policy Research and Education. (1995). *The attack on affirmative action: A racist diversion from solving America's true problems*. Leonard, J.

*Johnson v. Transportation Agency of Santa Clara County, CA.*, 480 U.S. 616 (1987).

*Kirwan v. Podberesky*, 38FF.3d 147 (4th Cir. 1994), *Cert. Den.*, 115 S. Ct. 2001 (1995).

Leonard, J. (1990). The impact of affirmative action: Regulation and equal employment law on Black employment. *Journal of Economic Perspectives*. 4(4) 47–64.

*Local 28, Sheet Metal Workers v. EEOC*, 478 U.S. 421 (1986).

Martin, L. (1991). A report on the glass ceiling initiative. U.S. Labor Department, U.S. Government Printing Office.

Minority Business Enterprise Legal Defense & Education Fund, Inc. (1995). Exploding the big lie: The truth about affirmative action. (Position Paper).

Myers, S. L., (1995). Affirmative action in higher education. Whites go on the offensive. Emerge, 6(9), 48–52.

Nondiscrimination in federally assisted programs; Title VI of the Civil Rights Act of 1964; Notice of final policy guidance, 59 Fed. Reg. 36, 8756–87762 (1994).

Robinson, G. M. (1995). The challenge of social change: A historical analysis of affirmative action. Unpublished research paper, Michigan State University, Lansing.

Rosser, R. F. (1991). Response to Office for Civil Rights' release of proposed regulations on minority scholarships.

Semerad, R. D., (1990). Workforce 2000. U.S. Labor Department. Employment & Training Administration.

Smith, J. P. and Welch, F. (1984). Affirmative action and labor markets. *Journal of Labor Economics*. 2, p. 276.

Thompson, G. L. (1995). Affirmative action: Reverse discrimination? *Black Issues in Higher Education* 4, 32-34.

Thomas, R. R. (1990). From affirmative action to affirming diversity. *Harvard Business Review*, March\April, 191.

*United Steel Workers of America, AFL-CIO and Kaiser Aluminum & Chemical Corporation v. Weber, et. al.* 443 U.S. 193 (1979).

*University of California Regents v. Bakke*, 438 U.S. 265, 407 (1978).

*Wards Cove Packing Co. v. Atonio*, 490 U.S. 642 (1989).
Williams, M. L. (1990). Letter to Fiesta Bowl concerning illegality of race-based scholarships.
Winston, J. A. (1990). Equality, Diversity and Opportunity. Civil rights and affirmative action in the 1990s. Keynote address of the 17th Annual Conference of the American Association for Affirmative Action, Los Angeles, California.
Winston, J. A. (1995). Letter to college and university legal counsel to confirm that the Department of Education's policy guidance on race-targeted student financial aid has not changed as a result of the U.S. Supreme Court's decision in *Adarand Constructors v. Pena* or the Supreme Court's decision not to hear the University of Maryland's appeal in *Podberesky v. Kirwan*.

Linda Flores and Alfred A. Slocum

# 4
## *Affirmative Action: A Path Towards Enlightenment*

Affirmative action, torn, tattered and tethered, now little more than a mere shadow of its former presence, may well face its death knell. After some 25 years of experimentally confronting almost 400 years of racial discrimination and gender bias, it is unlikely that a fresh new crop of minorities will enter the academy or the ranks of skilled professions, craft guilds, apprenticeships, and small businesses (*Adarand Constructors, Inc. et al. v. Pena*, 1995).

Governor Pete Wilson of California has abolished all affirmative action programs within the state (American Council on Education, 1995). It is proposed that access to higher education in California be based solely on test scores and grade-point averages.[1] No other factors are to be considered despite concerns about test reliability. At the national level, the so-called "Contract with America" of the Republican Party (which now controls both the House and the Senate) calls for the end of affirmative action as a wrong-headed liberal Democratic experiment. President Bill Clinton himself gives faint praise to affirmative action when he argues "mend it, but don't end it" (American Council on Education, 1995). Thus, affirmative action now lies gasping on fallow ground, the unfortunate victim of its own success. We examine the beneficial fruits of this now-poisoned tree with the hope, quite frankly, of resuscitating the debate on its appropriateness.

Recently, a great deal of time, money, and energy were spent in an attempt to influence the nation's judgment on the appropriateness of entering into the General Agreement on Trade and Tariffs (GATT) and the North American Free Trade Agreement (NAFTA) international business accords. The issues were hotly debated, but when all was said and done, and the accords had been signed and the matters had been put to rest, it became apparent that the decisions had been based on something other than the facts. In truth, there simply was no factual data available on the issues presented. We, as a nation, had been asked to make a leap of faith. No such leap is necessary, however, when it comes to affirmative action. But while the field is replete with data, apparently it is not a welcome harvest. For the debate over affirmative action all too often centers on unfounded yet highly appealing negative assumptions. This chapter aims to give short shrift to these assumptions and to set the facts of affirmative action squarely on the table in an effort to demonstrate that, in its relatively short life, affirmative action has harmed few, served many, and continues to benefit us all.

The most frequently heard assumption about affirmative action is that for every preference given, someone is denied a benefit to which he or she is entitled and therefore becomes a victim of "reverse discrimination." This is clearly not the case. Ample opportunity is provided through the courts and administrative procedures to redress grievances alleging discrimination in any form. Yet, relatively few claims alleging reverse discrimination have actually been filed. More significantly, however, is the fact that only a minuscule number of reverse-discrimination claims have been determined to warrant relief (Blumrosen, 1995).

The term "reverse discrimination" is almost as old as the concept of affirmative action itself, and it has served to promote—sometimes subtly, and at other times overtly—the notion that all affirmative action, by its very nature, must wrongly injure someone. While almost all benefits discriminate, in that they bypass some and not others, being bypassed is not the same as being wrongly discriminated against. The graduated income tax is an obvious example: Those earning lesser incomes are given the benefit of a lower tax rate, which incidentally increases the burden carried by those with higher incomes. This is but one of myriad examples of incidental discrimination which go unquestioned and unchallenged by the American public. Clearly, it is only wrong to target a group for discrimination without justifying the resultant benefit to society, particularly when the targeted group is a constitutionally protected class. If there is no resulting benefit, such discrimination cannot be justified. But, an analysis of the benefit side of the distribution equation does not put an end to the panoply of unjustifiable assumptions surrounding affirmative action.

Race as the basis for bestowing preferential benefits on a class to remedy past discrimination has been attacked as woefully unfair because individual class members, it is argued, may never have felt the sting of racial discrimination—at least not at the hand of those who may suffer as non-class members. Consider the academy. Racial preferences as a factor considered in professional school admissions allows all members of the racial class to obtain the benefit simply as a consequence of their race, even though they may have benefited from an upper-middle-class life. The argument contends that this is wrong simply because they are not disadvantaged, that is, as individuals they have not been the victims of past racial discrimination. Clearly, this is not the case.

It is no secret that, through slavery, the very foundations of this country embodied the concept of woefully disparate treatment solely as a consequence of race. All blacks—and no one but blacks—were brought here as slaves; they were all treated similarly. They were forced to exist under the absolute worst of circumstances. The consequential damage to the class of blacks that endured such treatment is immeasurable, and however great the inflicted injuries, they were imposed on the class (*Scott v. Sanford,* 1857; The Civil Rights Cases, 1883; *Plessy v. Ferguson,* 1896). Consequently, the remedy for such class injuries must be made available to all class members. Since the injury was a class injury, the remedy must therefore be a class remedy as well (Kinoy, 1967).

However, the Court's recent decision in *Adarand* denies this reality. Stating that the Fourteenth Amendment speaks to individuals, not groups, the Court determined that since race-based mandates are group classifications, they do not fall within the purview of the Fourteenth Amendment (*Adarand Constructors, Inc. et al. v. Pena,* 1995). The effect of this determination is to severely limit Congressional power to compel conduct in furtherance of a perceived governmental need.

This is the work of an overzealous Court which insists upon viewing the Fourteenth Amendment in isolation, rather than as a natural extension of the Thirteenth Amendment. As the first of the Wartime Amendments, the Thirteenth Amendment abolished slavery and all of its "badges and incidents" (U.S.Constitution, amend. 13). Congress is thus authorized to assure the mandate. Indeed, the Thirteenth Amendment covers even private actions of race discrimination unlike the Fourteenth, which employs the all-too-familiar language "nor shall any state deny to any person the equal protection of the laws" (U.S. Constitution, amend. 14, sec. 1).

The easy question then becomes whether the badges and incidents of slavery were in fact race-based. Whites, whatever their station, were not permitted to serve as slaves; at worst they were indentured servants for a term and not for life as was the lot of slaves. The distinction between the two was justified by the allegation of "Negro inferiority" (*Scott v. Sanford*, 1857). Race alone was the dispositive factor, and it was universally applied. The notion of so-called "Negro inferiority" is slow to die. It surfaces periodically to the exaltation of some and the chagrin of others. Is it really conceivable that the Fourteenth Amendment bars group protection, and as a consequence, race-based Congressional remedies? Is the Fourteenth Amendment just another example of Congressional ineffectiveness or, more likely, is the Fourteenth Amendment an extension of the Thirteenth requiring the elimination of slavery's race-based residue? The historical evidence points unerringly to the latter, providing ample support for affirmative initiatives designed to undo the legacy of slavery (Kinoy, 1967).

So, race-based affirmative action efforts do have a basis in the Constitution. How these efforts bestow benefits upon others who are not members of the targeted class is the purpose of this chapter. To do so, we return briefly to the GATT and NAFTA accords where the debate was prospective, focusing on what might happen. An interesting aspect of the GATT and NAFTA debate centered upon why the accords as an untested venture were likely to work. Proponents of the accords were not certain why they worked, but they were absolutely certain that they do, simply because of diversity in production and market expansion. In support of this contention the development of the modern automobile industry was reviewed.

Detroit's Big Three domination of the automobile industry from the early 1920s through the very early 1970s began with assembly line innovations which launched a dynasty, and ended with a distinct brand of Detroit chrome styling and monstrous horsepower. Automobiles were produced on a "take-it-or-leave-it" basis, with limited liability on the part of manufacturers. Automobile markets, at that time, were basically provincial. The huge gas-guzzling "Detroit Iron" was suitable for the concrete-clad roadways of an expansive American landscape, but it was relatively worthless in most foreign markets, where both gasoline prices and terrain were ill-suited to the excesses of the American automobile. Reliability only meant the car would probably get you where you were going, unless you had accumulated 65,000 miles of road use, at which point the vehicle was ready for recycling in the used steel markets. Enter the Japanese and the entire automobile scene was never to be the same again. Engine size decreased; gas mileage increased; performance improved; selection increased; markets expanded, losing their provinciality; and reliability became the watch word of the day, extending the expected life of the automobile to well over 100,000 miles. In response, the automobile industry—including Detroit's Big Three—improved dramatically as diversity entered the manufacturing process. The general principle at work here is a simple one: Diversity benefits everyone. Increase the size of the pool and expand the criteria from which you draw and, all other factors being equal, the outcome of the operation will be significantly improved.

There are many other examples in such areas as professional sports and the arts where exclusiveness has given way to diversity with dramatic results and impressive track records. Surely, the automobile industry was only one of several examples of the benefits of diversity that could have been promoted by the supporters of GATT and NAFTA. In fact, we contend that the benefits of diversity, achieved through affirmative action, to the nation as a whole and to individuals who are not members of the target population are so significant and dramatic that affirmative action could have successfully been substituted for the automobile industry in the arguments to bolster support for GATT and NAFTA.

Affirmative action initiatives were designed to incorporate previously disenfranchised groups into the body politic in an effort to reverse racial discrimination in this country which has endured hundreds of years of struggle. Since higher education has served as the engine for dismantling the status quo, it is useful to examine what higher education has wrought over these 30 years of affirmative action efforts in specific areas. To that end, we will look at higher education itself, but we will also examine those areas that have been affected by the beneficiaries of the higher educational process. Accordingly, this chapter will explore the nature of the benefits derived from affirmative action for those who are not members of the target population in the labor market, higher education, and the economy. In each of these areas, we outline the prevailing conditions preceding the advent of affirmative action, discuss in some detail the affirmative action mechanisms employed, and then critique the particular enterprise under review in its present posture by measuring the positive effects, if any, of affirmative action.

## Labor

The big issues in labor prior to the 1960s centered on the collective-bargaining process and those organizational rights deemed essential to counterbalance the one-sided aspects of the labor-management relationship of the pre-Depression era. Shortly after the Great Depression and in some measure because of it, Congress enacted one of the most significant pieces of present-day federal legislation, the National Labor Relations Act (1935). More commonly known as the Wagner Act, the Act attempted to place labor and management on equal footing by guaranteeing employees the right to form labor organizations, to address the terms and conditions of their employment through such organizations, and to engage in concerted activities in furtherance of those rights. Those rights were effectuated by establishing a number of unfair labor practices. The National Labor Relations Board (NLRB) occupied center stage, a creature of legislative authority, empowered to enforce unfair labor practices and representational provisions of the Act. The Act was subsequently fine-tuned in 1947 by the Taft-Hartley Act and again in 1959 by the Landrum-Griffin Act, amendments which successively expanded worker freedom. Significantly, the Taft-Hartley amendments contained the first restrictions on union activities, notably the proscription against the closed-shop agreement which required employers to hire only union members. The Landrum-Griffin amendments, passed on the eve of the civil rights era, focused on the undemocratic conduct of unions in their internal affairs by providing for a bill of rights for union members. Thus, in three major legislative cycles spanning some 25 years, Congress struggled to strike a balance of power between the forces of labor and management (Morris, 1971).

Within the ranks of labor, however, social issues were affecting the most fundamental aspect of the work force that this federal legislation did not address and for which there was no hue and cry. To begin with, racial discrimination was rampant. Blacks and Hispanics often were denied membership in the union, thereby depriving them of significant job opportunities.

While one of the unfair labor practices set forth in the Taft-Hartley Act was an employer's interference with a worker's effort to join or organize a union, it was clear that Congress was concerned with the delicate balance that existed between its perception of the real parties at issue. No language addressed the possibility, indeed the likelihood, of union discrimination against segments of the rank and file, with the major exception being the noncommunist-affiliation requirements that were imposed on union officers. Consequently, the manner in which the rank and file were treated by the union hierarchy mirrored the social pecking order of the day—slavish adherence to both racial and class distinctions (*N.L.R.B. v. Local 106, Glass Bottle Blowers*, 1975; *N.L.R.B. v. Mansion House Center Management Corp.*, 1973; *Peterson v. Rath Packing Co.*, 1972; *Brotherhood of R.R. Trainmen v. Howard*, 1952; *Steele v. Louisville & Nashville R.R.*, 1944).

Moreover, nepotism within the union's ranks was all too prevalent. Not only did hiring personnel employ their own relatives, but point systems were created which served to increase the possibilities of employment for those applicants who were related to workers already on the job. The role this practice played is obvious: It served to preserve the status quo regardless of who was doing the hiring.

Similarly, although hiring criteria were imposed for all jobs, those criteria were often unrelated to the job requirements (*Sprogis v. United Air Lines, Inc.* 1971; *Laffey v. Northwest Airlines, Inc.*

1983; *AirLine Pilots Assoc., Internat'l et al. v. United Air Lines, Inc.*, 1979). For example, to be an airline stewardess, the criteria were "young, female and attractive." This meant that no males could serve in this capacity; unattractive women had no chance; older women could forget about it; and even attractive young women knew that their term of employment would be short-lived. This job was hardly a career, for a career carries with it at least the hope, if not the expectation, of longevity. Moreover, what was offered was offered to a limited few.

Another example is the police academy. In New York City, for example, in addition to standardized test scores, the criteria for employment on the police force included height requirements. This requirement was challenged by Puerto Rican residents on the grounds that Puerto Ricans tended to be shorter than others, and virtually all Puerto Ricans were shorter than the criteria imposed. In effect, the height criterion served to exclude all Puerto Ricans from the police force (*Guardians Ass'n of the NYC Police Dept., Inc. et al v. Civil Service Commission of the City of NY*, 1977). In this pre-affirmative action era, the result was not surprising. The City of New York could hire whomever it pleased, and conversely refuse to hire all others who fell outside its rather arbitrary criteria.

Despite its laissez-faire approach to matters of union hiring and promotion, neither Congress nor the judiciary entirely shied away from issues of race. Congress had effectively addressed the racial question in the armed forces, housing, public accommodations, employment, and certainly voting rights (The Civil Rights Act, 1964). It was Congress that had expressed the view that past racial discrimination ought to be dealt with affirmatively.

It was in this setting that a blockbuster of a decision handed down by the United States Supreme Court burst on the labor landscape in a manner destined to alter the nation's work force from its pursuit of the status quo like no other single event in American history. To the extent that *Plessy v. Ferguson* (1896) had its *Brown v. Board of Education* (1954) and *Swift v. Tyson* (1842) had its *Erie v. Thompkins* (1937), the status quo had its *Griggs v. Duke Power and Light Co.* (1971)—and eclipsed them all. It was a stunning victory for those seeking to alter significantly the status quo and provide greater access to the work force for all.

The Duke Power and Light Company, a North Carolina utility, established hiring criteria which included the completion of a high school education. It did so with the full and certain knowledge that no blacks residing in the area from which the utility might reasonably expect to obtain its work force had achieved this level of education. Consequently, no blacks were eligible for employment. Suit was brought against the utility alleging racial discrimination because of the disparate impact the criterion had on blacks, even though requiring a high school education was racially neutral on its face.

The Court in *Griggs* determined that, unless the employer could show a legitimate business purpose or a rational relationship between the employment criterion and the task to be performed, a disproportionate impact on a protected class, in this instance race, would render the hiring criteria racially discriminatory. As a consequence of the utility's wrongful conduct, the Court mandated an affirmative plan to remedy the effects of past discrimination.

In trial courts throughout the country racial minorities who had been ostracized from craft unions, limited in hiring and promotion opportunities, and in general relegated to the most menial and laborious tasks, lay claim to a preferred right to redress these past abuses simply by pointing to practices having a "disproportionate impact" on blacks and other racial groups. That decision significantly altered the relationship between the employer and the rank and file. It now appeared that hiring and promotion had become a nondelegable duty. Employers could no longer play Pontius Pilate. They now found themselves confronting a new science in the business of hiring and promoting—psychometrics. Employers had to either reevaluate their hiring and promotion criteria in light of the tasks to be performed or risk a series of lawsuits alleging discrimination. The American work force would never look the same again. The uninterrupted continuum of the status quo work force had been broken.

Desegregation of the work force began in earnest because many employers were vulnerable to the disparate-impact claim. Prior to the 1960s, it was no secret that there were "white men's jobs" and "black men's jobs." And the jargon made no mention of women, who at that time constituted some 30 percent of the nation's work force (Bureau of the Census, 1995). So it is interesting to look at the two examples provided—airline stewardesses and police officers—because prior to affirmative action both positions were gender-based and regarded by most to be racially discriminatory. The police, however, were a little better than firemen, who justified their racial policies with the statement, "After all we have to sleep together."

However, after the Griggs decision, police departments were placed under siege. The number of lawsuits brought alleging discrimination in hiring and promotion and seeking an affirmative action plan to remedy the situation were legion. Many large cities, particularly those subjected to "white flight," now enjoyed black leadership and many were willing to attack the issue head on. They developed affirmative action plans setting forth "targets" or "goals" in percentages of the work force to be filled by hiring and promoting racial minorities. Those bypassed, mostly white males, struck back alleging reverse discrimination.

There is little doubt that the very nature of policing altered as the conflict unfolded. In applying principles of psychometrics to police employment policies, it became necessary to define just what police officers do and what demonstrated skills are required to perform those duties. Knowledge and fitness rose to the fore. In addition, a new concept emerged—community policing which stressed that police effectiveness is greatly enhanced when law enforcement has a rapport or is familiar with the community in the area for which it is responsible (Wykoff & Skogen, 1993). Further, such rapport is more easily obtained when at least some members of the law enforcement group are of the same race or gender. It is not now nor should it ever be a requirement that blacks confront blacks, whites confront whites, and women confront women. However, there can be little doubt that the quality of policing is enhanced when police officers have something in common with the public they serve.

The knowledge and fitness skills required for policing were equally significant in changing the face of policing from its traditional white male composition. Test scores had always been instrumental in the hiring process, but the questions raised about test validity resulted in a reassessment of the particular tests being used. Questions pertaining to the tests' correlation with the tasks to be performed, cultural biases, and the weight accorded test results abounded. In many jurisdictions, questioning led not only to changes in the tests themselves, but in the outcomes as well. Consequently, many blacks, for example, scored higher than they had previously, thereby improving their rankings. Improved testing methods along with affirmative action programs which established targets and goals brought about significant changes in police populations.

Fitness played a dual role. As the focus on police hiring and promotion qualifications shifted to the skills required to accomplish the policing tasks at hand, the impact was also felt by police officers who were already on the job. The fat, pot-bellied police officer eating an ice cream cone of Norman Rockwell fame became an artifact of the past. Rigorous training and testing consisting of long-distance running, calisthenics, boxing, and weightlifting became an integral part of police training. However, fitness for its own sake may not have been the only motivation.

Women had begun to challenge this male bastion with an earnestness that defied rebuff. Fitness requirements excluded women from participation, and it was alleged that the fitness standards had been purposefully set too high to permit female applicants to pass. In one instance, weightlifting was deemed to be the culprit. Female candidates for the New York City fire department were required to lift significant weights and run great distances along with their much larger male counterparts, often resulting in serious injury. Serious questions began to surface challenging the necessity for such training. Just how much weight does a fireman lift and run on the job? The so-called fitness training had to be restructured (*Berkman v. New York City Fire Dept.*, 1983).

Neither firemen nor the "Blue Line" of police are exclusively masculine; women in uniform are commonplace. Indeed, the benefits of affirmatively addressing the exclusion of blacks and women from playing a significant role in firefighting and law enforcement reverberated in other areas. Recall the old size requirements of the police departments. They are a relic of the past. The short white police officer says, "Thank you, affirmative action," and we should all join. We have a much improved police force. Its members are fit. Community policing, once thought to be no more than a cover for police intelligence, plays a necessary and positive role in law enforcement from which we all benefit.

The airline industry reveals a similar story. Older women and men are now commonplace as flight attendants. Even the name has changed, denying a gender base and avoiding the identification as sex object. Today, the woman in the cockpit is not serving coffee to the pilot—she is the pilot. It is hard to find a gender-based occupation in the post-affirmative action era.

Gone today are the myriad artificial requirements which served principally to exclude racial minorities and women. Criteria such as educational achievements (*Griggs v. Duke Power & Light Co.*, 1971), license, performance or experience requirements (*Maldonado v. Yellow Freight Systems, Inc.*, 1975), arrests and conviction records (*Gregory v. Litton Systems, Inc.* 1970), garnishments and other financial criteria (*Johnson v. Pike Corporation of America*, 1971), less-than-honorable discharges (*Gregory v. Litton Systems, Inc.*, 1970), among others, have now been largely eliminated where no job-related nexus can be demonstrated. In doing so, access by minorities and women has been expanded to job opportunities which had heretofore been foreclosed to them. And to the extent that whites shared the height, weight, size, and other characteristics typical of the previously excluded groups, they, as well as society, benefited from the improved selection criteria.

The word "qualifications" is a nebulous term. In the pre-affirmative action era, it was often said by employers, "We take the most qualified." That statement was made while wholesale exclusion was more the practice than the exception. Consequently, the efficacy of that statement was questioned by affirmative action and psychometrics, and labor as we knew it would never be the same again. Yet, the echo of that defensive statement is heard today when opponents of affirmative action demand "a return to a meritocracy." The fact is that the meritocracy of the past never existed. All too clearly, labor practices and policies today are based upon merit to a much greater extent than they ever were.

The face of labor will never look the same again. But it's more than a question of appearances or who gets the paycheck. While these may be important aspects of labor's imprint, they are by no means the most important. The quality of the products produced has been greatly improved since the advent of affirmative action, as has the quality of the labor force itself. Diversity does improve the quality of the product in more ways than one.

## Higher Education

It is almost impossible to talk about affirmative action in higher education without first commenting on the state of public education in the United States in the mid-nineteenth century. While the country had yet to throw off the oppressive yoke of *Plessy v. Ferguson* (1896), its stranglehold on blacks had begun to weaken. In 1948, after 75 years of silence on civil rights issues, Congress, with the impetus provided by President Harry S. Truman (Executive Order, 1947) integrated the armed services. And there was more movement toward a more equitable society. *Sweatt v. Painter* (1950) was decided, granting Sweatt, a black man, admission to the all-white University of Texas Law School. It is perhaps in this precarious Humpty Dumpty setting of the Plessy "separate but equal" doctrine that, more than the opinion itself, permitted so many to read the opinion in *Brown v. Board of Education* (1954) and speak of its promise.

In Brown, black school children challenged the claimed right of the states of Kansas, South Carolina, Virginia, and Delaware to maintain segregated public schools on the grounds that "segregated public schools are not 'equal' and cannot be made equal . . ." and therefore, they as blacks, were being denied the equal protection of the states' laws (*Brown v. Board of Education*, 1954). The decision in *Brown* "promised" to overcome the most deeply rooted aspects of racial segregation by eliminating the concomitant psychological impact on its primary victims. Long after the completion of the socializing educational process, the psychological impact of segregated public schools on blacks, its primary victims, contributed significantly to both a continuation of disparate treatment and poor performance.

Congressional action in desegregating the armed forces did not go unnoticed by the Court, which noted in *Brown* that the educational process had affected performance in the newly integrated armed forces. The implication was clear: If blacks and whites were to share similar roles and responsibilities, they must have similar or equal educational opportunities. Yet, in the decade that followed, *Brown's* promise was called into question. The Court seemed to backtrack with its "all deliberate speed" decision (*Brown v. Board of Education*, 1955). However, if the Court's concern about blacks' educational afterlife became muted with its "all deliberate speed" pronouncement, higher education saw blacks and other racial groups facing a mid-life crisis and spoke in a loud voice.

Universities responded to the immediate need to improve performance. But, the segregated public school systems challenged in *Brown*, along with the de facto segregation of track systems, gerrymandering and other divisive public school programs left many blacks ill-prepared to compete with whites for college admission. Could a decision to wait with "all deliberate speed" for the effect of *Brown* to bring about parity in the admission process be justified?

At the undergraduate level, many institutions begged the question. They developed "open-enrollment" admissions programs and admitted all who applied. Others developed special admissions programs, giving first blacks and then others a preference. The preference, a factor in the admission process, was often given solely on the basis of race without a showing by the applicant of personal injury due to past discrimination. Criticism of these preferences surfaced almost immediately, challenging the universal application of the preference to all members of the targeted racial group. "Societal discrimination" was argued to be too great an abstraction to be remedied by such extreme measures.

Some admissions programs guaranteed a specific number of seats for those specially admitted. These special admissions programs became the focus of attention as opposition mounted against a "return to a quota system," a system particularly offensive to Jews, who had suffered as a group under quota systems.

The first challenge to these types of special admissions initiatives to reach the United States Supreme Court came in *DeFunis v. Odegaard* raising the issues of racial preferences in the admissions program used at the University of Washington Law School (*DeFunis v. Odegaard*, 1974). The case, however, was never decided by the Court because Marco DeFunis was admitted to law school before the matter could be decided. But such was not to be the case for Allan Bakke, a white applicant who had been denied admission to medical school by the University of California and 12 other medical schools. Bakke challenged the right of the medical school both to take race into account in its admissions process and to set aside one-sixth of its entering class for the sole occupancy of racial minorities as violating the Fourteenth Amendment (*Regents of the University of California at Davis v. Bakke*, 1978). One commentator remarked on the outcome:

The Supreme Court of the United States has ordered that Allan Bakke be admitted, in the upcoming academic year, to the medical school at the University of California at Davis. His attempt to compel his admission has ended. But it was never suspected that the emotional, political and economic furor that surrounded this single piece of litigation existed primarily because of the extreme concerns of a nation for one single individual's personal ambitions and goals. Rather, the advent of the affirmative action concept parallelled an ever-increasing deficit in this country's balance of payments resulting in a devalued dollar, a spiralling inflationary economy, accompanied by high unemployment, and increased interest in professional education, all culminating in extreme concern over the division of America's limited largess.

"Middle America," in assessing its circumstances, had concluded that their perceived rewards for having "done the job traditionally required," were being frittered away by high taxes on the one hand, and stripped away entirely by the incursion of "affirmative action" into such previously sacrosanct areas as higher education, seniority rights as well as hiring and promotion, small business opportunities, and public works contracts on the other. Yet, from the perspective of America's racial minorities, a socio-economic debt long overdue stood in jeopardy of being abandoned just at the moment when it appeared meaningful relief might be at hand. Virtually the entire nation looked to the Court for justification of its beliefs that heartfelt wrongs, permeating all of society, would be vindicated through this litigation. At least someone had to be right (Council on Legal Education Opportunity, 1978).

In a close decision, the Court found the special admissions program at Davis' medical school to be unlawful. And although it expressed the possibility of the program's constitutionality if a "compelling state interest" had been demonstrated, the Court rejected reducing the historic deficit of traditionally disfavored minorities in medical schools, countering the effects of societal discrimination, and increasing the number of physicians practicing in under served communities.

The clear implication from the decision could only be that group remedies were not per se unconstitutional. The Court was fragmented on this issue. Mr. Justice Powell cast the swing vote on this issue; programs mandated by the judiciary after a finding of past discrimination were certainly safe, while voluntary programs were subject to strict scrutiny.

It is argued in this chapter that the "state interests" proffered in *Bakke* are more than sufficient to justify the continuation of special admissions. Prior to the advent of special admissions programs, institutions of higher education determined questions of admission in an autonomous and unfettered manner. Preferences, as discussed in Chapter 5 by Hurtado and Navia, although not based on race, were routinely given to alumni children in return for monetary gifts, and to other applicants at the request of the dean or other campus officials.

In contrast, exclusion based on gender and race was commonplace. Yet, the Court found in Allan Bakke's favor without Bakke ever showing that he was discriminated against by the University of California, Davis medical school, "solely because of his race" while 84 other white applicants were admitted. It would seem that Bakke's denial of admission was based, at least in part, on other factors. This comparison of preferences clearly suggests that preferences based upon race are being used to justify a return to admissions practices which exclude blacks, other minorities, and to a lesser extent women. If not, why did the Court dismiss the "compelling interest" of offsetting both the historic deficit of traditionally disfavored racial minorities from medical schools and societal discrimination as well? Is it not compelling to right such egregious wrongs?

Notions of morality may not have been persuasive to the Court, but the pragmatics of the other justifications—physicians practicing in under served communities and diversity in the classroom—should have sent Bakke packing. In the abstract, with race removed from the equation, would medical schools have an interest in the nation's health care needs to the point of considering them when making admissions decisions? Such considerations have routinely figured in medical school admissions decisions. And, while some health care needs are greater than others, any health care risk serious enough to jeopardize the health and well-being of the population, or some significant portion of it, most certainly constitutes a compelling state interest at least for some.

Just how under served are these communities and how significant is the affected population? If no physician is available to a community comprising a particular racial group, it would certainly justify taking race into account as a factor to be considered in the admissions process. There is a greater probability that the physician most likely to fill the void will be of the same race as community members. To those communities, the need is compelling. But what about disease control? It would only take one epidemic emanating from any one of these under served communities to demonstrate how the nation as a whole benefits if these needs are addressed. Hindsight would demonstrate just how compelling the need had been. The argument is not that health care providers must be of the same race as the patients, but rather that underservice based on race justifies a racial solution. It is interesting to note that alumni preferences have never been challenged—and the recipients of virtually all of those preferences are white. Consequently, blacks and other racial minorities are not and cannot be in competition for those seats, to say nothing of women. The benefit of reducing significant health care risks to the nation is certainly greater than that of preserving the status quo through alumni preferences.

The last of the compelling state interests—diversity within the student body—is certainly not the least significant. In *DeFunis v. Odegaard*, one of the stated justifications for special admission to law school was the importance of racial minorities having an input in those decision-making processes that govern their lives. It was pointed out that 70 percent of the members of Congress had attended law school (Council on Legal Education Opportunity, 1974). Further, the DeFunis record reveals that the University of Washington Law School had implemented curriculum changes based on student input. This process reflected the University's acknowledgment that much of the "law" is grounded in public policy. Courts frequently cite student law review articles. Returning to *Bakke*, is there any reason to believe medical schools are less influential in setting health care policy? While this is no doubt an important question, the more crucial question remains whether educational quality is improved by diversity.

To the extent that educational quality can be measured by the degree to which expressed concepts are challenged, diversity is an all-important ingredient. The argument has been made that affirmative action in higher education has accomplished little more than to allow blacks and other racial minorities to "step up in class" and attend schools for which they are not qualified. Without affirmative action, they could have attended lesser-ranked schools and avoided all of the controversy. The image created by this argument reveals its flaw at first glance: The top schools would be all white while the number of minority students would increase as school rankings decrease. The status quo would thus remain the order of the day. And not only would the power of policy-making be locked in the ivory towers of the top-ranked schools, the quality of education at the top would suffer enormously from its myopic perspectives.

There is then this particularly interesting aspect to affirmative action in higher education. Those minorities specially admitted to the higher echelon Ivy League schools, for example, would not be barred from higher education altogether. Their scores and academic credentials are competitive with a host of other schools with arguably lesser reputations. Indeed, recent litigation involving The Citadel of South Carolina revealed that the average SAT score of Citadel students is around 350 (Mandelbaum, 1995). Those specially admitted to Harvard and Yale are certainly eligible to attend places like the Citadel unless, of course, you are female. But again, the point is that each educational institution that affirmatively addresses the question of diversity in its student body enjoys a robust and enhanced exchange of ideas, thereby improving the quality of education enjoyed by all.

To return for a moment to the GATT and NAFTA debates, it would have been almost impossible to get the Detroit "Big Three" to voluntarily agree to give up significant market shares. Those accustomed to a monopoly are never fans of competition and are not persuaded by improved product arguments. But the benefits are undeniable by whoever uses the product. Diversity in the classroom does improve the quality of education for all, well beyond the benefit of getting to know one another in preparation for life after graduation.

Fortunately for the nation, although the promise of *Brown v. Board of Education* was never realized and the education of blacks and Hispanics in public schools still lags behind all others, the *Bakke* decision did not result in the wholesale dismantling of special admissions programs in higher education. Sure, there were some retreats. Many schools, for example, narrowed their open-enrollment admissions policies yet still considered race as a positive factor in admissions. However, the numbers of blacks enrolled in predominantly white institutions dropped for any number of reasons, one of which was a decrease in the availability of financial aid. In support of affirmative action special admissions programs, many schools set aside significant sums of money to finance the education of racial minorities. It made little sense to admit the grandchildren of former slaves to the nation's most prestigious, and often most expensive, educational institutions and expect them to be able to afford the high costs. However, financial aid funds distributed on the basis of race were also attacked, ultimately successfully. It was determined that no schools receiving federal funds could designate financial aid funds for targeted racial groups (*Podberesky v. Kirwan*, 1994).

But neither *Bakke* nor setbacks in financial aid could topple higher education's response to hundreds of years of educational deprivation. Those institutions that continue their special admissions programs continue to meet the compelling needs previously described—and the benefits accumulate with each entering class. It is indeed arguable that the conscience of America resides in higher education's approach to affirmative action, and although the benefits to the nation are enormous, it is no surprise that the attacks continue. Still, higher education's professional schools deserve the nation's gratitude for taking the moral high ground in responding to *Brown's* promise, giving credibility to the claim of a free democratic society. Such is not the case, however, for public education, now wallowing in an abysmal state of segregation and dysfunction.

## Business And The Economy

It is also no surprise that the initial challenges to affirmative action occurred in higher education, while the later landmark challenges were in the public works arena. The shift was an important one because from all indications the initial challenges were as much about class as they were about race. As noted previously, no one argued that the nation's racial minorities were not entitled to the benefits of higher education; the question was simply, where? The argument accepts notions of elitism. But as the economy tightened, markets shrank as a consequence of foreign competition, downsizing resulted in high unemployment, and the nation focused more than ever on monetary issues. Hence, the fight shifted to the lucrative opportunities of public works and the construction industry. Business was as much affected by affirmative action as labor and higher education.

Local, state, and federal governments spend tens of billions of dollars each year on public works (Public Works Employment Act, 1977). Consistent with the national effort to provide equal opportunity to all citizens, many state and local governments took the federal government's lead and affirmatively supported minority businesses. Race became a factor in the bidding processes. Soon the race "factor" became a "set aside," with local and state governments typically setting aside 10 percent of their public works projects for minority-owned businesses.

At the outset, affirmative action plans formulated by public agencies met with court approval. In a series of cases, the courts upheld affirmative action plans that set hiring goals or ratios for minority tradesmen in government-financed construction projects. The First Circuit in *Associated General Contractors of Massachusetts, Inc. et al. v. Altshuler et al.* in 1973, recognized that public authorities have a broader discretionary power to remedy past discrimination than that of the judicial branch. When it came to public works, the courts considered the public policy aspects of affirmative action and found them to be best addressed by the policy-making entities of government.

The Altshuler court set forth the premise of governmental action to remedy affirmative action, stating that:

> It is by now well understood . . . that our society cannot be completely color blind in the short term if we are to have a color blind society in the long term. After centuries of viewing through colored lenses, eyes do not quickly adjust when

the lenses are removed. Discrimination has a way of perpetuating itself, albeit unintentionally, because the resulting inequalities make new opportunities less accessible (*Associated General Contractors of Massachusetts, Inc. et al. v. Altshuler*, 1973).

Many states took these matters seriously. Some passed legislation requiring all state agencies to develop, implement, and administer affirmative action programs (N.J.S.A. 11A:7–1 to 13). In 1979, the Supreme Court in *United Steelworkers of America v. Weber* upheld an affirmative action plan that did not serve as an "absolute bar to the advancement of white employees." The consequence of a contrary ruling finding reverse discrimination would have turned all anti-discrimination laws on their heads and made a mockery of the new national policy to remedy past discrimination.

But set asides raised different questions, or the same questions directed toward different facts. In the *Bakke* case, one of the 50-odd amici briefs filed was the work of the American Subcontractors Association (1978). The association raised questions difficult to answer under the Weber rationale. Public works, it argued, constituted an almost $40 billion industry of which 10 percent had been set aside for minority subcontractors. Therefore, as the argument went, some four billion dollars of business and job opportunities were being denied whites and, as such, set aside programs posed an absolute bar to all white employees, at least of nonminority firms. The most obvious flaw with this analysis is that all whites were not barred from set-aside job opportunities. The argument assumes that minority firms did not and do not hire whites. But it is common knowledge that they did and do. Consequently, the "bar" that occurs from set-asides, if there is one, is certainly not absolute where race is concerned. As far as employees are concerned, there is no race-based discrimination at all.

At the same time, all white-owned businesses, based on the lack of minority owners, were deprived of a designated piece of the public works pie—a significant piece at that. They did not like it. And, as other markets tightened, they liked it even less. Some almost made a game of it by creating companies—holding companies and partnerships that were established under minority ownership. It was a lot like "Monopoly." If politics makes the strangest of bedfellows, minority set aside programs cannot be far behind.

Some entrepreneurs played set aside "Monopoly" as a "shell game." Which corporation housed the minority owner? Some of it was fraudulent and some of it was merely stretching the administrative envelope of set aside administration. It seemed that those who could "work the system" benefited while those who could not, such as inexperienced minorities who had little opportunity to familiarize themselves with the administration of government contracts, did not. Within the ranks of the inexperienced minorities, recent college graduates did best. Business partners took on a new look—the new look of diversity. Beneath all of the acrimony of challenge and cries of unfairness, a new rapport began to develop in business. Whites and the nation's racial minorities were thrust together as a consequence of set-aside programs. Whether it was the business of acquiring "partners" to declare as minority owners of new or reorganized business entities, or hiring minorities as subcontractors, whites and a multitude of racial minorities did business. And, as the economy bulled and beared, tensions ebbed and flowed.

There were cries that fraud was rampant, that many alleged minority firms were in reality all-white-owned, masquerading under puppet minority regimes. Several prosecutions alleviated some of the tension, but it was not enough. Once again, hard times were settling on the nation and the pressure to gain access to all of America's largess continued to heighten. Yet, it is ironic that these matters all came to a head at the citadel of racial segregation—Richmond, Virginia—where a public works set-aside program requiring that 30 percent of its public works contracts be awarded to minority contractors was in place to remedy past discrimination. In *Crosen v. City of Richmond* (1989), a plumbing contractor challenged the constitionality of the set-asides.

Justice O'Connor crafted a strange decision, alleging a tension between The Fourteenth Amendment's equal protection clause and race-based measures by the city of Richmond to ameliorate past discrimination. As "Wartime Amendments," the last enacted before the ink could fully dry on the first, the Thirteenth and Fourteenth Amendments had similar if not identical purposes: the elevation of blacks to full-fledged citizens. Now, according to Justice O'Connor, remedies based on race and targeting the very group the Amendment intended to benefit, are barred by the language of the emancipating Amendment and its progeny. Her specific ruling in *Crosen* imposed a strict scrutiny standard and then determined that the standard was not met, thereby holding the set-aside program imposed by the city of Richmond unconstitutional.

Justice O'Connor justified her conclusion with the argument that no factual basis for alleging racial discrimination was adduced at trial, but merely allegations of societal discrimination (*Crosen v. City of Richmond*, 1989). Justice Marshall, in his dissenting opinion, countered that the majority opinion failed to distinguish between present and past discrimination. He argued that where past discrimination results in the "continuing exclusion of minorities from an historically tight-knit industry, a contrast between population and work force is entirely appropriate to help gauge the degree of exclusion" (*Crosen v. City of Richmond*, 1989). Justice Marshall later described the decision as "... [taking] a broad swipe at affirmative action making it very hard for any state or city to fashion a race-conscious remedial program that will survive its constitutional scrutiny" (Marshall, 1989).

While the dark clouds of doom gathered, anticipating an affirmative action wipe-out, many government decision-makers surprised affirmative action supporters and opponents alike by holding the line and doing nothing but awaiting a challenge to their own programs. While *Crosen* did not cause the immediate dismantling of public works set-asides, the blue skies of remediation for past discrimination were just about gone—but not without leaving its indelible imprint on American society.

The principal beneficiaries of affirmative action in higher education had teamed up with the minority labor force and tapped into one of America's most lucrative markets. The failure of *Crosen* to shut down affirmative action in public works had no small impact on the economics of the black populace. Studies show that in the last decade, the per-capita income of blacks in America virtually soared in comparison with any prior decade in this century (Smith & Welch, 1989). Clearly, all blacks did not benefit. The gap between upper and lower income blacks widened significantly, but there can be no argument that the combined effect of affirmative action in higher education and public works, in tandem, changed the economic lives of many blacks dramatically.

The overall question then becomes, at whose expense? Were white contractors driven into bankruptcy? There is no evidence of that. Were they driven from the business into other crafts and professions? No data supports that conclusion. White contractors could better diversify than fledgling minority firms, and they did so where necessary to ensure their survival. Clearly, while minorities benefited from minority set-asides, whites indirectly fell into enormous benefits as well.

There is little doubt that the benefits of the civil rights movement in general and affirmative action, in particular, increased the wealth of blacks and minorities, even if that new-found wealth was not evenly distributed. The new-found "wealth" of blacks and other minorities, however, clearly had a spillover effect because it was either spent or invested, creating new markets. Black and minority purchasing power became a target of the advertising industry. The once all-white models advertising clothes, hair products, and even such high-priced products as automobiles suddenly became integrated showing black and brown consumers enjoying life through the use of promoted products.

Advertising markets expanded. Product promotion explored new advertising frontiers. Sales increased as a consequence of this market expansion beyond what they would have been had the new market thrust not taken place. Inventories had to be replaced because of this newly found purchasing power. Automobiles, appliances, clothing, and housing inventories were greatly affected. Keynsian roundabout economic theory came to the fore. As inventories were being replaced, job opportunities opened up and the economy as a whole expanded. While other factors, such as corporate raiding funded with "junk bonds" in the eighties, may have offset some of the suggested gains of affirmative action, the collapse of financial wizardry has nothing to do with the suggested benefits of affirmative action. Affirmative action, in a much smaller sense, had become the "New Deal" of the last quarter of the Twentieth Century, benefiting all.

## Conclusion

As the sham of *Plessy v. Ferguson's* separate but equal doctrine shuddered under the stunning blow of *Sweatt v. Painter*, compelling a black's admission to the all-white University of Texas—just before its final collapse under *Brown's* assault—the plight of public education was hardly predictable. Education, it was thought, would be the panacea for America's racial problems, and so the nation spoke of *Brown's* promise. But that promise has never been realized. Ironically, instead of the long-awaited educational utopia, making the "promised land" a reality, public education has become America's killing fields for blacks and other racial minorities.

The failure of public education to respond positively to segregationist demands for the continuation of class subjugation based upon race through private school havens for the white elite, voucher systems for the middle class, gerrymandered school districts conforming to racially controlled real estate configurations, and the significant underfunding of minority school districts has placed higher education in its current posture of apologist for the attempted academic genocide of black and minority youth at the public school level. Fortunately, higher education has been able to rise to the occasion and continues to do so.

However, many institutions essential to the fabric of American life are determined to address the race question affirmatively, once given their lead by the judiciary in *Brown* and *Griggs*. And, to the extent that the judiciary became the catalyst in the formation of the complex affirmative action compound, higher education has become the main ingredient fueling the demands of America's economic engines. Every facet of affirmative action in labor (and politics for that matter) relied at least in some measure on the affirmative steps taken in higher education to include, or rather embrace, blacks and other racial minorities as participants in the educational processes of higher education. Affirmative action in higher education allowed America's racial minorities to participate in those decision-making processes that govern their lives. And, indeed they did; affirmative action in labor encompassed almost every field imaginable, including the hierarchy in higher education. Diversity in higher education, both in faculties and the student bodies, soon became its own reward!

As a result of affirmative action, far more equitable standards were set in virtually every aspect of American life. Gone were the days of routinely arbitrary hiring practices, gender-based exclusion, unfair employment criteria, unfair and insensitive academic curricula, and too many class distinctions to count. And, it is essential to remember that the nation was struggling desperately to take the moral high ground and redress grievances which had accumulated for centuries. The moral question of racial discrimination is no small piece of business; it is very difficult to assume an international role of leadership on such issues as human rights while we as a nation wallow in our own nightmare of racially motivated class distinctions.

The ultimate effect of affirmative action, however, distilled into buying power for America's minorities and economic growth for all Americans. Yet, thus far these benefits have failed to dissuade the opposition, which seeks to scrap affirmative action and desires a return to the status quo ante of separate but equal with all of its inequities, but this time under the guise of race-neutral criteria. Should the opposition succeed, the results will be nothing short of disastrous for all Americans.

Affirmative action is a stop-gap measure still awaiting *Brown's* promise to give all of America's children an equal, quality education so that as adults they can all compete on a race-neutral level playing field. Until that time comes, fundamental notions of fairness dictate: It was race that got us into this mess, and it will be race that gets us out.

## REFERENCES

*Adarand Constructors, Inc. et al. v. Pena*, 63 LW 4523 (June 12, 1995).
*Air Line Pilots Assoc., International et al. v. United Air Lines, Inc.* 480 F.Supp. 1107 (E.D. N.Y. 1979).
American Council on Education, *UC Regents Abolish Race-based Policies*, 44 Higher Educ. & Nat'l Aff. 14 (July 24, 1995).
American Subcontractors Association, Amicus Curiae in *Regents of the University of California v. Bakke*, 438 U.S. 265 (1978).

*Associated General Contractors of Massachusetts, Inc. et al. v. Altshuler et al.* 490 F.2d 9, 17 (1st Cir. 1973).
*Berkman v. City of New York*, 536 F.Supp. 177 (E.D. N.Y. 1982, aff'd, 705 F.2d 584 (1st Cir. 1983). Excessive training was not limited to fire departments however. State police in New Jersey were severely criticized for imposing boxing as training criteria. Female cadets were forced to "box" with their much larger male counterparts. Such activity was hardly a part of on the job requirements.
Blumrosen, A. *How the Courts Are Handling Reverse Discrimination Claims*, 1995 D.L.R. 56 (March 23, 1995).
*Brotherhood of R. R. Trainmen v. Howard*, 343 U.S. 768 (1952).
*Brown v. Board of Education*, 347 U.S. 483, 488 (1954).
*Brown v. Board of Education*, 349 U.S. 294 (1955).
Bureau of the Census, Statistical Abstract of the United States—1995, 115th Edition.
The Civil Rights Cases of 1883, 109 U.S. 3 (1883).
Cose, E. *The Rage of a Privileged Class* (1993).
Council on Legal Education Opportunity. *Allan Bakke v. Regents of the University of California*, Vols. I-VI, Vol. VI, 463 (Slocum, A. ed.).
*Crosen v. City of Richmond*, 488 U.S. 469, 498-500, 542 (1989).
*DeFunis v. Odegaard*, 416 U.S. 312 (1974).
*Erie v. Thompkins*, 304 U.S. 64 (1937).
Executive Order 9981, 3 CFR, 1947 Supp.
*Gregory v. Litton Systems, Inc.*, 316 F. Supp. 401 (C.D. Cal. 1970).
*Griggs v. Duke Power and Light Co.*, 401 U.S. 424 (1971).
*Guardians Ass'n of the NYC Police Dept., Inc. et al. v. Civil Service Commisssion of the City of NY*, 431 F. Supp. 526 (S.D. N.Y. 1977).
*Johnson v. Pike Corporation of America*, 332 F. Supp. 490 (C.D. Cal. 1971).
Kinoy, A. *The Constitutional Right of Negro Freedom*, 21 Rutgers L. Review (1967).
*Laffey v. Northwest Airlines, Inc.*, 740 F. 2d 1071 (D.C. Cir. 1983).
Landrum-Griffin Act, 73 Stat. 519 (1959).
*Maldonado v. Yellow Freight System, Inc.*, 10 FEP 1290 (C.D. Cal. 1975).
Mandelbaum, S. ACLU Women's Rights Project, Counsel for Sharon Faulkner, Unpublished Keynote Address Delivered at the Symposium, *The Next Generation of Women's Issues*, Honoring Ruth Bader Ginsburg at Rutgers Law School on April 11, 1995.
Marshall, T. *Remarks at the Second Circuit Judicial Conference 1* (September 8, 1989).
Morris, C. J. *The Developing Labor Law*, Vol. 1 (1971).

National Labor Relations Act, 49 Stat. 449 (1935).
*N.L.R.B. v. Local 106, Glass Bottle Blowers*, 520 F.2d 693 (6th Cir. 1975).
*N.L.R.B. v. Mansion House Center Mngmnt Corp.*, 473 F.2d 471 (8th Cir. 1973).
N.J.S.A. 11A:7-1 to 13.
*Peterson v. Rath Packing Co.*, 461 F.2d 312 (8th Cir.1972).
*Plessy v. Ferguson*, 163 U.S. 537 (1896).
*Podberesky v. Kirwan*, 38 F. 3rd 147 (4th Cir. 1994).
Public Works Employment Act of 1977, 42 U.S.C. sec. 6701 et seq.
*Regents of the University of California v. Bakke*, 438 U.S. 265 (1978).
*Robinson v. Lorillard Corp.*, 444 F.2d 791.
*Scott v. Sanford*, 19 How. 393 (1857).
Smith, James P., and Welch, Finis R. *Black Economic Progress After Myrdal*, 27 J. Econ. Lit. 519 (June 1989).
*Sprogis v. United Air Lines, Inc.*, v. 444 F.2d 1194 (7th Cir. 1971).
*Steele v. Louisville & Nashville R.R.*, 323 U.S. 192 (1944).
*Sweatt v. Painter*, 339 U.S. 629 (1950).
*Swift v. Tyson*, 41 U.S. 1 (1842).
Taft-Hartley Act, 61 Stat. 136 (1947).
*United Steelworkers of America AFL-CIO-CLC v. Weber et al.*, 443 U.S. 193, 208 (1979).
U.S.C.A., Title 42, secs. 3601 et seq., 2000a, 2000e-5, 1973.
U.S. Const. amend. 13.
U.S. Const. amend. 14.
Wycoff, M. A., and Skogan, W. K. *Community Policing in Madison: Quality from the Inside Out. An Evaluation of Implementation and Impact* (December 1993).

---

## NOTE

1. The proponents of this measure may be surprised at the likely beneficiaries of such a decision. *The New York Times* Magazine Section, Sunday, September 10, 1995 states, "At the University of California at Berkeley, 42 percent of the freshman class is Asian-American. Next year, given the state's ban on affirmative action, thus awarding admission solely on grades and test scores, that number is expected to be 53 percent." Additionally, it is no secret that those who are responsible for producing and administering standard-

ized tests such as the SAT, LSAT and MCAT for higher education such as the Educational Testing Service (ETS) argue against the sole use of test scores to determine eligibility for admission. Interestingly white males (along with Asians) score highest on the math side, but women do not take a back seat on the verbal side. Consequently, white males will surely be the victims of an abandonment of affirmative action as a consequence of raw score dependency.

Sylvia Hurtado and Christine Navia

# 5
## Reconciling College Access and the Affirmative Action Debate

Early posturing for the 1996 Presidential elections placed state and federal affirmative action policies at the center of public discourse, drawing higher education institutions somewhat unwillingly into a battle framed largely by political interests and less by the problems of inequity that these policies were developed to help resolve. Designing equitable policies and the reexamination of existing policies to address society's difficult problems are a healthy form of public discourse that require careful examination, self-criticism, and continual improvement as the times change. However, this is not how discussions of affirmative action, as it relates to the role and function of higher education, have been framed. The discourse on affirmative action, like so many issues dealing with racial/ethnic issues, is rife with misconceptions and ill-conceived notions regarding how the policy works (or fails to work) in actual practice. We address some of these misconceptions as they apply to college access and admissions practices, illustrate the political nature of the debate using issues that arose surrounding the University of California Regents' vote to eliminate affirmative action, and attempt to highlight important gender and racial/ethnic group inequalities that still exist as part of the need to continue to ensure access to higher education. Reviews of affirmative action programs and policies in higher education should be conducted, not because we view them as suspect but because we wish to determine how we can effectively work toward resolving some of the persistent problems confronted by our communities.

The main question obscured by the affirmative action debate is the same question higher education historian John Brubacher posed in a 1965 book, the *Bases for Policy in Higher Education*: "Higher education for whom?" Underlying many of our contemporary policies is an unstated assumption regarding who is entitled to attend higher education and which types of institutions they should have the opportunity to attend. Indeed, while decisions regarding whom to serve have become central to the mission of many institutions, increasing equal opportunity in college access now means providing more students with choices to attend a variety of high quality institutions (Southern Education Foundation, 1995). However, the fact that we have not arrived at a collective consensus regarding college access and the representation of various segments of our population is both a testament to the longstanding currency of Brubacher's question and a powerful indictment of how the value of our previous attempts to answer his question has diminished over time. In devising new strategies to meet the demands of the coming millennium, institutions must evaluate their educational goals and mission, including their commitment to ensuring opportunity for women and racial/ethnic groups. Gender and racial/ethnic inequalities persist in our society and higher education's role remains key in working toward the elimination of these problems.

## Misconceptions Regarding College Access and Affirmative Action

Nearly every form of affirmative action geared toward improving the educational opportunity for students of color and women has endured public scrutiny. Admissions criteria and financial aid awards based on race have received the lion's share of attention for their perceived bias against white students (Jaschik, 1995). Although conservative politicians have perpetuated misconceptions about affirmative action, perhaps a major part of the problem is that higher education institutions have not effectively communicated their educational goals and related admissions practices to the general public. Individual institutions have lost legal challenges to affirmative action practices in admissions and the awarding of scholarships because they have failed to communicate how these practices are tailored to remedy past discrimination evident at the institution or to achieve a diverse learning environment that is consistent with the educational mission of the institution (Bazluke, 1995). Clearly establishing diversity as a legitimate educational goal is an important step, but there are other issues that require our attention. We address some of the key misconceptions in relation to college access in order to help refocus discussions among educators on the important issues that remain to be addressed by higher education institutions. In addressing these misconceptions, we pose key questions that underlie some common assumptions about affirmative action for students. When one closely examines the underpinnings of the arguments made against these policies, what one finds is a foundation riddled with false assumptions about the historical and ethical moorings of higher education, its meritocratic practices, and the role of race and gender in college access.

## Is Affirmative Action Consistent With the Way Higher Education Has Historically Operated?

Some believe that campus affirmative action programs are unfair because they undermine the meritocratic history and spirit of higher education. In other words, offering a student admission to a college or university based on anything other than academic qualifications violates the historical precedent of access based on merit. However, access to higher education has never been based exclusively on academic merit, rather colleges have historically favored those with the most financial resources. As Laurence Veysey (1965) points out in *The Emergence of the American University*, institutions of higher education were often created to serve very distinct social classes, namely the sons of wealthy donors and businessmen, the clergy, and educators for a growing population. As a result, wealth and status became one of the preconditions for gaining access to college. So much so, Veysey writes, that the purpose of higher education in the 1800s was defined predominately as a "means of confirming one's respectable place in society" (p. 4). Therefore, the role of higher education was to maintain the social order. Access to elite institutions ratified one's social status, and restricting access for women and students from different income and racial/ethnic groups became an accepted practice because these groups were intended to play less prominent roles in society (Thelin, 1985).

This is not to suggest that the notions of competition and merit were foreign ideas to those involved in higher education during the 1800s. Rather, admission to colleges and universities was based upon less meritocratic criteria than is currently assumed to be true today. Wealth played a major role not only in the development of higher education during the 1800s but also in determining who would partake of it. Although college admissions became more closely tied to meritocratic principles, in the movement from elite to mass higher education during this century, wealth nevertheless continues to influence college access in important ways. Families from high socioeconomic backgrounds have typically been better able to invest in learning activities that develop their children's academic and nonacademic talents, send their children to the best secondary schools in the country, and obtain better college counseling. More recently, these advantages have been reinforced by a shift from a public model of financing higher education to one that is based on a private model where higher tuition is replacing state taxpayer support. This shift has altered the types of colleges that students from different income levels apply to and attend (Hauptman, 1993). In addition, college admissions offices at many elite colleges continue to give preferential treatment to both alumni children and "development cases," or students from families that have the potential to make significant financial contributions to the college. In effect, these practices continue to bestow the benefits of access through ascription rather than through purely meritocratic means. Yet, factors that sustain the privilege of advantaged students in college admissions receive no criticism nor are these other forms of preferential treatment deemed antiethetical to the way colleges operate.

The introduction of affirmative action programs in college admissions and the expansion of student financial aid were attempts to make the benefits of college opportunity available to those who had been previously excluded from higher education. However, Cornel West (1994) notes that "every redistributive measure is a compromise with and concession from the caretakers of American prosperity" (p. 94). In the same manner, affirmative action in college admissions is a redistributive measure which was a compromise between those who demanded greater access to higher education in the 1960s and exclusive institutions that conceded space in their entering classes to new groups of students. Expansion in financial aid programs during this era was an incentive or a "carrot" that could make such a compromise work, whereas an enforceable affirmative action policy represented the "stick." Institutions that did not comply with principles to prevent discrimination or remedy past discrimination could risk the loss of federal funding for student aid and research. As part of a compromise, however, the two redistributive measures were designed to be consistent with the way that colleges and universities operated. Institutions retained the autonomy to admit whom they wished, and more importantly, to continue a preferential system of admissions that also established academic merit as the central criteria for admission. Together, affirmative action and financial aid placed a college education within the reach of more students and encouraged institutions to learn how to evaluate the potential of students from different backgrounds. Ultimately, institutions began to acknowledge the benefits of both redistributive measures because they contributed to a vision of higher education that not only more accurately reflected society but also placed institutions at the forefront of social progress in terms of diminishing the hierarchy of race, class, and gender relations in society.

Inherent in the arguments made against the use of race/ethnicity, specifically as a factor in college admissions, is the assumption that the use of race is inconsistent with the way the admissions process normally works. More specifically, the use of race is believed to subvert an otherwise fair and objective admissions process. Part of the problem with such an argument is that it is simply not true. All candidates, including those admitted with affirmative action as a consideration, are first evaluated according to some acceptable level of prior academic achievement and future academic and leadership potential. Furthermore, there are a plethora of objective[1] and subjective criteria that admissions officers use to determine if an applicant merits admission (Collison, 1992). The mix of race/ethnicity in the student body is an equally legitimate means of ensuring representation in a freshman class just as are considerations of geographic representation, the mix of specific academic majors, the balance of in-state and out-of-state residents, the number of athletes, etc. These forms of preferences in admissions practices, including the preference for racial diversity, can withstand legal challenges because they are intended to serve an educational purpose (Bazluke, 1995). Today, a major educational goal of many institutions is to create a multicultural environment for student learning. To achieve that goal, these institutions must both attract and maintain a diverse student body.

The other problem with this argument is its implication that admission to college is based solely on academic criteria. While an individual's academic record is extremely important, there are still a variety of ways of assessing student potential that require subjective evaluations by experienced admissions staff. Moreover, no single criterion can accurately predict a student's future academic performance. Institutions that place unusual emphasis on academic criteria eventually select candidates based on very fine numerical gradations, which are neither statistically nor substantively meaningful (Crouse & Trusheim, 1988). Furthermore, this approach to admissions does not consider an applicant's potential for learning and growth. As Astin (1994) attests, it is possible for a student with a mediocre academic record to learn and develop in college as much as a student with a strong academic record.

In sum, institutions of higher education do not admit students solely on the basis of standardized scores or high school transcripts but often use a range of information that attests to a student's unique qualities. To argue that institutions should begin to do otherwise only serves to reduce students to "inputs" and "outputs" with little consideration for other salient considerations such as persistence, maturity, and potential for growth among individuals (Astin, 1994; Dey & Hurtado, 1995). Moreover, such a stance does not take into account institutional needs and goals for creating a diverse learning environment which represents the type of society students will encounter after graduation. It is important to note that because the debate regarding affirmative action has been the most contentious surrounding admission to the highest selectivity institutions, many institutions and students have been left outside the debate in higher education. Those institutions that depend on racial/ethnic enrollments for economic survival or that have redefined their mission to serve a diverse student population are shut out of the discussion, even though we may learn from the challenges they face as they successfully achieve access for a broad segment of the population.

## Who is "Qualified" for Admission?

The question of who is qualified for admission is raised primarily in discussions about access to elite colleges whose reputations facilitate access to top jobs and elite graduate schools. The fact that some of these undergraduate institutions turn away up to 85 percent of their applicants further attests to their desirability among college-bound students. It is important to note while many college-bound students are qualified to attend some type of college, very few are eligible to meet the specific admissions criteria of a highly selective college. Only a small portion of the nation's students would qualify under a system with strict cutoffs for academic eligibility; as a result, the composition of the student body on many campuses would look quite different under such a system. A national study of 1992 college-bound seniors showed that only about 6 percent of this cohort met five criteria considered to be representative of highly selective colleges, including: a high school GPA of 3.5 or higher, a score of 1100 or higher on the SAT, credits in the appropriate coursework, positive teacher evaluations, and participation in two or more school-related activities (Owings, McMillen, Burkett, & Pinkerton, 1995). Using these criteria, which are more heavily weighted for students' academic characteristics, the data show women were more likely than men to meet all five criteria, as are Asians and students from the highest socioeconomic backgrounds. The number of white students admitted might remain the same if these criteria for eligibility were employed—as was projected for the University of California system (Lively, 1995)—but the number of white males would probably decrease. Black, Hispanic and Native American students are less likely than white students to meet all five criteria and therefore would also decrease, but these groups are also more likely to come from low-income families, as well as racially segregated and resource-poor high schools. Thus, it is not simply historical discrimination that warrants a remedy in higher education, but the current inequalities which continue to have a persistent effect on students' chances for college opportunities.

Spurred in part by affirmative action, specific admissions practices and policies have served to ensure better representation of racial/ethnic students through the evaluation of nonacademic criteria in conjunction with academic criteria. These nonacademic criteria include motivation, success in overcoming adverse situations, extensive work and family responsibilities, as well as potential for leadership in their respective communities based on nonacademic accomplishments. At the same time, however, emphasizing specific criteria has also served to ensure better representation of white males. This is because the admissions criteria, as outlined in Owings et. al. (1995), are typically not given equal weight at most selective colleges.

In effect, use of specific admissions criteria gives preferential treatment to specific groups of students. For example, even though women (including women of color) typically earn higher grades in both high school and college than their male counterparts, a college that emphasizes standardized scores tips the balance in favor of males because they typically achieve relatively higher SAT scores (Owings, et al., 1995). In addition, overdependence on the SAT as an admissions criterion has been shown to have an adverse effect on African-American and low-income applicants (Crouse and Trusheim, 1988). Emphasis on criteria that give greater weight to verbal over mathematics scores in admissions or in the awarding of scholarships (such as the National Merit Scholarship) excludes many students whose first language is not English, particularly affecting Asian and Latino students. Further, nonacademic criteria such as athletic achievements and participation in particular leadership activities work to the advantage of male students and put both women and many academically oriented students at a distinct disadvantage. Takagi (1992) documents how using various criteria at elite institutions makes some Asian students appear to be less attractive candidates to admissions officers, even though their scores and high school grades exceed those of white students. Clearly, different gender[2] and racial/ethnic groups are favored when a college's admissions practices emphasize particular academic and nonacademic criteria. While admissions officers may believe that a substantial portion of their admissions procedures are blind to applicants' sex, race, and income, admission criteria are not blind to these various groups. Selective colleges that acknowledge these biases in criteria can work out these complexities by taking into consideration a wide range of information on each candidate and selecting students who excel along several dimensions.

Thus, while some critics of affirmative action contend that there is an objective definition of a qualified student, the notion of who is qualified for admission to a particular college is not straightforward. Most selective institutions have a broad definition of an ideal student that places relatively strong weight on students' personal characteristics, including leadership, overcoming adversity, and unique talents which might contribute to the educational environment. A well-rounded candidate for admission is someone who has excelled not only at academics but is also judged to have significant nonacademic accomplishments which go beyond involvement in typical high school activities. The ideal "well-rounded student," with significant accomplishments in both academic and nonacademic arenas, is rare and highly recruited. Since very few students meet this ideal, what admissions officers really seek is a well-rounded student body which gives a college considerable latitude in selecting among admissions candidates based on unique personal qualities that ensure a balance of academic and leadership potential in an entering class. Most applicants to highly selective institutions can reliably do the academic work required of them, and so it is these unique personal characteristics that receive significant weight (particularly at private institutions) and allow admissions officers to select candidates consistent with the educational goals of the institution. Under such multifaceted criteria, assertions that affirmative action leads to the admission of unqualified students are difficult to substantiate because most females or students of color typically meet a variety of admissions criteria.

## Is Affirmative Action Harmful to Students?

Some studies show that affirmative action may create a social stigma for women and people of color in their admission to colleges and universities. The social stigma of being a minority student in college is very real, but other research suggests this has more to do with a context where members of the organization are unfamiliar with individuals from particular minority groups (Kanter, 1977). A longitudinal survey of college life for the top Latino performers on the PSAT, a test used to identify top academic candidates in the junior year of high school, revealed that approximately 43 percent felt that most students at their four-year college thought that all minorities were special admits (Hurtado, 1994). The same study showed that approximately 68 percent of top Latino SAT performers thought that most students at their college knew very little about Hispanic culture and, not surprisingly, about 29 percent stated that many Hispanic students felt like they did not fit in on their campus. These data suggest that even the most talented racial/ethnic students are subjected to misconceptions regarding their abilities and culture, and sometimes even hostility, all of which affect their sense of belonging in college. The social stigma associated with minority status appears to have less to do with affirmative action policy, however, than with general stereotypes and attitudes towards gender and racial/ethnic differences. This notion of being unqualified is linked with a recurring historical belief that women (Solomon, 1985), nonwhite racial/ethnic groups (Gould, 1981), and low-income groups (Herrnstein & Murray, 1994) are genetically inferior in intelligence. Since social constructions of inferiority and beliefs about cultural differences predate the implementation of affirmative action policies, the dismantling of these policies is not likely to eradicate the deeper problem of longstanding stereotypes or institutionalized racial, ethnic, gender, and class discrimination.

Still, there are others who claim that affirmative action leads to unfair exclusion of many white students who are then forced to attend second- and third-choice schools. An analysis of recent national data indicate that this is clearly not the case for undergraduates. Table 1 shows the percentage of students beginning postsecondary education for the first time in 1990, by racial/ethnic

**Table 1.** College Applications and Acceptance At First-Choice College by Race/Ethnicity

| Student Race/ Ethnicity | Applied to One College | Applied to More Than One College | Accepted At First-Choice[a] Institution |
|---|---|---|---|
| African American | 56.5 | 43.5 | 50.1 |
| Native American | 57.2 | 42.8 | — |
| Asian American | 51.9 | 48.1 | 53.7 |
| Latino | 74.7 | 25.3 | 62.6 |
| White | 60.1 | 39.9 | 61.7 |

*Source*: Beginning Postsecondary Student Study 1990-92, National Center for Education Statistics.
[a]Analysis controlled for students who applied to more than one four-year college;—denotes sample size too small for reliable statistics.

group, who applied to one or more colleges. It shows the percentage of students who stated they are attending their first-choice institution, among those students who applied to more than one four-year college. Asian American students and African American students were somewhat more likely than white students to apply to more than one college and yet they were least likely to be accepted at their first-choice institution. An overwhelming majority of Latinos (75 percent) apply to only one college; of the few who applied to more than one college, they were about as likely to attend their first-choice institution as white students. White students do not appear to be disadvantaged in the admissions process. In fact, of all groups, African Americans and Asian Americans were most likely to report having to attend second- and third-choice institutions. Furthermore, Latino and Native American students are highly concentrated in community colleges (Carter & Wilson, 1992), low-cost institutions with low selectivity which are close to their respective communities but less likely to lead to a baccalaureate degree. Thus, the data show distinct racial/ethnic differences in terms of those who apply and are accepted at their first-choice institution.

The assumption that large numbers of minority students are obstructing white students' access to college is also erroneous. If anything, affirmative action has intensified competition among institutions for only the most academically able minority students. In fact, many selective colleges continue to admit only a limited number of minority students despite steady increases in the numbers of minority applicants. The potential use of caps or ceilings in relation to the admission of minorities has been best documented with regard to Asian American enrollments at selective colleges, where admission rates have not kept pace with the rising number of applications (Tagaki, 1992). Although admissions officers typically deny employing such ceilings, and they have not been legally challenged, their practices in effect produce restrictions on enrollments of various racial/ethnic groups. In other words, admissions personnel maintain a level of consistency in the freshman class from year to year by keeping in check the numbers of students with particular academic and nonacademic characteristics.

Therefore, in years when the applicant pool is judged to include fewer minority students who rate highly along admissions criteria, fewer minorities are typically admitted. The overall strategy among selective college admissions has been to increase the quality and quantity of the applicant pool from which only a few will continue to be selected. Still, among all other groups that receive some form of preference in admissions, (e.g., athletes, alumni children, development prospects, candidates from underrepresented regions) frustrated white students are quick to blame the relatively small numbers of students of color for their failure to gain admission to a selective college. This expression of entitlement and scapegoating should be mitigated by the sobering reality that, regardless of race/ethnicity or gender, the competition for access to selective institutions has increased and moreover, that these institutions bolster their reputations by rejecting the vast majority of their applicants.

## Does Race Matter?

Perhaps the most insidious assumption embedded in anti-affirmative action arguments is that gender or racial/ethnic background is unimportant or insignificant in acquiring societal benefits. In short, it is assumed that an individual's race and gender does not and should not matter. Yet, as history shows, race/ethnicity and gender has often had serious implications for an individual particularly in terms of the quantity and quality of educational and employment opportunities made available to him or her (Solomon, 1985). Furthermore, there is evidence to suggest that little has changed in this regard. People of color with the same level of educational attainment continue to earn significantly lower wages than their white counterparts (US. Department of Commerce, 1992 as cited in Nettles & Rodriguez, 1993) and endure more job bias and discrimination while in the workplace (Kielman, 1995). Both white and racial/ethnic college students are aware of these problems. In a 1989 survey, approximately 88 percent of students attending four-year institutions stated that they thought racial discrimination was still a major problem in America (Hurtado, 1992).

In terms of access to college, we have seen considerable growth in student participation rates for all racial/ethnic groups. At the beginning of the 1990s, the percentage of high school graduates (aged 18 to 24) who enrolled in college was 41 percent compared with 32 percent in 1972 (Carter & Wilson, 1992). However, Table 2 shows that while the college participation rates rose for African American and Latino students, the gap between these groups and white students actually increased over the two decades. In fact, the gap in the college participation rate between white and African

**Table 2.** Percentage of High School Graduates Participating in Higher Education, 18-to-24 year olds

| Student's Race/ Ethnicity | Percentage of Participants in Higher Education | | Percentage of Difference between Whites and other Groups | |
| --- | --- | --- | --- | --- |
| | 1972 | 1991 | 1972 | 1991 |
| All Races | 31.9 | 41.1 | — | — |
| African American | 27.1 | 31.5 | −5.2 | −10.2 |
| Hispanic | 25.8 | 34.4 | −6.5 | −7.3 |
| White | 32.3 | 41.7 | — | — |

*Source*: Carter & Wilson, 1992. *Minorities in Higher Education*. Washington, DC.: American Council on Education. Data are unpublished tabulations for October 1991 and from the US. Department of Commerce, Bureau of the Census, *Current Population Reports, School Enrollment—Social and Economic Characteristics of Students: October 1990*, Series P-2-, No. 460.

American students almost doubled, and the gap between Hispanic and white student participation rates increased slightly since 1972. These data suggest that a persistent problem exists in increasing college access for African American and Latino students. This problem merits serious academic study and innovations in both policy and practice. It is not clear how much more inequality we can endure in terms of these attainment gaps before they start to undermine our economic productivity, erode our basic democratic processes, or yield unusually high prison populations.

Given evidence of the growing gap in college participation rates between white and African American students, the assertion that white students are disadvantaged under the current system is highly questionable. The only way to assert such a claim is to deny that race has anything to do with acquiring societal benefits, except under affirmative action policies. Yet this is precisely the claim many opponents of affirmative action make, particularly when it comes to the discussion of their own personal achievements. To illustrate this point, consider the argument that University of California Regent Ward Connerly put forth to justify his appointment to the Board of Regents. Connerly, an African American Republican, stated that he was not appointed to the Board of Regents because he was Black but because he had been a friend of Governor Wilson for 26 years and contributed over $120,000 to the Governor's political campaigns since 1990 (Lively, 1995). In this context, gaining access to benefits and decision-making positions through personal connections and financial advantage is perceived as legitimate, perhaps because this is how we expect that the political world works. However, Connerly's justification raises some serious questions. Since when are appointments to the University Board of Regents based on political contributions? How is this type of appoinment consistent with the philosophy of working hard to "move up the ladder" on the basis of individual effort that Connerly claimed was part of his own upbringing? Why is such a process more acceptable than conceding that Wilson had carefully considered the symbolic and political importance of Connerly's race, along with other criteria, in making his appointment to the Board?

Cornel West (1994) states that the quest for black middle-class respectability based on merit, or criteria other than race, cannot be overestimated in the new black conservative movement:

> The need for black conservatives to gain the respect of their white peers deeply shapes certain elements of their conservatism. In this regard, they simply want what most people want, to be judged by the quality of their skills, not the color of their skin. But the black conservatives overlook the fact that affirmative action policies were political responses to the pervasive refusal of most white Americans to judge black Americans on that basis (p. 78).

Connerly's proposal to require the University of California to select a larger proportion of students (from 50 to 75 percent by 1997) on solely academic criteria was consistent with the need to gain respectability and eschew race. His initial proposal to the Board reflected even more stringent reliance on academic criteria. Both proposals, however, gave little consideration to the fact that affirmative action programs were designed to work with evaluations of academic merit to ensure that California's rapidly growing underrepresented populations, which face considerable barriers in access to the elite tier of public higher education, could gain equal footing with others who had advantages in college access.

What these issues reveal is that race does, indeed, matter. It matters because we continue to have persistent gaps among racial/ethnic groups in academic attainment, in access to particular types of colleges, and in admissions criteria which work to the advantage of some groups and to the disadvantage of others. Paradoxically, as was illustrated in the case of Ward Connerly, it appears that race matters most to those who claim it should be less important. Furthermore, opposition to affirmative action arose just as the top-tier public institutions in California began to reflect the diverse population of the state and women became the majority in undergraduate institutions. Such rapid demographic change in the state's population, and its reflection in higher education, may have caused alarm among those who have historically had the privilege of access. Moreover, it was also a politician's racially divisive approach that took precedence in the UC Regents decision to end affirmative action, rather than concrete evaluations of how the institutions had met their goals for the educational interests of the state's rapidly growing, diverse population. It is to this event that we now turn.

## Access to Higher Education as a Zero-sum Game of Politics

The current debate over the use of race/ethnicity and gender in the college admissions process tends to reduce a complex and multifaceted issue into a simplistic, dualistic matter. Affirmative action is characterized as only right or wrong, fair or unfair. As a consequence, the pursuit of higher education is also reduced into an elite zero-sum game where students are pitted against each other in competition for admission to elite colleges or universities. Those students who are offered admission are considered winners while those who are denied that same opportunity are considered losers. Not only does this neglect our common destiny which is based on the adequate training of students from all racial/ethnic groups, but it is also an irresponsible way to deliberate and evaluate the efficacy of something as important as educational policy. Perhaps the best way to illustrate the problems with this dualistic approach is to discuss its shortcomings in light of the events that occurred at the University of California.

In what was labeled as a "major retreat" from justice by Chief of Staff Leon Panetta and other members of the federal government, the University of California Board of Regents decided to eradicate all campus affirmative action programs based on race or sex in July 1995 (Ayers, Jr., 1995). According to Regent member John Davies, the decision was based upon the fact that the Board had "learned that this tool does more harm than good" (Schwartz, 1995). Yet, according to information relayed via internet about the public session and various newspaper accounts of the vote, there was considerable opposition to Davies' assertion from faculty, students, and staff within the university system (Ayers, Jr., 1995; Witt, 1995). In particular, Dean Haile Debas of the University of California at San Francisco School of Medicine provided testimony which argued the contrary: A study conducted by the School of Medicine revealed that many of the Latino and African American graduates had returned as physicians to their respective communities to establish their medical practices.

If the debate over affirmative action had been cast in anything other than the terms of a zero-sum game, there might have been a chance for Debas and Davies to discuss the particulars of the medical school's approach to admitting and educating students of color. However, under the rules of a zero-sum game, compromise or the possibility of a mutually beneficial alternative does not exist. This is unfortunate, for Debas' study embraced the types of outcomes many public policymakers dream of—one that is mutually beneficial for the individual, for higher education, and for a state in need of improved health care in particular communities.

What also became apparent was that the Board of Regents voted against affirmative action before conducting a thorough assessment of the implications and consequences the policy reversal would have on the university system and its students. In fact, the Regents voted against campus affirmative action programs and then instructed both faculty and university leaders to "come up with something that will achieve . . . diversity" (Schwartz, 1995). One must question the logic behind so readily inviting intervention by the federal government, which could have potentially placed students in jeopardy of losing their federal financial aid as well as millions of dollars in research funds. Additionally, there was no alternative plan for achieving diversity whose financial costs had been evaluated at the time of the vote. Campuses were told to end programs or revise policies and then search for an alternative approach that would achieve diversity.

This action defied the fiduciary responsibility of the Regents and also smacked of extreme political maneuvering. Using divisive racial politics in the week prior to the vote, Governor Wilson stated on national television that admission to the University of California was not based on merit, but on race and gender—an intentional fabrication to stir up the debate that was to follow at the Regents meeting. In the week following the Regents' vote, Wilson presented himself as a champion of white and Asian interests in this battle but could not articulate a clear position on other forms of preferential treatment in admission. As a result, he not only revealed his lack of knowledge regarding multifaceted admissions criteria, but also made the articulation of a sound University admissions policy seem insignificant.

Governor Wilson, via the UC Board of Regents, was virtually handed an ideal topic to convert into a battle of state autonomy over federal intervention that he hoped would escalate and become key in his bid for the presidency. Shortly after the Regents' vote, Wilson reported in newspapers that he would not be intimidated by the threat of a federal government investigation of University programs and policies, essentially calling their bluff in terms of actual enforcement of affirmative action. Although the battle regarding affirmative action was won by Wilson's supporters, Wilson ultimately proved not to be popular enough to gain the financial support necessary to become a strong 1996 presidential contender.

These facts reveal another fundamental flaw in the zero-sum game approach: There are only two consequences of importance—that of winning and losing. The consequence that often receives the most attention is, not surprisingly, related to winning. That there may be negative consequences for the opposition is assumed to be a legitimate part of the game and is therefore tolerated. Suddenly changing the direction on the University's affirmative action policies, particularly the long-term goals regarding student recruitment and admissions, was a win for Wilson. However, the consequences of the decision plunged a University system (including a new president, administrators, and faculty) into a quandary about what to do next. If they changed their practices, would they be in violation of federal guidelines? Could they work around the Regents' decision and still keep their jobs? Could they defer[3] admission to an increasing population of nonwhite racial/ethnic students who, no doubt, would seek admission to the University in the coming years? The President of the University of California, appointed in 1995, wished to delay implementation of the ban on race preferences until 1998 to allow administrators time to develop new procedures for incoming undergraduates, but met considerable resistance from the Regents and the Governor and was forced to retract his decision and submit an apology (Schmidt, 1996). These were unusual events for a new president and can only be understood in a political context: Several of the Regents and the Governor were also in the midst of promoting a state ballot measure banning affirmative action. In sum, what matters most in a zero-sum game is winning. Just as a zero-sum game is not conducive to compromise or the consideration of consequences unrelated to winning, it is also not conducive to the discussion of larger, more important issues like institutional mission and purpose.

As the following quote from Regent Roy Brophy to the Chairman of the Board indicates, it seems this held true for the University of California system as well. He said:

> Your Board managed to circumvent the president. Your Board managed to circumvent the chancellors, and also to circumvent the faculty and you managed to circumvent the students. I would also say staff too . . . What bothers me more than anything else is for us to circumvent the best people we have . . . I only hope in the future that we keep it in mind that if we are going to do something like this let's not have a quick vote and shake hands and go home. We must plan for the future, in the future, that everyone is involved in the process . . . (Schwartz, 1995).

As a final point, the zero-sum game approach to evaluating higher education policy is also limited because it fails to take into account history or the notion of restitution for injustices committed in the past. In all the rhetoric that has been bandied about regarding affirmative action, there has been virtually no mention of history, historical injustices or the role that the university system may have played in perpetuating those injustices. The assumption is that we are beyond the vestiges of an exclusionary past. However, by all indicators, we have a long way to go toward eliminating the vestiges of historical discrimination and achieving the goals of equity in college access.

## Renewed Commitment and Articulation of Goals for College Access

The discussion of misconceptions and zero-sum politics leads us to a central question: If we are not concerned with student welfare, educational purpose, responsibility, history or compromise, then what is the current debate over the use of race and gender in the college admissions process truly concerned about? Underlying many of our contemporary policies is an assumption regarding whom we believe is entitled to higher education opportunity and what kinds of colleges should remain for the elite or the masses.

Part of the reason that we have not been able to arrive at a consensus regarding Brubacher's question, "Higher education for whom?" has to do with the zero-sum manner in which we have approached the issue of college access. It also has to do with the effects of time and the tests of our commitment. Circumstances have changed considerably for higher education since 1965. Most notably, there is a different student population to educate with varying levels of preparation for college (Dey & Hurtado, 1995), tighter fiscal restraints to contend with (Callan, 1993), and greater societal expectations of higher education to meet the educational needs of its citizenry without a significant increase in resources (Zusman, 1994). Consequently, in an era of growing economic uncertainty, the fervor for redistributive measures to ensure educational opportunity has also diminished. In sum, as the needs of society and individuals have changed, so too has our ability to definitively answer who higher education ought to serve and why. This is a time for higher education institutions to clearly articulate their goals for college access and review procedures, not because affirmative action has been portrayed as an attack on American values by politicians, but because it is part of a reasonable plan for educating students.

One result of affirmative action policy is that today more institutions acknowledge the educational value in having a diverse student body, faculty, and administration. The institutions in the State of California have not abandoned this value but they now must find new ways to achieve greater equity in access before they suffer the economic and social consequences of educating too few. The Regents of the University of California have placed great faith in their institutions to work toward increasing diversity without the "stick" and with a shrinking "carrot." While there is talk about focusing on low-income students, a social category some find more acceptable than race/ethnicity or gender, most admissions practices and programs already serve these students. Perhaps more importantly, the numbers of low-income students who apply to top-tier institutions have dropped dramatically in the last decade as tuition increases and changes occur in the distribution of federal and state financial aid. Moreover, these declines have resulted in a greater gaps among students based on background: Depending on race/ethnicity, students from high-income families are now eight to thirteen times more likely to attain a baccalaureate degree by age 24 than students in the lowest-income quartile (Mortensen,1990). Tinkering with student-aid programs and doing away with affirmative action programs effectively eliminates key redistributive measures to promote equity in higher education and essentially reinforces the belief that higher education ought to be for the few.

As consequence, some contend that eradicating affirmative action would mean "that racial and sexual discrimination would return with a vengeance" (West, 1992, p. 95). Yet, because these policies were in place, most discrimination is not likely to be so overt. At the same time, eliminating affirmative action will not make our social problems disappear; race and gender inequalities continue to permeate our thinking, practices, and social interactions. What is needed is a renewed commitment to make higher education available to broad segments of the population because both the historical and the continuous inequalities among groups continue to affect our attitudes and interactions with individuals in these social categories. As Audre Lorde (1984) has stated, "we have no patterns for relating across our human differences as equals. As a result, those differences have been misnamed and misused in the service of separation and confusion" (p. 115).

## Strategies for a New Era

Higher education institutions have a definitive role to play in addressing this separation and confusion by educating students about social and cultural differences and taking the lead in reframing the issues underlying the debate on affirmative action. Institutions must take a more active role in the shaping of public policy, or as in the case of the University of California system, risk being subjected to its vagaries. Linking activities and practices with clear institutional goals is the first step in creating an institutional strategy that reflects priorities for creating a diverse learning environment.

One way institutions could address some of the misconceptions surrounding affirmative action, racial issues, and social stigma is through the educational process itself. While most campuses have focused on increasing the diversity of their faculties and student bodies, campuses have neglected the important dimension of improving intergroup relations and attitudes. Institutions can build bridges across communities of difference by engaging faculty and students in dialogue activities inside and outside of the classroom which address long standing conflicts, stereotypes, and problems in intergroup relations. Engaging members of the local community also develops public support for the institutional goals of creating a diverse learning environment.

A second way for higher education institutions to eliminate misconceptions is to be less secretive about admissions procedures and openly convey to potential applicants and their parents the realities of weighing various institutional goals in the admissions process. This would entail an honest discussion of how difficult it is to be admitted to a selective college without a combination of unique qualities that is consistent with the college's educational goals and needs. Such an approach would also recognize the anxiety many students and their parents experience about getting into the right college and their concerns about postcollege career possibilities. Rather than contributing to this unhealthy anxiety, institutions should identify ways to reduce this tension.

Even more importantly, admissions officers should conduct analyses of their own affirmative action efforts and engage in frank discussions about their progress toward eliminating inequality in college access and what they can expect to achieve on their campuses in the coming years. This would also enable admissions officers to identify specific strategies which may be highly effective in increasing the number of underrepresented students on their campuses. While some politicians claim that higher education has achieved its goals through affirmative action, there is little evidence regarding which goals were met nor how they were attained. Many campuses that have made a commitment to diversity should report what they have accomplished, acknowledge the obstacles they have faced, and take the lead in promoting and disseminating successful strategies for achieving diversity goals.

In addition, higher education institutions and their admissions offices should assess the extent to which they have relied upon affirmative action as the primary means for diversifying their campuses and student bodies. The use of racial preferences in college admissions is a legal way to ensure diversity, but more documentation may be necessary in terms of providing information on historical and continuous barriers that women and different racial/ethnic groups face in gaining admission. Admissions officers at selective colleges must also acknowledge the biases that result from employing specific criteria for different groups and address them by considering a wide range of information on each candidate, and then selecting students who excel along several dimensions. Moreover, as with all other types of preferences in admissions, institutions must be able to articulate how their selection practices are consistent with the institution's mission and goals. The goal of educating a diverse student body is not only important to educational processes within the institution, but also extends beyond the campus community to the larger social goals of decreasing inequality, improving race relations, and increasing economic productivity and civic participation among broad segments of society.

Institutions can also engage in creative problem-solving to devise additional methods of diversifying their campuses. For example, cooperative agreements regarding course and degree work with secondary schools, community colleges and four-year colleges that have high proportions of women in underrepresented fields or students of color could be established. Coordinated planning and effort across sectors may result in new ways to improve the preparation of students prior to college and increase student progress through the educational pipeline. As a final strategy, maintaining cooperation and dialogue with other institutions facing similar pressures for maintaining diversity in a changing financial and political climate might also inspire the development of new strategies for achieving educational goals.

We must renew our commitment to determining whether higher education is for the few or for the many. Which answer is chosen depends upon how we approach the question. We cannot pick one over the other because it is consistent with our own needs and interests as the current affirmative action debate would suggest we do.

That is simply too easy. In order to answer Brubacher's question and answer it fairly, we must take into consideration what the purposes and goals of higher education should be, whether or not these purposes and goals are consistent with the overall goals and needs of society, whether they are consistent with the needs of individuals, and understand the implications and consequences of our choices. In other words, we have to honestly assess our past, plan for the future, and honor the needs of both the individual and society. Balancing these concerns will require goal clarification, innovations in institutional approaches, and sustained effort.

## REFERENCES

Astin, A. W. (1994). Educational equity and the problem of assessment. In M. Justiz, R. Wilson, & L. G. Bjork (Eds.), *Minorities in higher education* (pp. 44-63). Phoenix, AZ: ACE-Oryx Press.

Ayers, Jr., B. D. (1995, July 24). Obstacles arise to switch by California on diversity. *The New York Times*. pp. 1–2.

Bazluke, F. (1995). Affirmative action at the crossroads: Legal parameters governing racial preferences in college admissions and financial aid programs. Presented at the University of Vermont Division of Continuing Education, Fifth Annual Legal Issues Conference, October, 1995.

Brubacher, J. S. (1965). Higher education for whom? In *Bases for policy in higher education*, (pp.1-19). New York: McGraw-Hill.

Callan, P. M. (1993). Government and higher education. In A. Levine (Ed.), *Higher learning in America*, 1980-2000 (pp.3–19). Baltimore, Maryland: Johns Hopkins University Press.

Carter, D. J., and Wilson, R. (1993). *Minorities in higher education, Eleventh annual status report*, 1992. Washington, D.C.: American Council on Education.

Collison, M. (1992, February 5). Colleges have done a bad job of explaining affirmative action to students, critics say. *The Chronicle of Higher Education*, pp. A37–A38.

Crouse, J., and Trusheim, D. (1988). *The case against the SAT*. Chicago: The University of Chicago Press.

Dey. E. L., & Hurtado, S. (1995). College impact, student impact: A reconsideration of the role of students within American higher education, *Higher Education*, Vol. 30, pp. 207–223.

Gould, S. J. (1981). *The mismeasure of man*. New York: Norton.

Hauptman, A. M. (1993). *Higher education finance issues in the early 1990s* (Consortium for Policy Research Report Services RR-027). Rutgers, NJ: Consortium for Policy Research in Education.

Herrnstein, R. J., & Murray, C. (1994). *The bell curve: Intelligence and class structure in American life.* New York: The Free Press.

Hurtado, S. (1994). The institutional climate for talented Latino students, *Research in Higher Education*, Vol. 35 (1), 21-41.

Hurtado, S. (1992). Campus racial climates: Contexts for conflict, *Journal of Higher Education*, Vol. 63 (5), pp. 539–569.

Jaschik, S. (1995, April 28). A valuable tool or bias in reverse? *The Chronicle of Higher Education*, pp. A14–A16.

Klieman, C. (1995, July 30). Job bias is rampant, blatant, EEOC chief says. *The Chicago Tribune*, p. 1, Section 8.

Lorde, A. (1984). *Sister outsider: Essays and speeches.* Freedom, CA: The Crossing Press.

Lively, K. (1995, July 28). Preferences abolished: U. of California regents vote to end affirmative action in hiring and admissions. *The Chronicle of Higher Education*, pp. A26–A28.

Mortensen, T., & Wu, Z. (1990). *High school graduation and college participation of young adults by family income backgrounds 1970 to 1989. ACT student financial aid report series 90-3.* Iowa City, IA: American College Testing.

Owings, J., McMillen, M., Burkett, J. & Pinkerton, B. D. (1995). *Making the cut: Who meets highly selective entrance criteria?, Statistics in Brief* (April), National Center for Education Statistics 95–732. Washington, D.C.: U.S. Department of Education, Office of Educational Research and Improvement.

Rodriguez, E. M. & Nettles, M. T. (1993). *Achieving the national education goals: The status of minorities in today's global economy.* A policy report of the State Higher Education Executive Officers Minority Student Acheivement Project, May. Denver, CO: State Higher Education Executive Officers.

Schmidt, P. (1996). U. of California chief won't delay ban on race preferences. *The Chronicle of Higher Education*, XLII (22), p. A29.

Schwartz, J. (1995). [Excerpts from the University of California Regents meeting were sent out over internet July 25, 1995].

Solomon, B. (1985). *In the company of educated women.* New Haven, CT: Yale University Press.

Takagi, D. Y. (1992). *The retreat from race: Asian American admissions and racial politics.* New Brunswick, NJ: Rutgers University Press.

Thelin, J. R. (1985). Beyond background music: Historical research on admissions and access in higher education. In J. Smart (Ed.), *Higher Education: Handbook of Theory and Research*, Vol. 1, 349–380.

Veysey, L. R. (1965). *The emergence of the American university.* Chicago, IL: The University of Chicago Press.

West, C. (1994). *Race matters.* First Vintage Books Edition. New York: Vintage Books.

Witt, H. (1995, July 30). At U. of California, a new set of rules. *The Chicago Tribune*, p. 1, Section 1.

Zusman, A. (1981). Current and emerging issues facing higher education in the United States. In P.G. Altbach, R.O. Berdahl, & P.J. Gumport. (Eds.), *Higher education in American society* (3rd ed.), (335–364). Amherst, NY: Prometheus Books.

## NOTES

1. Evaluating student academic achievement and potential is not a clearly objective enterprise in that admissions officers must consider grades offered by high schools of varying quality, courses of varying academic rigor, as well as whether standardized scores accurately predict achievement for particular populations of students. Moreover, different admissions committees may take into account whether significant experiences have impacted a student's record of academic or leadership accomplishments.

2. While gender was historically used as a category to exclude or limit admission (Solomon, 1985), it is not typically used as an affirmative action category in admissions with the exception of a few fields that actively seek to recruit and admit more women who are underrepresented (e.g. math, science, engineering).

3. The University of California does not formally reject applicants, it *defers* their admission. While the effect of deferring an applicant, essentially leads to the student enrolling elsewhere or not attending higher education, the original thinking behind this view is that any student may eventually become UC eligible.

Caroline Sotello Viernes Turner
and
Samuel L. Myers, Jr.

# 6

## *Faculty Diversity and Affirmative Action*

In 1965, President Johnson outlined many of the ideas behind affirmative action. He stated:

> You do not take a person who, for years, has been hobbled by chains and liberate him, bring him up to the starting line of the race, and then say, "You are free to compete with all the others," and still justly believe that you have been completely fair.

The idea of promoting diversity to remedy past discrimination was directed to the professorate in 1973, when the American Association of University Professors endorsed the use of affirmative action in faculty hiring. Faculty retention was not addressed at this time. Today, after several challenges to affirmative action practices, particularly questioning college admissions policies and higher education race-based scholarships, a review of all federal laws involving affirmative action is taking place. Thus, affirmative action is said to be "on the line" (*Chronicle of Higher Education*, April 25, 1995).

### *Review of the Literature on Faculty Diversity*

A review of the literature on faculty of color in higher education reveals a number of common themes, including documentation and discussion of the continued existence of underrepresentation of faculty of color in American colleges and universities. Some studies (Schuster, 1990; Thomas, 1987; Carter and Wilson, 1991; Adams, 1988; Blackwell, 1988) indicate that the problem of underrepresentation of faculty of color is one of supply and that the answer is to increase the number of doctorate recipients from communities of color. While an important part of the solution, this approach fails to address the barriers within academia that hinder the recruitment and retention of faculty of color.

Researchers have identified several barriers to the recruitment and retention of faculty of color: 1) *isolation/lack of mentoring opportunities*. Faculty of color find themselves outside the informal networks of the department. (Boice, 1993; Blackwell, 1989; Spann, 1990); 2) *occupational stress*. With men and women of color underrepresented in academe, the desire of universities to have minority representation on committees places formidable responsibilities on minority faculty. (Menges and Exum, 1983; Smith and Witt, 1993); 3) *institutional racism*. Minority faculty find that research on minority issues is not considered legitimate work, particularly if research is published in journals that are not "mainstream." Faculty of color voice a common concern that their work is undervalued and that they are treated differently in the academy than their peers. (Nakanishi, 1993; de la Luz Reyes and Halcon, 1988; Mitchell, 1982; Granger, 1993; Padilla and Chavez, 1995). Olivas (1988) describes these higher education institutions with their continued exclusionary practices as "segregated citadel(s)."

Despite years of affirmative action policies, much of the literature that examines the status of faculty of color in higher education reports continued underrepresentation and racial/ethnic bias in the academy.

## Recent Study on Minority Faculty Development

In our recent study for the Midwestern Higher Education Commission (MHEC) completed in May 1995, we reported that underrepresentation of faculty of color among the professorate continues, that racial and ethnic bias remains a concern for many faculty of color (untenured or tenured) participating in this study, and that a lack of institutional commitment undermines faculty success on many Midwestern campuses. While many exemplary programs exist, our study underscores the importance of addressing two areas of concern: 1) the supply of faculty of color and 2) the academic workplace environment for minority faculty. This essay presents an overview of the study findings. Research design and discussion of the details of data collection and analysis can be found in the technical report (Myers and Turner, 1995).

This study was designed to provide the necessary background and planning information to propose a specific set of strategies that the MHEC might adopt in order to enhance recruitment and retention of faculty of color at membership institutions in the Midwest. MHEC was established in 1991 by the Midwestern Regional Education Compact, an interstate statutory agreement among several states. Current compact members are Illinois, Kansas, Michigan, Minnesota, Missouri, Nebraska, Ohio, and Wisconsin. One of the goals of the MHEC is to develop a plan to expand minority faculty in underrepresented academic disciplines in both public and independent colleges, universities, and community colleges throughout the Midwest. We present study results for African Americans, Latinos, and Native Americans—groups which are traditionally covered by affirmative action legislation.

Information for assessment of the patterns of underrepresentation, the causes of underrepresentation and the strategies for remedying minority faculty underrepresentation at MHEC member institutions comes from many sources. There are three principal sources of data used in our discussion. The first is the Public Use Micro Sample Census data, which permits an analysis of the patterns of underrepresentation and of the market factors that contribute to underrepresentation. A second data source is a collection of interviews with minority faculty and administrators in MHEC member institutions, designed to elicit information about minority faculty concerns and recommendations for increasing retention and improving recruitment. A third data source consists of the results from a mailed survey of faculty development programs sent to all MHEC member institutions. The survey was designed to examine existence of faculty development programs and institutional barriers to recruitment and retention of minority faculty.

## Patterns of Underrepresentation

The 1990 Census Public Use Micro Sample (PUMS) represents a sampling of all long census returns including information on industry and occupation for employed persons. We used this data set to define a subset of faculty members. The subset consists of persons, 24 to 70, with occupations listed as postsecondary teacher, not in school, and reporting the industry classification of "college or university." The PUMS counts are generated from self-reports of faculty employment. Accordingly, the definition can include both full-time and part-time employment.

When measured in comparison with the percentage of the population ages 24 to 70, representation among higher education faculty in Midwestern Higher Education Commission (MHEC) states demonstrates the following:

1. The percentage of African American faculty members in MHEC states (3.7 per cent) is considerably less than half the percentage of African Americans ages 24 to 70 in the population (9.5 percent).

2. The percentage of Native American faculty members (0.2 percent) is half the percentage of Native Americans ages 24 to 70 in the population (0.4 percent).

3. In seven MHEC states the percentages of Latino faculty were less than the percentage of Hispanics ages 24 to 70 in the population.

This data shows that African Americans, Native Americans, and Latinos are clearly underrepresented among the faculties in MHEC member states.

More refined comparisons also reveal substantial minority faculty underrepresentation. When the percentage of minority faculty among minority M.A.'s and Ph.D.'s is compared to the percentage of all faculty among M.A.'s and Ph.D.'s, one finds ratios of .39, .50, and .77 for African Americans, Native Americans, and Latinos in the Midwestern states sampled. This means that when compared to all qualified persons in the member states of the MHEC, qualified African Americans are only four-tenths as likely to be faculty,

Native Americans are only half as likely to be faculty, and Latinos are but three-quarters as likely to be faculty.

Further analysis of the data revealed that the central *cause* of the underrepresentation of minority faculty is not the underrepresentation of minorities covering Ph.D.'s. Consistent with the finding that even among highly trained minorities, minority faculty are underrepresented, the evidence suggests that some other factor—perhaps internal to the university setting itself—must be conspiring to prevent full and equal representation of minorities among faculty.

Qualitative data from minority faculty themselves reveal a possible clue.

## Faculty Concerns and Recommendations for Remedy

*Interview Data.* In our interviews with fifty-five individual faculty, and our interaction with nine faculty in two focus groups, we gleaned potent information about minority faculty perceptions of a "chilly climate" on many MHEC member campuses. The key concerns expressed by the minority faculty were:

- Racial, gender, and ethnic bias
- Isolation, and unsupportive work environment
- Lack of information about tenure and promotion
- Language/accent barriers
- Lack of mentors and lack of support from superiors

White faculty may share these same concerns.

This summary will report data specific to racial and ethnic background. Racial and ethnic bias was the most frequently mentioned challenge in the interviews and focus groups. It is useful to "unpack" this piece of baggage in an attempt to understand the manifestations of racial/ethnic bias perceived by most faculty of color interviewed for this study. Numerous personal experiences underscore the problem of racial and/or ethnic bias:

> And I've heard some anecdotal things with one of my friends that was told very straight-in-the-face, you might

say . . . He was going for a provost position and the president of that place said, well you know, you should try this other place. There's more (minorities) there . . .

Related to the feeling of racial bias is the perception that minority faculty members must work harder than whites and that they must be twice as good to be just as equal. Being in the "spotlight," these minority faculty members feel they are under almost constant scrutiny. They believe that they must be at their best at all times and must exceed what whites do in a comparable situation. To achieve within the normal realms of expectation might be construed as lacking the necessary drive to become a successful faculty member:

The competence of minority faculty is more apt to be questioned and challenged, it makes it more difficult.

Rightly or wrongly, many of my non-minority colleagues, they are never 100 percent sure that a minority person is here because they are good at what they do or because of affirmative action.

Being very conspicuous is an added burden to the minority faculty person and creates great discomfort for them. They feel diminished in their professional capacity and long to be recognized first for their academic credentials.

It's like you get this look and all of a sudden you think to yourself, that's right, I'm black. That's right I'm a person of color. And, so, they're not seeing me the way I see myself. They see that [color] first and then get their little shock . . .

Those interviewed do not want to be seen as a showpiece or for others to think that standards were lowered to hire them. The existence of affirmative action policies often is used to discount or discredit faculty of color:

It's just like when they trot me out for the minority students and then they trot me back in. It's the same notion, they trot me out when they need attention brought to renovation, and then they trot me back in when they no longer need me.

I think that one of the challenges is to prove that you don't have your job because you were an affirmative action hire, that you're not a token.

One person really got mad at me . . .He was resentful that I was hired . . .he thought it was solely on my race.

You know, students sometimes ask, well do you think you got your job because of affirmative action?

You feel like a token, I always feel like that, feeling like a token. The token Indian.

Many respondents also remarked that research on minority issues was not valued:

But the chair said, get rid of this Indian stuff, when he looked at my vita. . . and I looked at him [and said] I'll do anything else that you want me to do. . . but I can not give that up . . .

or, that they were expected to handle minority affairs;

Issues of pedagogy and cultural diversity and gender are not the province of just women or just faculty of color. I think that happens too often and that puts the faculty of color person or woman on the spot, to kind of convince or persuade—be this change agent . . .

The faculty members feel the added pressure, but are caught in a "catch 22" because minority issues are also important to them.

> It's time consuming . . . almost every committee wants you to be on it. It gives you opportunities at the same time.

Being one of few minority faculty members or the only minority faculty member on a campus presents a problem. Although most of these faculty members continue to function well in this situation, some of them said that it presents a special problem:

> I've gotten tired of going to faculty meetings and being the only African American there.

One informant believes that the small numbers of minority faculty at many institutions perpetuate the notion that minorities cannot achieve as highly as whites in academia:

> And I think that the paucity of black professors and administrators in these kinds of settings reinforces the presumption people have that we're out of place and it leads to all kinds of ironic, comical, and downright restrictions on life chances for blacks and other minorities in these kinds of settings.

Racially based bias appears to be pertinent to all of the minority groups that were a part of this study. Uniformly, the minority voices claim that the university represents an unwelcoming environment where the talents and aspirations of people of color are not always fully valued. These interview data do not prove that the chilly climate causes underrepresentation of minority faculty, but they provide convincing testimony of the pervasiveness of that problem.

## Recommendations from Faculty

From our interviews we gleaned an alternative set of strategies that focus on retention of minority faculty by improving prospects for tenure and increasing satisfaction with academia. The main recommendations concerned the need for better networks of minority scholars, for better mentoring, and for support for research and publications.

*Networking.* Networking is a way to combat the isolation that so many minority faculty reported. It is also a way to connect with others from institutions throughout the Midwest. Through this connection informants suggested that an organized sharing process would encompass both the professional and personal areas affected by academic life. The following quotes are ethnically grouped, yet they share a common thread of wanting to reach out and share their experience with other faculty of color.

### African American

Yeah, the first thing that pops into my mind is the whole notion of networking information, connecting with those faculty members of color who are out there—and maybe even some faculty members who are not of color could be part of the network, too, who have information, who are working on particular projects, who are at different stages of their academic careers—and the information, maybe it could be connected by Internet or E-mail. But, certainly, that sharing of the information. And with this whole new boom in technology, I think that would be a real doable thing.

### Native American

The following informant suggested "traveling in packs" as a metaphor for networking. This networking could be a way for faculty of color to be able to cope with being fringe members in an inherently racist society.

There does need to be support mechanisms. You need much more in terms of support systems . . . you need much more in terms of support systems because these environments are not of our culture, not of our world. Minority people, we are always fringe members of society, we're never fully accepted . . . This is America entering the 21st century, it's a racist society, period. That's an issue that many people don't want to address but that's the truth of it. So if there are going to be minority faculty there needs to be support for them. Sometimes 'traveling in packs' would help.

### Latino

These first two quotes echo the networking suggestions made by individuals in the other groups:

> That's helpful to get that networking and that kind of information disseminated at least throughout the region. Another might be additional funding to encourage people to go to different conferences to present . . .

*Mentoring.* According to a number of the informants, designing and implementing mentoring relationship systems would help new faculty of color become acclimatized to academia and to their individual institutions. There are suggestions that structures be created that would help department chairs and senior faculty facilitate the success of women and minority faculty. Each of the groups had comments about mentoring as a strategy:

### African Americans

> Well, get mentoring. That's definite . . . get as much mentoring—because if you are on a tenure track position and supposedly they are hiring you with the idea of tenuring you, then they should also be willing to avail you of the things that would support your packet. It's not just enough to hire them and leave it at that.

### Native American

> I particularly like the model which is used by—what is it? It's sponsored by the American Bar Association—Project CLEO, the Council for Legal Educational Opportunity in Washington, D.C. They run a summer institute which blends into a continuing mentoring relationship. A real

mentoring relationship. Not this: "Hi, let's get together, have lunch and tell me what you'd like." It's a real, structured mentoring relationship for law students. I think that's a wonderful model.

### Latino

If you could get something that would do what my mentor did for me, that would be the exact thing, but that's a difficult thing. My mentor became very instrumental and very important in my life . . . he took me on as a research assistant and so I did some research for him . . . and then he offered me a post-doc for two years. I co-authored with him. I had a really good mentor. He got me my first position . . . He's the one who gave my name to others and they put me on editorial boards. I will always be grateful to him.

*Support for Research and Publication.* In spite of renewed emphasis on teaching skills, the maxim of "publish or perish" still dominates the lives of academics. Indeed, there is always a need for continued research and conversation within the various fields. This presents a problem for new faculty for whom time is a scarce commodity. Each of the groups has suggestions for aiding new faculty:

### African American

So, I find myself doing research at the same time I'm going to school because I'm getting that message to that, you know, "publish or perish," you know, you hear it at the faculty meetings, but they say [to me] you're a new faculty, don't worry about it, but at the same time they say [to me] you'd better start worrying about it. I want to have a couple of things under my belt so when I finish the program, even though it's supposed to be tenure track, I've got a little insurance that they are going to say, 'Hey! We think we want to keep ya!' So, there is that unspoken pressure to be doing it all at the same time.

### Native American

We must have diversity in scholarship. Indians get censored even before we get in print. More outlets are needed to publish articles on minority concerns. An editor I know implied that research on Indians is second rate. Tribal sovereignty is not an interest of mainstream publications. But outlets to publish articles about minority concerns are growing, and growing with respect to respectability.

### Latinos

I would like to see something like the Spencer Grants for the Midwest region targeted to assist faculty members of color. I am thinking, what would help me? I need time to work on something. Time that is your own during the six year period. Buy out half-time or even a term. It is costly to implement but it would give us a leg up. This could be competitive and faculty could commit so they can't do other things. Try not to participate in other things on campus. Not increase involvement in other things. Time to focus on your own work would be extremely helpful.

These three strategies of networking, mentoring, and providing support for research and publications are cited widely in the literature as effective strategies for improving faculty retention. While these are obvious strategies that focus on keeping faculty once they are hired, they also have positive potential impacts for attracting them in the first place.

## Institutional Commitment

*Survey Data.* Institutional survey data reported here mirror individual respondent concerns. They show that there are many barriers to effective retention and recruitment among the member institutions. Some of the most telling evidence that there is much to be done in the MHEC states comes from the responses to the Faculty Development Survey. This survey was sent to all institutions of higher education in MHEC states. A total of 486 surveys were returned for a response rate of 68 percent. The results of the survey indicate that despite the fact that 77 percent of the institutions surveyed reported minority faculty recruitment and retention as a high or very high priority, most offer little organized support for these goals. Institutional barriers to minority faculty development include the following:

- There is an absence of direct administrative responsibility for minority faculty development.
- Few institutions have mentoring programs for minority faculty.
- Few resources are allocated for faculty mentoring (minority or otherwise).
- Support of faculty in recognition of diversity is lacking.
- Little money is spent on minority faculty development.
- There is a common perception that there are insufficient numbers of qualified minority candidates for faculty positions.

Specific results of the survey illustrate these findings:

1. Only six percent of the MHEC institutions have a special office for minority faculty professional development.
2. Only nine percent offer funding for minority faculty mentoring programs.
3. Only 20 percent offer (what they judge as) excellent support of faculty in recognizing diversity (such as supporting and valuing a faculty member's efforts to recruit minority students).
4. Fifty-four percent said that they allocate less than five percent of their faculty development budgets for minority faculty.
5. Respondents were asked what the primary obstacles are to recruitment of minority faculty in four areas: arts and humanities, science and engineering, social science, and

professional. Overall, the most common obstacle reported was insufficient numbers of qualified candidates. Respondents see a lack of qualified candidates as a barrier to recruitment within each area: 58 percent for arts and humanities, 59 percent for science, engineering, and technology, 49 percent for social science, and 48 percent for professional. This was the most common obstacle reported to recruitment of minority faculty in arts and humanities and science and engineering. The second most common obstacle reported overall was low representation (i.e., low numbers of minority faculty, staff, and students). This was the most common obstacle reported to recruitment of minority faculty in the social sciences. A third common obstacle was salary competition with other higher education institutions. This was the most common barrier reported to the recruitment of professional school faculty.

In summary, at least among the respondent institutions there are few mechanisms in place to improve minority faculty retention and recruitment. In part, this might be due to financial constraints and to the absence of administrative line responsibility for minority faculty recruitment and retention.

In addition to the "lack of qualified candidates" faculty employment obstacle, in a recent study Mickelson and Oliver (1991) contend that another obstacle to the employment of racial/ethnic minorities among the tenure track faculty ranks is underemployment or underutilization. The disproportionate hiring of faculty of color in part-time and nontenure track faculty positions may present other obstacles to having faculty of color in tenure track positions.

Mickelson and Oliver describe the effect or lack of effect of affirmative action on the faculty hiring process in this way:

> One policy used widely to increase the number of minority faculty members is affirmative action. Yet even the most rigorously enforced affirmative action programs have limitations because greater numbers of minority faculty per se are not their direct goal. Rather their primary objective is to open up the recruitment process by advertising widely and

stating explicitly employer's nondiscriminatory intentions. Affirmative action programs have been relatively unsuccessful in increasing the proportion of minority faculty in this country precisely because of the way in which qualified candidates are identified, screened, and selected for the short list ... An affirmative action policy is of little value if no minority candidates are selected for the short list ... (p.161)

Mickelson and Oliver contend that the traditional use of the "ranking of a candidate's graduate department and the recommendations of prestigious scholars" as proxies for the applicant's merit disadvantage many minority applicants, who for many reasons other than lack of talent, may have attended less prestigious institutions and may not have had the opportunity to work closely with prestigious faculty. Additional evidence is provided in the work of Turner and Thompson (1993) and Blackwell (1989). These studies discuss the lack of apprenticeship and mentorship opportunities for doctoral students of color in major research university settings.

## Questions of Stoking the Pipeline

Based on the data from this study, we recommended that the MHEC not limit its efforts to the production of minority Ph.D.s as a sole remedy to the underrepresentation of African American, Native American, and Latino faculty among member institutions. Such a strategy will not address the many concerns of existing faculty and will not pave a new path for future faculty of color whose retention problems will most likely remain severe. Instead, we recommended a focus on mentoring, networking, and research support to assure that minority faculty fulfill their potential and contribute to the intellectual future of our universities and colleges. There are benefits in this strategy that go far beyond the initial increase in retention rates. Future minority scholars contemplating careers in academia will be exposed to mentors and established research networks and will learn to expect quality support for research and publications. Only time will tell if our recommendations are followed.

The pursuit of a career in academia is not easy. There are rigorous requirements, both explicit and implicit. Persons of color face many additional obstacles that are not experienced by their white colleagues. The existence of these additional obstacles is given credibility by the fact that this view was expressed by nearly all of the participants in our interviews and focus groups. Whether they are tenured or tenure track, in the fields of science, social science, or humanities, at two-year or four-year institutions, similar experiences were reported. These informants can not be simply dismissed as disgruntled. It is significant that many "seasoned veterans" commented on the additional difficulties encountered by persons of color.

Nearly all of the informants remarked that faculty of color cannot wait idly by for the emergence of altruism in order to improve their situations. A focused strategy of assistance is needed. It is not a matter of reducing any of the existing academic standards. None of the informants expressed a desire for special treatment. What is necessary are strategies that help to level the playing field and thereby neutralize some of the extra burdens faced by faculty of color.

Many strategies have been suggested and several may be implemented. In many instances strategies go a long way to assist an individual as he or she struggles for success in academia. Even so, one underlying factor remains. What can be done about the obstacles presented by an unwelcoming and inhospitable college climate? In our analysis, racial/ethnic/gender bias stood out as the greatest challenge to success and well-being. Institutions must go a long way in order to transform the climate into one that encourages and nurtures all of its members. Faculty members of color have reported that they are willing and ready to do what is necessary to make themselves the best that they can be. They in turn need a promise and a commitment to change on the part of the institutions.

Although the mentoring, networking, and research support efforts will not eliminate racism or bias on college campuses, these efforts do hold promise for strengthening the capacity of minority faculty to help build a better university or campus climate. With minority faculty as coequal partners in restructuring the interactions that occur in the daily life of the academy, there is a better chance that the next generation will face less of the chilly climate that the current generation of faculty experience. The beneficiaries will be not only minority faculty, but students, staff, administrators, and faculty of all colors and ethnic backgrounds. This is the promise that higher education must embrace; this is the future that we can all build. Now is not the time to stop affirmative action policies but to fine tune them and press beyond present policy and practice in addressing racial and ethnic bias in the recruitment and retention of faculty of color in higher education.

## REFERENCES

Adams, Howard G. (January, 1988). "Tomorrow's Professorate: Insuring Minority Participation Through Talent Development Today." Engineering Dean's Council Student Pipeline Workshop. Washington, D.C.: American Society for Engineering Education.

Blackwell, James E. (June 1988). "Faculty Issues: The Impact on Minorities." *The Review of Higher Education, 11* (4), 417–434.

Blackwell, James E. (September 1989). "Mentoring: An Action Strategy for Increasing Minority Faculty." *Academe*, 75 (5), 8–14.

Boice, Robert. (March, 1993). "Early Turning Points in Professional Careers of Women and Minorities." *New Directions for Teaching and Learning*, 53, 71–79.

Carter, Deborah J., & Wilson, Reginald. (1991). *Minorities in Higher Education: Tenth Annual Status Report*. Washington, D.C.: American Council on Education, Office of Minority Concerns.

*Chronicle of Higher Education*. (April 25, 1995). "Affirmative Action on the Line." Volume XLI, Number 33, A11–A33.

de la Luz Reyes, Maria & Halcon, John J. (1988, August). "Racism in America: The Old Wolf Revisited." *Harvard Educational Review*, 58 (3), 299–314.

Granger, Marylyn W. "A Review of the Literature on the Status of Women and Minorities in the Professorate in Higher Education." *Journal of School Leadership*, 3(2), 121–135.

Menges, Robert J. & Exum, William H. (1983). "Barriers to the Progress of Women and Minority Faculty." *Journal of Higher Education*, 54 (2), 123–144.

Mickelson, Roslyn Arlin, & Oliver, Melvin L. (1991). "Making the Short List: Black Candidates and the Faculty Recruitment Process." in

Philip G. Altbach and Kofi Lomotey (Eds.) *The Racial Crisis in American Higher Education.* Albany: State University of New York Press, 149–166.

Mitchell, Jacquelyn. (February 1982). "Reflections of A Black Social Scientist: Some Struggles, Some Doubts, Some Hopes." *Harvard Educational Review,* 52 (1), 27–44.

Myers, Samuel L., Jr., & Sotello Turner, Caroline. (May 1995). *Midwestern Higher Education Commission Minority Faculty Development Project.* Technical Report. Minneapolis, MN: Midwestern Higher Education Commission.

Nakanishi, Don T. (March 1993). "Asian Pacific Americans in Higher Education: Faculty and Administrative Representation and Tenure." *New Directions for Teaching and Learning,* 53, 51–59.

Olivas, Michael A. (1988, May/June). "Latino Faculty at the Border: Increasing Numbers Key to More Hispanic Access." *Change,* pp. 6–9.

Padilla, Raymond V., & Chavez Chavez, Rudolfo. (1995). *The Leaning Ivory Tower: Latino Professors in American Universities.* State University of New York Press: Albany.

Schuster, Jack H. (June 1990). "Faculty Issues in the 1990s: New Realities, New Opportunities." *New Directions for Higher Education,* 70, 33–41.

Smith, Earl, & Witt, Stephanie L. (1993). "A Comparative Study of Occupational Stress Among African American and White University Faculty: A Research Note." *Research in Higher Education,* 34 (2), 229–241.

Spann, Jeri. (1990). *Retaining and Promoting Minority Faculty Members: Problems and Possibilities.* Madison: The University of Wisconsin System.

Thomas, Gail E. (Spring 1992). "Participation and Degree Attainment of African American and Latino Students in Graduate Education Relative to Other Racial and Ethnic Groups: An Update from Office of Civil Rights Data." *Harvard Educational Review,* 62 (1), 45–65.

Turner, Caroline Sotello Viernes, & Thompson, Judith Rann. (Spring 1993). "Socializing Women Doctoral Students: Minority and Majority Experiences." *The Review of Higher Education,* 16 (3), 355–370.

Bonnie E. Busenberg and Daryl G. Smith

# 7

## *Affirmative Action and Beyond: The Woman's Perspective*

Affirmative action is a policy obfuscated by emotionality, besieged by complex charges, and undermined both by the ignorance of its critics and the ambivalence of its beneficiaries. Some praise affirmative action as a politically imaginative way to pave the way for future equities in spite of current biases; others denounce it as a form of reverse discrimination which will ultimately be detrimental to progress toward equity in this country. Few understand exactly how affirmative action works or have the perspective to honestly evaluate its net effects after more than 20 years of implementation. For many, affirmative action is little more than a vague notion of advantages proffered by the government in retribution for prior discrimination—advantages given to women and minorities, diverse groups often referred to as a single homogeneous entity.

While it is true that women and minorities are both protected groups affected by affirmative action legislation, it is equally true that the two categories are by no means identical with one another with respect to their history of discrimination, their progress toward equity over the last 30 years, or their current employment status. This chapter will focus on women and affirmative action, examining the policy from the unique perspective of its effect on the progress of women in the university setting, yet mindful of the frequently overlooked reality that the experiences of white women are often in sharp contrast with those of minority women who must labor under the double jeopardy of gender and race discrimination.

## Women: The Step Children of Affirmative Action

In a very real sense, women were initially the stepchildren of affirmative action. The Executive Order which established affirmative action sought to ensure more immediate realization of the termination of occupational segregation by race which had been mandated by Title VII of the Civil Rights Act of 1964 (42 U.S.C.A. sec 2000e et seq., and regulations at 29 C.F.R. secs. 1604–1601, 1608.1 et seq.).[1] Lyndon B. Johnson's famous Executive Order 11246, issued on September 24, 1965, mandated that all companies wishing to do business with the federal government not only provide equal opportunity for all, but in addition, take affirmative action to bring their hiring in line with available labor pools by race in their locales. Specifically, that Executive Order required federal contractors (including public universities who contracted with the federal government) to "take affirmative action to insure that applicants are employed . . . without regard to their race, creed, color, or national origin and to take affirmative action to assure that employees and applicants for employment are treated without regard to these factors" (Yates, 1993). Women were not included as a protected class under this policy. It took two long, hard years of lobbying by feminists to include "sex" as a discrimination category so that unfair hiring practices with regard to women could be addressed. Women were only included in affirmative action mandates by Executive Order 11375, signed by Johnson on October 13, 1967. Executive Order 11375 extended Executive Order 11246 and required that affirmative action be taken to bring hiring of women into line with their availability in relevant labor pools.[2] The enforcement of the Executive Orders was given to the Office of Federal Contract Compliance Programs (OFCCP) of the Department of Labor.

The full impact of these executive actions were not fully felt in the academic world until five years later. Nineteen seventy-two was the pivotal year in bringing affirmative action measures to campuses. In that year, Title VII of the Civil Rights Act was extended to include all educational institutions. Additionally, the Equal Pay Act of 1963 was extended to cover executive, administrative, and professional employment. Finally, Title IX of the Educational Amendments of 1972 (20 U.S.C. sec. 1681 et seq., and regulations at 34 C.F.R. secs. 106.1 et seq., 45 C.F.R. secs. 86.1 et seq.), which prohibits sex discrimination in all educational institutions that receive federal funding, was also enacted. Its affirmative action provisions apply to the employment of workers as well as the admission of students. During the same 12 months, HEW issued guidelines to higher education for the implementation of Executive Order 11246 (Astin & Snyder, 1982). In these guidelines, affirmative action is defined as requiring assurance of employment neutrality through deliberate and positive efforts on the part of institutions to rectify existing inequities that resulted from past discrimination (Carnegie Commission on Higher Education, 1973). Since 1972, therefore, it has been reasonably clear that the obligation of colleges and universities to avoid discriminating against employees and/or applicants for employment because of their sex, as well as because of their race, and to take affirmative action to ensure that hiring practices are in line with the availability of women and minorities in the labor pools from which their employees are drawn, are approximately the same as those of any employer.

## Defining Affirmative Action

The phrase "affirmative action" was not defined in Executive Order 11264 and there has been much confusion over the exact meaning of the term. Additionally, there has frequently been a lack of differentiation between the legal meaning of the phrase and the moral imperative the words convey.

Many years ago, Greenawalt defined affirmative action quite loosely as "attempts to bring members of underrepresented groups, usually groups that have suffered discrimination, into a higher degree of participation in some beneficial program" (Greenawalt, cited in Cortese, 1992). This definition describes well those early, and mostly voluntary, affirmative action programs which outreached to minority members for college admissions, employment, and the awarding of contracts. In this, its broadest sense, affirmative action is "any measure beyond simple termination of discriminatory practices, which seeks to correct existent discriminatory patterns so that discrimination will not recur" (Maguire, cited in Cortese, 1992).

Unfortunately, higher participation rates for women and minority members were not achieved by open-ended implementation of the policy. Affirmative action has more recently, however, come to refer to a policy of preferences in decisions concerning educational and economic opportunities designed to change a historic pattern of discrimination in a particular institution, to remedy a general societal discrimination, or to achieve balance or diversity in line with contemporary demographic patterns. This understanding of the policy clearly differentiates it from anti-discrimination programs which attempt to discover overt misdeeds and rectify them. Affirmative action programs are designed as preemptive interventions which seek to modify hiring practices and ways of doing business so that some groups do not continue to benefit at the expense of other groups. Affirmative action in this sense is not about identifying flagrant discriminatory practices, but seeks to counteract more subtle, covert, and sometimes unconscious practices which systematically exclude qualified individuals from opportunities to enter, achieve, and contribute to the American work force because of their race or gender. In the words of President Bill Clinton, speaking in the Rotunda of the National Archives in July 1995 "Affirmative Action is an effort to develop a systematic approach to open the doors of education, employment, and business development opportunities to qualified individuals who happen to be members of groups that have experienced longstanding and persistent discrimination."

To comply with affirmative action regulations, colleges and universities nationwide have had to write affirmative action plans and to develop guidelines for recruiting and hiring faculty and administrators as part of their affirmative action compliance programs. The guidelines typically state that position qualifications must be approved prior to advertising a position, and mandate where and for how long the position will be advertised. The guidelines outline hiring procedures in some detail, and proscribe the creation of search or screening committees with the expectation that either the committees or their hiring administrators will enumerate the criteria used to select final candidates. Most guidelines include special approval requirements regarding recruitment procedures for positions where "underutilization" of women or minorities has been determined to exist. When qualified women and minorities are not selected for such positions, guidelines often require that the hiring unit submit a written justification of the decision to the institution's affirmative action officer and appropriate central administrators for review and approval before an offer is made to any other candidate. The purpose of such detailed affirmative action guidelines for universities is to ensure that all qualified women and minorities have equal opportunity to apply and be considered for available positions. The guidelines are complemented by utilization analyses which establish the number of women and minorities an academic unit could reasonably be expected to have, given its size. A utilization analysis also provides information on the corresponding current representation of women and minorities in the discipline of the academic unit and establishes the hiring goals where underutilization is determined to exist. It is clear that the focus of affirmative action regulations applied to colleges and universities is on process and procedures. The regulations do not interfere with, or attempt to control, decision-making processes concerning who will be hired into a department or institution.

Governmental intrusion into the higher education enterprise because of affirmative action policy has not been heavy-handed. No educational institution has ever lost its federal funding by virtue of its noncompliance with affirmative action measures. However, the regularization of the process of job searches which these measures have demanded has been one of the most significant contributions toward achieving equity in academic hiring. After affirmative action was implemented, no longer could deans and college presidents call up their acquaintances at other institutions, inquire about promising students, and hire without a competitive search. Reporting to affirmative action monitoring agencies has meant that all jobs have to be advertised and that records must be kept of applicants, interviewees, and job offers extended for a position. Hiring has thus become a public process, helping to break a cycle of intellectual inbreeding that existed at many schools and ensuring that more women and minorities are able to find out where the appropriate job openings are located.

## Should Affirmative Action Include Women?

There were many who thought in 1965, and many who think even now, that it was a mistake to include women in affirmative action legislation, that their inclusion diverts attention from the all important consideration of race issues, and that the discrimination they face was and is considerably less than that inflicted upon minority members. But is it appropriate to pit these two groups against one another? Would a more exclusive application of affirmative action measures result in its greater efficacy or a more ready acceptance of the policy? Shouldn't the dichotomous question "who has suffered more" be replaced by the more inclusive query "who has suffered discrimination at all and been excluded from their full rights as citizens?"

It is easily documented that women have long been the victims of both overt and subtle discrimination, particularly in the academic world. America's colleges were founded to educate young men. It was not until the period between 1865 and 1900 that women's colleges appeared, and that concomitantly many men's colleges began admitting women, making coeducation the model type of collegiate institution. Many of the most elite institutions, however, remained closed to women until some 30 years ago. Women who succeeded in graduating from college through the first quarter of the twentieth century were often excluded from graduate and professional programs. For instance, Mary Walsh, in her study of women and medical education, showed that institutions raised new barriers after the battle for access to medical training had apparently been won by women: quotas were imposed on admissions to medical schools, reinforced by still-smaller quotas on the acceptance of women interns, and by the refusal of some hospitals to admit women as interns or residents. There were even prohibitions against licensed women physicians' membership in certain medical societies (Clifford, 1993). Financial support for academic study was traditionally in short supply for women. Records indicate, for example, that while in 1920 women made up 40 percent of the graduate students at the University of Chicago, they received a mere 20 percent of the available fellowships. Women wanting to pursue careers in research often did so in the laboratories or intellectual circles of their fathers and husbands and rarely succeeded in obtaining a formal university appointment. A good example of this was the physicist and nobel laureate, Maria Goeppert Mayer. Mayer received her Ph.D. in quantum mechanics in 1930, emigrated to the United States with her American husband in that same year, but could work only as a voluntary associate at Johns Hopkins University because nepotism laws prohibited her from receiving a salary. She did not get her first salaried teaching job (at Sarah Lawrence College in Bronxville, New York) until 1942. Mayer participated on an equal footing with male colleagues on war research at Columbia University, but after the war when her husband and her wartime collaborators (e.g., Fermi, Urey, and Teller) were offered jobs at the newly created Institute for Nuclear Studies at the U. of Chicago with facilities at the nearby Argonne National Laboratory, Maria received only an appointment as associate professor and member of the institute, but with no salary.

Geneticist Barbara McClintock, the first U.S. woman to win a solo Nobel Prize (awarded in 1983 in the field of Physiology or Medicine for her discovery of transposable genetic systems or "jumping genes") suffered similar discrimination during her career. When she enrolled at Cornell University in 1919 hoping to study the breeding of plants, the genetics department would not accept her as a major because she was a woman, so her undergraduate degree was earned in the related field of botany. After she earned her doctorate in 1927, she held an instructor appointment at Cornell and then a series of research associate positions at the California Institute of Technology, at Cornell, at the Kaiser Wilhelm

Institute in Berlin and finally at the Carnegie Institute of Washington in Cold Spring Harbor.

Throughout her career, she was predominantly supported by grant funding. She held a regular position as an assistant professor at the University of Missouri for a short time, but quit when it became obvious there were no chances for advancement. Finally settling in at the independent laboratory, Cold Spring Harbor, where she lived and worked for over 50 years, her careful experimentation on maize pigmentation—which led to profound insights into genetic mechanisms—went largely unnoticed for three decades. Some say this is because conceptually she was so far ahead of her time; many believe her lack of recognition stemmed from her being a woman.

The lack of appointments available to Maria Mayer, Barbara McClintock, and countless others in past decades had nothing to do with inferior ability or dearth of productivity. It had everything to do with gender. Such blatant inequity among highly qualified people is at the heart of what affirmative action was meant to address.

Women have been historically underrepresented on faculties in the United States. A 1911 survey of women faculty in eighty-one state colleges and universities reported women to be about 9 percent of these schools' total faculty. They were most numerous in the fields of English, music, modern language, domestic science, and home economics, but in the natural sciences and mathematics, it was noted that women did not often rise above the rank of instructor. Studies of promotion patterns also yield strong evidence of discrimination. For instance, an examination of faculty promotion patterns from its opening in 1892 to 1969 at the private University of Chicago, showed that no woman had progressed through the ranks to full professor in the social sciences: all women full professors had attained that rank at another institution before being employed at the University of Chicago or had been promoted in departments which were almost exclusively female, such as Home Economics. As late as 1969, the University of Chicago had only 11 women full professors alongside 464 men of that rank. While search committees might have said that the female candidates were not equally as qualified as their male competitors in job searches, such explanations are questionable given the available pools of successful women faculty at other institutions during the same time period. The lack of proportionality in faculty hiring and promotion is a telling indicator of the discrimination traditionally experienced by women aspiring to academic careers.

While it is true that since 1900 the number of women faculty in American institutions of higher education has grown substantially, the proportion of women faculty compared to men faculty has been slow to change. Nationwide, women constituted 20 percent of the faculty in 1910. Their numbers grew slowly but steadily over the next three decades and reached a high point of 28 percent in 1940. But the representation of women on faculties plummeted in postwar years and recovered only slowly, so that even in 1970 women represented only 23 percent of the national professorate. The pre-World War II level of 29 percent female representation on faculties was finally regained in 1984 and has been slowly rising to the 36 percent level realized in 1994. But there is ample evidence in today's academy that women are still clustered in departments such as education and health care, and abysmally scarce in departments such as engineering and physics. Furthermore, they hold a much higher percentage of the part-time and nontenure track positions, and they experience salary inequities both within and across ranks and fields. In short, substantial evidence mandates the conclusion that women have a legitimate claim to protection under the law by virtue of the gender discrimination they have experienced in employment in higher education institutions.

## Current Status of Women in Academia

Although women could be considered the stepchildren of affirmative action, we all learned from the story of Cinderella that stepchildren can sometimes come out on top. In the 24 years since the full implementation of affirmative action measures in academe, women have clearly made progress—indeed they have made more progress than minority groups. According to 1993-1994 data from the National Center for Education Statistics (NCES), in 1993 women made up 56 percent of all undergraduates,[3] 53 percent of all graduate students and 41 percent of all first professional students. In 1992–1993 women received 55 percent of all the degrees awarded: 54 percent of all the bachelor degrees, 59 percent of the associate degrees, 54 percent of the masters degrees and 38 percent of all the doctorates. They also earned 40 percent of all the first professional degrees. While men continue to hold a majority of the faculty positions, women are making gains, with more than one-third (36 percent) of the 717,334 full-time and part-time instructional faculty employed by U.S. colleges and universities in 1992 being women. Bear in mind, however, that women make up more than half of the U.S. population and comprise 56 percent of all undergraduates and 53 percent of graduate students in the country. Currently, the profile of American faculties still does not mirror the face of the national student body. Women may be present in academe, but they are by no means equally represented among faculty ranks. Data from the National Center for Education Statistics indicate that in the fall of 1992, while women comprised 50 percent of the lecturers and 47 percent of the instructors in higher education, they made up only 18 percent of all full professors, 29 percent of all associate professors, and 43 percent of all assistant professors.

America has a large and diverse system of higher education. Among the more than 3200 colleges and universities within this system, women faculty are not equally represented at different types of institutions. Women have been and remain disproportionately located in the less prestigious community colleges (37.6 percent) and four-year colleges (29.3 percent). They are underrepresented in universities in general, with an overall presence of 25 percent, but at the major research universities, the percentage is even lower. A glimpse at the percentage of women by rank in relation to the total number of full-time faculty at the top twenty research institutions in the country at the end of the 1980s, revealed a sobering pictures of the dominant power coalition. Fifty-five percent of the faculty at these schools were male full professors. Only 4.6 percent of the faculty at the top twenty research institutions were female full professors (AAUP, 1987). The blatant inequity of voice and influence in decision-making is obvious.

Faculty of color are in a different, but even worse situation demographically within academe. Although the number of minority faculty members increased 48.6 percent in the decade from 1981 to 1991, they still make up only 12 percent of the nation's faculty (although minorities comprise about 21 percent of the U.S. population and approximately 31 percent of the total enrollment in institutions of higher education). These faculty are unevenly distributed among the professional ranks, comprising 17 percent of all lecturers, 15.1 percent of all instructors and 16.5 percent of assistant professors, but only 12.1 percent of associate professors and 10 percent of full professors. Moreover, the representation of minorities at the assistant professor level (the entry level of permanent regular positions) is not proportionately large enough to suggest that time alone will bring an appropriate realignment of representation within the ranks. The representation of minority faculty members at two-year institutions (14.5 percent), however, is not dramatically different from their average representations at universities (just below 13 percent). Unlike women faculty, the absence of minority faculty members is more noticeable at private liberal arts colleges where they comprise only 10.1 percent of the faculty.[4]

In administrative positions, according to the 1995 statistics from the College and University Personnel Association (CUPA), women now occupy almost one-half of the administrative positions in external affairs (48 percent) and student services (47 percent). However, according to the Office of Women in Higher Education (OWHE) at the American Council on Education (ACE), women occupy only 453 CEO positions at U.S. colleges and universities in 1995, accounting for only 16 percent of the total CEO population. As low as this number is, it represents a substantial gain of 58 percent over the past decade (Knopp, 1995). In administration, although far from having achieved equity, women still fare considerably better than minorities who account for only 16 percent overall of the nonfaculty professional staff at colleges and universities.

It remains uncertain what percentage of the advances that have been gained in the academy by women have been the direct result of affirmative action legislation. The social and political movements over the past thirty years which initially prompted statutes like the

Civil Rights Act and affirmative action programs have had inevitable effects on the conscience of institutions and the consciousness of victims of discrimination. Proponents of social justice have kept inequities in salary and job opportunities, in admissions to college, and in access to public programs in the public's eye. The women's movement in particular has strengthened women's position in the labor force and changed society's attitude about appropriate professions for women. All these factors, including affirmative action, share in the credit for the advances that have been realized. In many cases it is all but impossible to assign direct causality to any one factor.

While the status of women in the university is improving, gender equity is by no means at hand in the professional levels of academia. Admittedly, access to positions in the academy is heading toward gender neutrality, but promotions and advancement in academic careers for teachers and administrators are lagging. The infamous glass ceiling remains a reality in most college and university settings. Significant disparities between men and women still exist, despite gains made in the last two decades. Many of the degrees earned by women, for example, are in fields such as health professions and education (where 83 percent and 77 percent of the degrees, respectively, are earned by women) which have been traditionally dominated by females, whereas women received less than one-third of all degrees in fields such as engineering and related technologies and the physical sciences. Similarly, in 1992–1993, women still earned less than one-half of the first professional degrees in all fields except pharmacy (65 percent) and veterinary medicine (63 percent). Although they now represent 36 percent of all the instructional faculty, women are much more likely to be employed part-time than their male counterparts. For example, in the fall of 1992, 41 percent of all female faculty members were employed part-time, while only 29 percent of male faculty were employed part-time. Similarly, as already noted, women are more likely to be employed in lower level positions. Remember, in 1992, women made up only 18 percent of all full professors. Women faculty are also less likely than men to have tenure. Less than one-half (48 percent) of all female faculty had tenure status in 1994–1995, while 72 percent of the male faculty did. Some of this can be explained by age, i.e., there has been a greater influx of female faculty into academia in the last few years, and they have not come up for tenure yet. However, at least part of it has to do with the type of appointments offered to women. Eighty-one percent of all full–time female faculty members held tenure track appointments in 1994–1995 whereas 92 percent of their male counterparts did.

Rather than holding positions throughout a university, women tend to be concentrated in a few departments. For instance, in 1995 women made up nearly all (98 percent) of the faculty in nursing and more than one-half (56 percent) of those in education, while they made up only 6 percent of the engineering faculty and 23 percent of the natural sciences faculty. The earning power of women faculty members continues to drag behind that of men. Women tend to be clustered in fields which have the lowest average salaries, such as nursing, and to be noticeably absent from fields such as engineering which have the highest average salaries. This year, once again, the annual salary survey by the American Association of University Professors (AAUP) found that women faculty members continue to earn lower average salaries than their male counterparts at all levels, especially at the upper ranks where the average male faculty salary was 13 percent higher than the average female faculty salary at the rank of full professor.

In the administrative branch of American higher education, while women are approaching parity in total numbers employed in student and external affairs, the fact still remains that less than one-third of the chief officers in these areas are women. Specifically, only 31 percent of the directors of offices of student affairs, 29 percent of development offices and 25 percent of academic offices are headed by women. Statistics in admissions reflect the same phenomenon. While 62 percent of the admissions counselors in the country are women, and 57 percent of the associate directors of admissions are women, only 35 percent of the chief admissions officers are women. Salary discrepancies along gender lines are observed in administrative sectors as well as in the academic sectors. The 1995 CUPA survey showed that female chief admissions officers received lower salaries than their male counterparts at all types of institutions, and that this discrepancy could range from a high of 26 percent at doctoral institutions to a low of 10 percent at comprehensive institutions. Furthermore, although women have made gains in administrative positions over the last decade, on the average they are still employed at lower ranks and earn lower salaries than their male peers.

## Double Dilemma of Gender and Race

When considering the advances made by women in academia over the past two decades, it is critical to realize that the progress which has been made has benefited predominantly white women. The large subset of women in higher education who are minorities have not enjoyed the same relative success as their European American sisters. Of all the degrees awarded to women in 1992-1993, 78 percent were awarded to white women. Only 7.6 percent were awarded to African American women, 4.2 percent to Hispanics, 3.6 percent to Asian Americans and 0.6 percent to American Indian Women. Of the full- and part-time instructional faculty employed by U.S. colleges and universities, 36 percent were women. But 32 percent were white women and only 4 percent were women of color. Stop and think about that statistic for a moment: Only 4 percent of the teaching faculty in American higher education institutions are minority women. In light of a college and university student body which nationally has a 23 percent total minority enrollment and a minority women enrollment of more than 13 percent of the student body, and in light of the educational soundness of having a faculty which reflects the racial, gender, and intellectual diversity of the students it serves, the need for more faculty members who are women of color is obvious.

When the paucity of representation of minority women in faculty ranks is pointed out, two explanations are typically proffered: a) that qualified minority women cannot be found or b) that the women (particularly black women) have stepped back to give men (particularly black men) improved opportunity because racism and discrimination have had more serious repercussions for men than for women. Currently women minority members earn only 6 percent of the total number of doctoral degrees granted in the United States annually. One might think that because of affirmative action mandates, coupled with the limited number of minority women who hold doctoral degrees, those who do would have a distinct advantage in finding employment at colleges and universities across the country. But the experiences on the academic labor market of qualified minority women have not been found to be significantly different from those of other applicants for faculty positions, and there is no evidence to support that their absence from the market would benefit the experience of minority men (Smith, 1995). Instead, racial and gender stereotypes and prejudice converge for women of color in academia. Denied their own unique voice, they are being asked to identify with either their sex or their ethnic group, as if an experiential synergy does not exist between the two.

Statistics on the representation of minority women in administrative areas are only slightly better than those for faculty members. Among presidents and chief executive officers, 84 percent are white women, while only 16 percent are women of color, including 39 African Americans, 24 Hispanics, 2 Asian Americans and 7 American Indians. Clearly, to be a woman and to be a minority member is a double jeopardy for those seeking a career in academia.

## Contradictions and Paradoxes of Affirmative Action

In the last few years, anti-affirmative action sentiments have reached epidemic proportions in America. Executive and legislative branches at both the state and national level are engaged in efforts to dismantle the laws and programs implemented to augment the efficiency of the struggle against discrimination. The public is confused on at least two fronts: the practical outcomes resulting from the implementation of affirmative action and the ethical foundation for the policy. At least part of the confusion grows out of the identical language used with contradictory intent by proponents and opponents of the policy. Title VII of the Civil Rights Act of 1964 prohibits job-related discrimination on the basis of race, color, or religion, as well as national origin or sex. The Executive Order establishing affirmative action instructs institutions to "insure that applicants are employed . . . without regard to their race, creed, color, or national origin and to take affirmative action to assure that employees and applicants for employment are treated without regard to these factors." The intent of this legislation and executive action was to eliminate race and gender bias from employment, that is, to disallow the negative use of these factors in hiring decisions. Recently, Republican Senator Robert Dole of Kansas and Republican Representative Charles Canady of Florida have introduced the Equal Opportunity Act of 1995 to both houses of Congress. Using almost identical language as that contained in the Executive Order released more than thirty years ago, this act would also prohibit considering gender, race, or ethnicity in federal contracts, employment, and other programs. But the intent of this new act is to disallow the positive use of race and gender factors in hiring. The 1995 Equal Opportunity Act would end the existing Executive Order as well as the civil rights enforcement policies of past administrations. It is ultimately ironic that the same words can be used to dismantle discrimination in the first instance, and to ensure its continuation in the second. For in the absence of good hiring practices, neutral hiring policies inevitably maintain the status quo and result in little or no improvement in employment practices and statistics among minorities and women. Contradictory intent, obfuscated by uniformity of language, clouds the fundamental issue of equal job opportunity and confounds public opinion.

Another source of confusion stems from paradoxes inherent in civil rights/affirmative action policy itself. Although the Civil Rights Act of 1964 states that "nothing contained in this (law) shall be interpreted to require any employer . . . to grant preferential treatment to any individual or to any group," affirmative action requires employers and colleges (anyone wishing to do business with the federal government) to hire, promote, and/or admit minorities and women not without regard to their race, ethnicity or gender, but because of them. Herein lies the major paradox of affirmative action: it can be simultaneously attacked and supported by universal principles of justice. Arguments both for and against the policy can be presented from morally defensible positions. The basic conflict is over the implementation and regulation of individual rights. The purpose of law in this country is to protect individual rights; but the law itself derives from the obligation to respect the rights of others—the obligation to be just. This obligation for justness implies that where the law is not protecting rights but infringing on them, it may be right to break or reform it. Thus, the law can rightly be used to restore an equilibrium that has been broken or to correct an imbalance. From this point of view, affirmative action can be championed as a justifiable policy which is trying to correct the imbalances caused by several hundred years of discrimination. On the other hand, the law must be applied even-handedly because basic to American society is the assumption that individuals are fundamentally equal, and equality implies that no one deserves special preferences. Under this type of thinking, affirmative action, because it allows preferences, can be condemned as being immoral (Cortese, 1992). Should a society that seeks justice for its members give priority to the ultimate attainment of a just outcome, or scrupulously safeguard the principle of equality which in its practical application will work against and ultimately disallow the attainment of the goal sought after? The solution to the dilemma demands prioritization of outcome over process. In his opinion in the *University of California Board of Regents v. Bakke* case of 1978, Supreme Court Justice Blackman proposed a solution to the paradox of affirmative action in these words: "In order to treat some persons equally, we must treat them differently." His thesis was that history and experience has indicated that neutral policies, in fact, have little or no effect on employment equity. The removal of barriers, the prohibition of specific discriminatory procedures may put an end to overt racial and gender discrimination, but such passive measures rarely touch institutional racism and sexism embedded in the established operating procedures of an institution. It is precisely this institutional discrimination that can have the most profound implications. Without some type of active intervention for some groups in the short run, the idea of eventual justice for all would seem an unattainable myth.

Seventeen years later, public opinion seems to be turning away from this solution to the problem of how to end employment discrimination. In California, often the touchstone of the nation on social justice issues, bills have been introduced which seek to eradicate the legal bases for affirmative action measures in employment and education at every level. One would repeal all affirmative action requirements in hiring and promotion of personnel in state agencies, school districts, and community college districts. Another would prohibit postsecondary educational institutions from employing any type of discrimination and/or preferential treatment in faculty employment. A third would prohibit any educational institution in California, from kindergarten to the postsecondary level, from considering a person's race with respect to a decision to admit that person to the educational institution, to provide financial assistance to that person, or to evaluate that person's academic performance. Members of the Board of Regents, the governing board of the University of California system, recently backed the intent of these bills and voted to change their policies on affirmative action in admissions, hiring and contracting so that the use of race, religion, sex, color, ethnicity, or national origin are prohibited as criteria for admission or hiring. At the same time The California Civil Rights Act, a ballot initiative to amend the California Constitution to outlaw "state discrimination or preferential treatment" in public employment and education, is slated to appear on the state ballot if a sufficient number of signatures can be gathered. In Washington, President Clinton has ordered a full White House review of dozens of affirmative action programs now in force and hinted that those judged to be ineffective would be discarded, that he may propose "fine tuning" present programs, and that future federal affirmative action programs might be based on economic need rather than race. Currently, the nation is swaying toward focusing on process over outcome in its approach to confronting employment discrimination. It seems intent on dismantling affirmative action along the way.

## Is the Time Ripe for Dismantling Affirmative Action?

Affirmative action programs and legislation have existed in America for approximately 30 years. Opponents have many arguments as to why they should be eradicated. Perhaps the most emotional is that such programs represent a type of reverse discrimination against white males and that discrimination in any form is against the basic constitutional privileges upon which United States Government is built. The extent of bias against European American men seems to be regularly exaggerated by opponents of affirmative action. A recent study commissioned by the Department of Labor, drawing on court decisions and other employment data, found that fewer than one of every 30 bias cases decided by the courts involved a complaint of reverse discrimination. What's more, of the approximately 100 lawsuits claiming reverse discrimination that were decided between 1990 and 1994, only six were found to have merit. Similarly, statistics do not indicate any radical change in the social order of American colleges and universities in terms of total participation of white men in the higher education enterprise. A poll by *USA Today* concerning how affirmative action policies regarding gender had directly affected men revealed a striking answer of "hardly at all". Ninety-eight percent of the respondents said they had never been denied admission to school as a result of affirmative action based on gender. Ninety-three percent of the men reported they had never been passed over in a promotion which went to a woman. Ninety-two percent of the men reported that they had never had the experience where they were not offered a job which went to a woman. Furthermore, in a study carried out in 1995 by Smith in which 300 recipients of prestigious doctoral and postdoctoral fellowships were interviewed concerning their experiences in the academic labor market, it was found that while individuals had profoundly different experiences depending upon their field and a unique convergence of other factors, neither race nor gender, nor a combination of the two, were sufficient to determine this experience. Equivalent numbers of European American males, European American females, minority males, and minority females underwent similar experiences in the job search process (Smith, 1995). Evidence for widespread reverse discrimination caused by affirmative action is lacking. Nevertheless, conditions supporting gender equity can feel like a form of reverse discrimination when principles of affirmative action are making inroads into the exclusive privileges of access and promotion so long enjoyed by white males in this society. The attack on affirmative action may represent a response to this loss of privilege as opposed to a backlash caused by any type of true reverse discrimination.

Individuals facing frustrations in gaining access to university positions today may be tempted to use affirmative action as a scapegoat. It is true that affirmative action has played a significant part in opening up employment for qualified women and minorities in the higher education environment, thereby allowing more contestants onto the competitive playing field. But the idea that affirmative action is unfair because some innocent parties experience disappointment is at odds with traditional American notions of competition in situations ranging from sports to commerce. A universal reality of competition for a finite number of positions is that some candidates, though qualified, will be turned away. Qualification is no guarantee of selection in many situations, and decisionmakers are expected to make choices that advance the overall objectives of a setting, whatever that might be. The acceptance or rejection of a qualified applicant over another should not be controversial. There is nothing inherently unfair when white males lose to minorities or white women unless one has the assumption that a qualified white male is somehow entitled to prevail over qualified minorities and white women.

There are those who would argue that affirmative action measures have caused a bureaucratic nightmare, creating record keeping and reporting work disproportionate to the employment equity which has resulted from the effort. While it is true that regulatory agencies impose burdens on academic administration, it is equally true that before these regulations went into effect, colleges and universities were reluctant to voluntarily implement programs to combat discrimination in hiring and admissions. The public disclosure of the racial and gender balances among students and employees forced academic institutions to face the monocultural results of their traditional hiring practices, while the mandated reports detailing the nature of job opportunities and the pool of candidates who applied, necessitated new hiring procedures which fostered change of the status quo. If job search processes are no longer monitored, if public disclosure of gender and racial balances of employees are no longer mandated, what assurances are there that institutions will not return to the processes formerly employed?

One of the most honest arguments in favor of dismantling affirmative action is that, in fact, it has not proved to be the efficient vehicle to ensure employment equity that was initially hoped. Clearly, progress has been slow. But hiring in post-secondary education is a decentralized decision-making process. To influence or modify such a process requires administrative leadership and commitment, advocates of change among the faculty, a certain amount of constant external pressure, and a cultural context that fosters change (Hanna, 1988). Additionally, it is unrealistic to expect to undo three centuries of racial and gender discrimination in three decades or to make significant attitude changes in one-and-a-half generations. The change in hiring procedures mandated by affirmative action policy does not guarantee results. If, in fact, results could have been guaranteed, higher education would surely be in a better position with regard to racial and gender equity among faculty members than it currently is. The truth is that affirmative action, as it is currently configured, has never been adequate to the integrating and diversifying task at hand. But given the legislative initiatives and the customs of institutions, it has at least been a sincere attempt to keep colleges and universities publically accountable. At the same time, it has always been clear that more than the current affirmative action mandates is needed to effectively diversify institutions. This "more" includes a close examination of agreed-upon concepts of what is meritorious and what constitutes quality among faculty applicants.

## The Myth of Meritocracy

North Carolina Republican Senator Jesse Helms, no friend to affirmative action , says that it "flies in the face of the merit-based society [envisioned by] the Founding Fathers." Glynn Custred, coauthor of the proposed California Civil Rights Initiative, says that abolishing it will move us closer to a system of "advancement by merit" and ensure that people "get ahead by what they can do, not by who they are." Advancement by merit is a notion held dear in the American psyche, but in reality, America itself, and American higher education, have never been meritocracies. As Harley Shaiken, a UC Berkeley education professor has said, "The notion that we at one point had a system based on merit and then gratuitously introduced affirmative action rewrites history. It is a powerful and confining myth." Historically, if any merit system was in place, it was a system that admitted only white, Protestant, male "Americans." The system did not apply to women, to blacks, to Native Americans, to Irish Catholics, to Chinese Americans, to Japanese Americans, or to many other groups.

Today, informal systems of preference still mold much of American life, and take marked importance over merit. Kinship networks, for example, are very important in getting into skilled trade unions. In academia, scholastic "pedigrees," that is, association with particular schools, particular laboratories, or particular researchers can often be the critical factor in selecting applications for review or in choosing candidates to bring for interviews during a faculty search procedure. It is no secret either that family ties can make the critical difference in getting into an elite college. Even at some of the nation's most discriminating universities, "legacy" students, that is, children of alumni, are admitted at a much higher rate than non-alumni applicants despite having lower SAT scores. Harvard, for instance, over the last 10 years has had an admission rate for legacies between 35 percent and 40 percent, more than twice the overall admission rate of 15 percent. Stanford University admits alumni children at twice the rate of other applicants. At the University of Virginia, 57 percent of legacies are accepted, compared to a 36 percent overall (Lederman, 1995). In the Harvard freshman class of 1988, if legacies had been admitted at the same rate as applicants without alumni connections, the number of alumni offspring would have fallen by nearly 200, a figure that exceeded the total of African Americans, Mexican Americans, Puerto Ricans and Native Americans admitted as freshmen that year. The average SAT scores over a 10-year period of the legacy students at Harvard was 35 points lower than that of nonalumni students who were not athletes. A 1991 report by Berkeley's Institute for the Study of Social change noted that far more whites have entered the gates of the 10 most elite institutions through alumni preference than the combined number of all the African Americans and Chicanos entering through affirmative action (Woo, 1995). In the face of such considerations, arguments against affirmative action, which claim it contradicts the staunch meritocratic principles of American society, can hardly be taken seriously.

In academic searches for new faculty, administrators, and staff members, departmental search committees state that they are seeking the best-qualified candidate for the position they are seeking to fill. Opponents of affirmative action say that the policy undermines their determination to fill the position with the most meritorious person and promotes the hiring of individuals not qualified, or less qualified, by conventional standards. In the face of such arguments it is important to critically examine two issues: the objectivity of the process itself and the normative criteria used in the hiring process. Although faculty regularly defend the objectivity of their hiring process and selection criteria, it is obvious to anyone who has ever participated in a faculty or administrative search that there is much subjectivity involved in screening applications and deciding which candidates to recommend. In fact, intangible, unmeasurable characteristics, that is, judgments about a person's creativity, motivation to do research or provide leadership, teaching ability, and probability of "fit" in a department, weigh heavily in the process. It has been shown that, when left to their own resources, people are most likely to hire those with whom they have the most familiarity, that is, those who are most like themselves. In university settings overwhelmingly populated in decision-making roles by white male professors, affirmative action is critical to breaking this pattern of subtle subjective judgments against those who are of a different gender or race (Clifford, 1993). Given the subconscious tendency recognized by social psychologists, for people to hire those most like themselves (in outlook and culture, as well as in gender), the modest advantage bestowed by affirmative action simply serves to level the playing field and to allow the myriad other factors involved in selecting a new colleague (faculty member or administrator)—like research field, areas of expertise, teaching recommendations, basic personality, ability to integrate into the department— to take appropriate prominence in the final selection process.

Normative criteria, always called upon in merit-based arguments, need to be reviewed. Consider the case of a female candidate for an administrative position whose career has been interrupted and whose mobility has been limited for some years because of family responsibilities. She may have less exposure to the ladder of experience than a man whose career has proceeded without diversions, but her potential in terms of interpersonal skills and/or analytic ability may be greater. Her paper qualifications may not be as good, but is she necessarily inferior in terms of promise to excel in the position? Consider a woman applicant for a faculty position whose research centers on feminist or lesbian issues. She may not have publications in the traditional journals whose editorial policies do not address diversity concerns as intellectual interests. She may not be a graduate of one of the most prestigious schools in the country whose programs did not include her interests, and she may be perceived as a potential threat because she embodies a totally new viewpoint which she would introduce into the department. But her emerging scholarship may be exactly what is missing from a department's curriculum, and she can serve as a mentor and role model for the increasing population of undergraduates who share her intellectual point of view. Is such a woman a less qualified, less meritorious candidate than a male candidate whose research lies in a traditional area? Consider an older woman who has been geographically immobile for many years because of family considerations, and has held part-time and temporary teaching positions while continuing to publish and raise her family. If a regular, tenure-track position opens up at a time in her life when she is ready to return to the faculty full time, should she be a less serious candidate than a young doctoral recipient who has been able to hold postdoctoral positions at schools across the country. Finally, consider a minority woman faculty member who has devoted her initial years at a university to teaching, advising, and community service while also publishing, but in journals not considered mainstream. Should she be a less meritorious candidate for tenure than a person who has been disengaged from the life of the university in favor of pursuing research work? It all depends on the standards employed in decision-making. If criteria used in evaluation of applicants are not examined for their impact on women and minorities, the prejudices embedded in standard university hiring practices are unlikely to be admitted or overcome. At some point honesty demands an acknowledgement that white men in America have gained the advantage they hold through privileges awarded to them over the years by virtue of access to certain information, education, experience, and contacts through which they have gained unfair advantage. Affirmative action is not undermining merit in higher education hiring. It encourages critical inquiry into the definition of quality and qualifications of applicants. When we diversify the ways in which we identify talent and excellence, we will more easily accommodate diversity without the necessity of bureaucratic mechanisms which at their best are inadequate.

## Victory or Stigmatization

There is an argument presented in the literature that affirmative action must be abandoned because it stigmatizes its would-be beneficiaries in a manner they can never overcome. The important question to ask with respect to this argument is whether affirmative action is in any way responsible for such stigmas, or if they already existed and are exactly the reason that affirmative action is necessary. Indeed, placing competent women and minorities in positions where they can succeed and excel may be the only way to dispel such unfounded biases.

The stigmatization argument is used predominantly with regard to minority members. Women rarely claim stigmatization from the benefits they gain from affirmative action. This lack of stigmatization may be a phenomenon associated with numbers. There are many more women competing for jobs, and already in the academic work force, than minority members. Although not yet approaching equity in numbers with men, women are at least no longer tokens in most departments. In those environments, such as physics and math departments, where women are highly underrepresented, there is a much higher probability that a feeling may persist among male colleagues that a female colleague was hired "just because she was a woman," irrespective of her accomplishments. Stigmatization may also be a phenomenon associated with confidence. Thirty years into the women's movement, with prototypes of success available in virtually every profession and field, women themselves reject as laughable the idea that they are in some way less qualified than their male counterparts. In a tight job market, in an open competition among many qualified candidates, far from feeling stigmatized that gender has given them an edge over their competitors, they are grateful for the small advantage it may bestow, particularly given that many of their other qualities may be undervalued. The greater danger now is that white women will deny the help they received from affirmative action and in so doing undermine its potentially positive effects on others.

## What Has Limited Progress?

Why hasn't better progress been made in two decades of affirmative action? The limited progress achieved since the implementation of affirmative action mandates may be partially attributable to the overall depressed faculty labor market in the 1970s and 1980s, and the dearth of qualified women and minorities in particular fields such as business and engineering that were experiencing growth. An alternative explanation for the slow progress focuses on attitudinal barriers. As any administrator knows, it is possible to be within procedural compliance of the law and not be hiring within the spirit of the law. It has been implied in a wide variety of publications that there are significant numbers of administrators and faculty who resist the spirit of affirmative action efforts and are willing to have progress slowed as a result. Another explanation involves implementation problems. It is often quite challenging and time consuming to identify available women and minority candidates in a field and to implement truly effective methods to advertise positions. Yet another possibility to consider in explaining the slow and modest effect of affirmative action policies in higher education settings is that the legalistic affirmative action guidelines drafted and implemented by many colleges and universities actually work against the moral underpinnings of the policy. Sometimes the guidelines induce even well-intentioned search committee members and hiring administrators to making hiring decisions that effectively place at a disadvantage persons the guidelines were intended to help. Because of the need stressed in the guidelines to document "defensible" selection decisions, the emphasis in searches can switch from finding the "best qualified" candidate from a qualitative point of view, to a heavy reliance upon those criteria which are more easily quantifiable, for example, the number of publications, years of teaching experience and other "facts" contained in the candidate's paper credentials. A process which relies heavily on quantifiable paper credentials in the initial phases can truncate a thorough review of a candidate's qualifications and result in a large number of women and minority candidates not surviving the screening and interviewing process. Affirmative action guidelines, as interpreted at many large universities, tend to focus on preparing for a possible compliance agency review, not on facilitating the addition of women and minority members to their faculties (Higgerson & Higgerson, 1991). At the same time that the threat of compliance agency review may curtail the fulfillment of the intent of affirmative action policy, in a perverse way the lack of effective enforcement of affirmative action mandates also acts as a disincentive to accomplishing the goals of the policy. As already mentioned, although the threat looms large and ominous, no college or university has been reported to have lost federal funds because of failure to comply with affirmative action regulations.

An assessment of changes in the overall views of faculty members, as well as adjustments in faculty attitudes and practices with respect to diversity in educational and curricular matters, indicated that during the 1970s and 1980s teachers at American colleges and universities had become more aware of—and committed to—

issues of race and diversity on campus and in the larger society. In the study, conducted in 1989 by Milem and Astin (1993), three-quarters of the U.S. faculty members surveyed felt that colleges should be actively involved in solving social problems and over 60 percent considered it personally important that they help promote racial understanding and racial equity. Such a result would predict significant and growing support for affirmative action measures among the American professorate. But American faculty are notorious for being simultaneously socially liberal and academically conservative. Only about a third of the faculty members surveyed supported affirmative action (preferential) hiring for minority or women faculty and that percentage did not change appreciably between 1972 and 1980 (Milem & Astin, 1993). It was no surprise, therefore, when the researchers reported their finding that while faculty attitudes had changed over the 16-year period between 1973 and 1989, institutional hiring practices had not.

## Why Women Need to Continue to Back Affirmative Action

Amidst the wave of political conservatism washing over America, support for affirmative action is dissolving on every front. In the African American and Latino communities, some scholars of color are trying to distance themselves from the policy. Among women too, support is slipping for a variety of reasons. Among white, middle-class women in particular, a generation is coming into its own which has not experienced the gender discrimination so commonly encountered by others in the past. Understandably, the current generation does not appreciate the effects of affirmative action with the same intensity as did their aunts and mothers. But at this junction in time, instead of abandoning support for affirmative action, it is vitally important that women reflect on recent history and rally behind the policy. They need to remember the encouraging numbers of women in academia which existed in the 1930s, numbers that predicted an equitable future. But changes in national politics and society at large (namely the return of men from the

World Wars) stymied progress for 40 years. Political changes could rapidly reverse the progress acquired step by step in the last 30 years as well. Women need to stress the importance of process in affording opportunity for all and champion the continuation of public disclosure of racial and ethnic balances to serve as a check on the efficacy of these processes. They need to remember that while affirmative action measures have opened up access to many academic positions, women are still in a minority status in the top decision-making position of universities. Until equity is reached at this level, the resolution of struggles concerning hiring, promotion, and tenure will still be an uphill battle.

In a less selfish vein, women also need to continue their support of affirmative action in order to help their minority colleagues, both male and female, make progress against the institutional discrimination that has thwarted their entry and progress into the academy. Those women who have gained access and hold positions in the mainstream life of colleges and universities need to continue to acknowledge their accomplishments under affirmative action, to make sure other minority groups follow in their footsteps, to motivate minorities—especially women—and serve as role models to convince them that the struggle toward equality can be waged and won. They should serve as the conscience of their department, reminding others of the value of diversity and the moral imperative toward equal opportunity. Affirmative action has never been adequate to realize true diversity in the professional ranks of academe, but there is a danger that its dismantling would signal permission to institutions that they could back away from the beneficial procedures the policy motivated them to initiate.

Rather than allowing inadequacy to be an excuse for dissolution, women need to realize that affirmative action policies must not be limited to bureaucratic and legalistic imperatives. To effectively achieve diversity of participants in higher education, women will have to voluntarily expand the dimensions of affirmative policy, and continually question the standard criteria used for the evaluation of quality. They must be at the forefront of the movement to reconceptualize excellence to include a more varied array of achievements and contributions. They need to exert leadership not only in defining excellence, but in reframing the relationship between academic excellence and affirmative action, keeping before the public eye their steadfast belief that the implementation of affirmative action measures does not mean an inevitable dilution of quality among the faculty.

The inclusion of persons of many ethnicities in academic careers is a goal best achieved by people of all ethnicities working together. Similarly, to achieve true gender equity in academe—for women of color as well as for white women—all women must work together to recognize and break down the racial tensions and barriers that exist among themselves and then to respect their obligation to others who have suffered even more profound discrimination than they. If women remain committed, united, and courageous, they may hold the key that can open the door to diversity for everyone, and change the face of higher education in America.

## REFERENCES

Astin, H., & Snyder, M. (1982, July/August). Affirmative Action 1972–1982: A decade of response. *Change, 14,* no.5, 26–31.

AAUP Annual Report on the Economic Status of the Professions (1989). High education goals: Low salary increases. *Academe,* March–April.

Carnegie Commission on Higher Education (1973). *Opportunities for Women.* Carnegie Commission Report, New York: McGraw-Hill.

Clifford, G. J. (1993). "Shaking Dangerous Questions from the Crease: Gender and American Higher Education." in Glazer, J., Bensimon, E., & Townsend, B. *Women in Higher Education: A Feminist Perspective.* Needham Heights, MA: Ginn Press, 135–173.

Cortese, A. (1992). Affirmative action: Are white women gaining at the expense of black men? *Equity & Excellence, 25,* 77–89.

Hanna, C. (1988). "The Organizational context for affirmative action for women faculty." *Journal of Higher Education,* 59, (4), 390–411.

Higgerson, M. & Higgerson, R. (1991). Affirmative action guidelines: Do they impede progress? *CUPA Journal, 42,* 11–14.

Knopp, L. (1995). "Women in higher education today: A mid-1990s profile." *Research Briefs # 5.* Washington, D.C.: American Council on Education.

Lederman, D. (1995, April 28). The special preferences are not limited to blacks. *The Chronicle of Higher Education, XLI,* 33, A16–A18.

Milem, J., & Astin, H. (1993). The Changing composition of the faculty: What does it really mean for diversity? *Change, 25,* 21–27.

Smith, D. (1995). The pipeline for achieving faculty diversity: debunking the myths. Unpublished manuscript.

Vetter, B., & Babco, E. (1987). *Professional Women and Minorities: A Manpower Data Resource Service.* Washington, D.C.: Scientific Manpower Commission.

Woo, E. (1995, April 30). Belief in meritocracy an equal-opportunity myth. *Los Angeles Times,* p. A1, A24–A25.

Yates, W. (1993). Equity management: Affirmative action for the 21st century. *Change, 25,* 40–43.

## NOTES

1. Title VII of the Civil Rights Bill (42 U.S. C. A. sec. 2000e et seq., and regulations at 29 C.F.R. secs. 1604-1601, 1608.1 et seq.) applies only to employment and prohibits job-related discrimination on the basis of race, color, or religion, as well as national origin or sex, by any employer with 15 or more employees. It mandates fair practices in hiring. As amended in 1972, it applies to public and private educational institutions, training, supervision, and termination.

2. Exclusion of women from equity legislation is nothing new in American history. In fact, women were almost excluded from inclusion in the epic Civil Rights Act of 1964 which sought to end discrimination in the United States. In early drafts of that act, discrimination on the basis of race, color, religion, and national origin were prohibited, but there was no mention of the prohibition of discrimination on the basis of gender. Indeed, a southern Congressman added the category of "sex" to the Civil Rights Act, not out of recognition of the second-class status that women had long endured, but because he thought that this amendment in the language might kill the bill. Much to his dismay, and the contrasting delight of the burgeoning feminist movement, the bill passed prohibiting discrimination on the basis of race, color, religion, national origin, **or gender** (Tobias, personal communication 1994).

3. Interestingly, of all women enrolled in college, almost one-half (45 percent) were over the age of 24.
4. Faculty statistics in this section, unless otherwise noted, are from the U.S. Department of Education for Fall of 1992, as quoted in the September 1995 Almanac Issue of the *Chronicle of Higher Education*.

Robert A. Rhoads

# 8

## Toward A More Inclusive Vision Of Affirmative Action: Improving Campus Environments for Lesbian, Gay, and Bisexual People

A few months ago when I was working as a researcher at Pennsylvania State University, a group of lesbian, gay, and bisexual faculty and staff asked me to speak with them about my research on the coming out experiences of gay college students (Rhoads, 1994). The group, which served as both a source of support for members as well as a social network, wanted to learn more about the difficulties gay students face in academe. As the discussion progressed and as I shared the many stories of harassment and discrimination I had heard from students, the mood of the group gradually shifted from one of curiosity and concern to one of frustration and disappointment. The conversation also took a new turn as individuals began to reflect on their own experiences of marginality and their general dissatisfaction with the progress—or lack of progress—that we have witnessed in academe. A gay associate professor spoke about his fear of being out in his department: "There is always some type of decision or control that someone has over your life that they can use against you if you're gay. Like teaching assignments. They can make sure you get all the bad ones." A lesbian assistant professor talked about the power students have to make her life difficult: "If the students find out that I'm a lesbian, they may not sign up for my classes. If no one signs up for my classes it looks like word has got around that I'm a bad teacher."

Another faculty member voiced his frustration about how slowly things have changed over the years. "Yeah, the students have gay-pride rallies, but it's still not safe for them or for us to walk down the street at night." Everyone at the meeting seemed to agree that visibility was very important, but that it could also be quite costly. As one staff member pointed out, "A career is a huge investment. You just can't throw caution to the wind like the students sometimes do."

One might suspect that our college and university communities—as "ivory towers" of intellect—would be bastions of equality where persecution of individuals based on sexual orientation is nonexistent. Such is not the case. Research demonstrates that heterosexism and homophobia are rampant on American campuses. John D'Emilio speaks to this issue:

> Despite the changes in the last two decades, gay people are still swimming in a largely oppressive sea. Most campuses do not have gay student groups. Most gay faculty members and administrators have not come out. Even on campuses that have proven responsive to gay and lesbian concerns, progress has often come through the work of a mere handful of individuals who have chosen to be visible. . . . There are still many campuses in the United States where no lesbian or gay man feels safe enough to come out. From a gay vantage point, something is still wrong in the academy. (1990, p. 17)

Although D'Emilio points to the general problem of hostile campus environments, a number of specific campus assessments provide more concrete evidence. Arthur Reynolds (1989) reports that gay men rate the climate at the University of Virginia lower than straight men in regard to emotional support. Jane Low (1988) notes that students at the University of California at Davis rate campus intolerance of homosexuality as more serious than racial intolerance. At several universities, investigations of campus climates found that lesbian, gay, and bisexual students are significantly more likely to face harassment and discrimination than heterosexual students (Herek, 1993; Nelson & Baker, 1990; Nieberding, 1989). In separate studies conducted at Pennsylvania State University, Anthony D'Augelli (1988, 1989b) discusses high rates of victimization among lesbian and gay students, faculty, and staff, with 75 percent reporting that they had been verbally threatened and 25 percent reporting that they had been threatened with physical violence.

My intent in this chapter is to examine the experiences of lesbian, gay, and bisexual students, faculty, and staff with the broad agenda of affirmative action in mind. Affirmative action may be understood in two ways. First, there is the narrow, legalistic conception of affirmative action reflected in Title VII of the Civil Rights Act of 1964 which prohibits employment discrimination on the grounds of race, color, religion, sex, or national origin. From a legal standpoint, the employment opportunities and social advancement of lesbian, gay, and bisexual people are not included as part of affirmative action as it is presently understood. However, there is another conception of affirmative action rooted in the progressive ideals of democracy and the notion that a just society offers certain opportunities (such as education and employment), rights, and protections to all people regardless of personal or group characteristics. John Rawls (1971) talks about this conception of society in his theory of justice as fairness and is akin to the principle of equal opportunity—the idea that all individuals ought to have an equal chance to compete for jobs as well as other social benefits (Greene, 1989). And Philip Quinn (1993) discusses a similar conception of affirmative action when he juxtaposes it with multiculturalism. Whereas a legalistic interpretation of affirmative action pertains only to discrimination based on race, color, religion, sex, or national origin, a broader philosophical interpretation is concerned with discrimination based on a wide array of characteristics including sexual orientation. Certainly, there is no denying the pervasive discrimination, harassment, and general loss of liberties faced by lesbian, gay, and bisexual people in educational and employment settings. The fact that sexual orientation is not part of the legalized version of affirmative action necessitates that colleges and universities adopt their own localized view of affirmative action based on its deeper philosophical roots. Of course, the assumption I make here is that colleges and universities ought to be concerned with creating just campus communities.

The issues faced by lesbian, gay, and bisexual people are different from many of the struggles racial and ethnic groups face (although there are some similarities) and need to be understood within specific social and cultural contexts. In the case of this chapter, the context is higher education. With this said, I want to first describe the sources of discrimination and harassment faced by people of diverse sexual orientations and how visibility may be seen as a response to ignorance and hostility. I discuss heterosexism and homophobia and why coming out is so important in battling these insidious forms of discrimination. I go on to contextualize some of the experiences of students, faculty, and staff and follow with a brief summary discussion. I then offer recommendations that colleges and universities ought to consider if they are to truly embrace affirmative action as justice and opportunity for all.

## Heterosexism and Homophobia

To understand the nature of the hostile campus climates lesbian, gay, and bisexual people face, one must come to terms with the underlying roots of discrimination directed against such individuals. What I refer to here is heterosexism and homophobia. Heterosexism, notes Richard Friend, is "the belief that everyone is, or should be, heterosexual" (1993, p. 211). He goes on to add:

> Based on the assumption of universal heterosexuality ... a systematic set of institutional and cultural arrangements exist that reward and privilege people for being or appearing to be heterosexual, and establish potential punishments or lack of privilege for being or appearing to be homosexual. Heterosexism is prejudice against homosexuality which is maintained by a pervasive set of societal institutions that sanction and promote this ideology (p. 211).

Similarly, Audre Lorde (1985) describes heterosexism as "a belief in the inherent superiority of one pattern of loving over all others and thereby the right to dominance" (p. 3). The dominance of heterosexist ideology and culture contributes to homophobia.

On college and university campuses, heterosexism gets enacted in multiple ways. For example, policies that offer benefits to "spouses" almost always include only opposite-sex couples (presumed to be heterosexuals). In fact, Lee Badgett (1994) reports that only about 30 colleges and universities offer health care benefits covering same-sex partners. And professors who offer examples in class using opposite-sex couples effectively render invisible same-sex partnerships as heterosexuality gets reinforced. Likewise, when professors and professional staff make comments about "homosexuality" being an example of "deviant" or "sick" behavior, a statement is made about the positioning of heterosexuality as the defining form of sexual orientation and identity.

Heterosexism is not the only source of discrimination evident on college campuses. Homophobia also is pervasive. Lorde describes homophobia as "a terror surrounding feelings of love for members of the same sex and thereby a hatred of those feelings in others" (1985, pp. 3-4). Likewise for Friend, homophobia is seen as "the fear and hatred of homosexuality in one's self and in others" (1993, p. 211). Whereas heterosexism relates more to a set of ideologies pervasive throughout a culture, homophobia is the acting out of heterosexist beliefs and attitudes.

There are numerous examples of homophobia on college and university campuses. Incidents of homophobia range from conservative student groups protesting the official status and rights of lesbian and gay student groups to students being physically and verbally assaulted at fraternities, residence halls, and in locker rooms. Lesbian, gay, and bisexual faculty and staff who come out may put their jobs in jeopardy at institutions where fear and disdain are deeply rooted and protective clauses are absent. Furthermore, in today's high-tech age it should come as no surprise that computerized messages have become a source of homophobic jokes and hate speech. At one university, a student went so far as to offer a rationale for killing homosexuals. Study after study of campus climate unearths similar findings: Lesbian, gay, and bisexual people face daunting challenges during their educational and professional years in academe.

## Coming Out

Coming out is the process of disclosing one's sexual orientation; it typically begins with self-acknowledgement and expands outward to others in what is often termed self-disclosure (Nelson-Jones & Strong, 1976). Gilbert Herdt (1992) talks about how coming out marks the rite of passage to a lesbian, gay, or bisexual identity. Because we live in a society in which nearly everyone assumes people to be heterosexual, coming out is a never-ending process; no matter how many people know about one's sexual orientation, there will be others to whom that individual will have to come out.

For many people, coming out is not only a step in the development of a positive sense of identity, it is also a means of battling heterosexism and homophobia (D'Augelli, 1989a; D'Emilio, 1992; Rhoads, 1994, 1995b). The belief is that increased visibility is a step toward greater tolerance and understanding on the part of heterosexuals. A significant body of research supports this claim (Gentry, 1987; Glassner & Owen, 1976; Grieger & Ponterotto, 1988; Hansen, 1982; Wells & Franken, 1987). The idea that increased visibility leads to greater tolerance and acceptance is one reason why public events such as gay-pride rallies or marches are believed to be so important.

Coming out has a metaphorical quality to it in that one "comes out" by leaving "the closet." The closet symbolizes the oppression of lesbian, gay, and bisexual people who have been forced to remain silent (and invisible) about their sexual orientation—and their sexual identity. As Eve Kosofsky Sedgwick maintains, "The closet is the defining structure for gay oppression in this century. . . . For many gay people it is still the fundamental feature of social life; and there can be few gay people, however courageous and forthright by habit, however fortunate in the support of their immediate communities, in whose lives the closet is not still a shaping presence" (1990, p. 68). The closet provides safety from harassment and discrimination, but at the same time limits one's ability to develop a positive sense of sexual identity. Michelangelo Signorile speaks to this issue in the introduction to his book *Queer in America:* "The closeted, as captives, suffer such profound psychological trauma that they develop a relationship to their closets similar to that of hostages to their captors" (1993, p. xviii). When expressions such as "keep it private" or "sexual orientation is a personal matter" are uttered by heterosexuals, what they are saying in effect is that lesbian, gay, and bisexual people ought to remain closeted.

Although coming out (and necessarily leaving the closet) may be an avenue for confronting heterosexism and homophobia, it can take a heavy toll. In what follows, I highlight some of the experiences students, faculty, and staff face as they come out or consider coming out in college and university settings. I also discuss why many decide to stay in the closet.

## The Experiences of Lesbian, Gay, and Bisexual People in Academe

As a researcher, I tend to adopt ethnographic strategies because of the depth of understanding such methods can provide. Ethnography in particular and qualitative research in general offer researchers opportunities to describe the experiences of others in rich detail. Ethnographic and qualitative methods offer a glimpse into someone else's life. This is why I borrow primarily from such methods as I discuss the lives of lesbian, gay, and bisexual students, faculty, and staff.

### Faculty and Staff

Over the past four years I have been involved to varying degrees in research related to lesbian, gay, and bisexual faculty and staff. One of the things that stands out when I think about their academic lives is the diversity of their experiences. This diversity in part relates to great variation in the visibility faculty and staff choose to enact. In many ways, visibility is the defining feature of their social lives. In discussing the idea of visibility and its significance, I highlight the life and work of Adrienne Rich, who discusses her experience as a lesbian working in academe:

> I have been for ten years a very public and visible lesbian. I have been identified as a lesbian in print both by myself and others; I have worked in the lesbian-feminist movement. Here in Claremont, where I have been received with much warmth and hospitality, I have often felt invisible as a lesbian. I have felt my identity as a feminist threatening to some, welcome to others; but my identity as a lesbian is something that many people would prefer not to know about. And this experience has reminded me of what I should have let myself forget: that invisibility is not just a matter of being told to keep your private life private; it's the attempt to fragment you, to prevent you from integrating love and work and feelings and ideas, with the empowerment that that can bring (1986, pp. 199–200).

Rich highlights a persistent dilemma that many individuals face: the notion that their identity as a gay or lesbian can somehow be kept separate from their professional life. This same standard is rarely if ever applied to heterosexuals. How many times have we seen pictures of husbands or wives on someone's office desk? How many times have we observed someone's opposite-sex spouse call or stop by the office to go to lunch? How many times have we witnessed an opposite-sex partner accompany a colleague to a professional conference or convention? Are these examples of the separation between personal and professional spheres? I do not mean to suggest that heterosexuals have failed in enacting the separation between the personal and the professional. What I suggest instead is that the professional is often the personal and the personal is often the professional. In other words, the division of public and private lives is a forced dualism that does not reflect the reality of people's lives.

In an article in which she documents the life of an untenured lesbian assistant professor, Estela Mara Bensimon (1992) criticizes the notion that we can somehow separate our personal life from our work. Bensimon highlights how Julia (a pseudonym) must restrict her behavior because of views that others may hold about her personal life, views that may be used against her. Julia comments on her fears:

What concerns me most right now is my career. I must protect that. And I don't want to be rejected at the human level. I don't want negative relationships with the people I work so closely with on a daily basis. I don't want them to have reasons to dislike me. In my field, it's a very small world, everyone knows everyone, everyone talks to everyone (p. 105).

Bensimon notes that, "Julia's statement exemplifies the interlocking nature of oppression and the struggle for survival. As an assistant professor who is a woman, lesbian, and untenured in an institution that is male and heterosexual-dominated, Julia is subject to simultaneous sources of oppression that regulate her conduct in the public sphere" (p. 105). Because of the attitudes heterosexuals hold about homosexuality, faculty such as Julia are forced to maintain a dual identity—one for the world of work and one for their private life. In their discussion of college administrators, Maura Cullen and Jim Smart (1991) report that many professionals are forced to maintain such a "dual identity." They point out that, "When conversations arise involving the personal self, the gay, lesbian, or bisexual individual either refrains from participating or creates stories in an effort to belong to the majority group" (p. 180). This is done out of fear of being "fired, demoted, overlooked for promotions, or ostracized and harassed by colleagues" (p. 181). The following statements by Julia provide insight into the fear Cullen and Smart highlight: "It made me nervous to attend the lectures that were part of the Lesbian and Gay Scholarship Series. Once one of my undergraduate students saw me there. She had been assigned to go to the lecture by another professor. It made me nervous. It is such a repressive place. . . . I went home and wondered what she might think" (Bensimon, 1992, p. 106). One of the tragedies of course is that Julia lives a life in which she is not only judged on the basis of her professional competence and ability, but her sexual orientation as well—which ironically many of her condemners say is a "private matter." It seems then, that the private and professional must be kept separate only when it is convenient for those who make such decisions.

Similar pain and anguish as that experienced by Julia is described by other lesbian, gay, and bisexual faculty and staff. In an article in which he highlights conflict over the implementation of a sexual-orientation clause at a large university, William Tierney (1993) contextualizes some of the fears faculty experience. A gay untenured faculty member described feelings he lives with on a daily basis: "You feel the pain of oppression, of knowing, of having mirrored back to you every day that you're different and that there are people who want to hurt you, and deny you basic human rights" (p. 150). A lesbian faculty member commented, "You have to be very cautious about 'coming out' to the wrong people. It is hard to know when it is safe to be who you are" (p. 150). A second lesbian faculty member added, "Professionally I would be frightened to be open about my lifestyle. Having a president who doesn't want to include a sexual-orientation clause makes me fearful of being found out. What concerns me most right now is my career. I must protect it" (p. 150).

Tierney argues that colleges and universities cannot remove themselves from important social and political issues such as gay rights and at the same time argue that they support academic freedom. The failure to support the rights of lesbian, gay, and bisexual faculty and staff through, for example, the adoption of a sexual-orientation clause is to condone an environment in which certain individuals are silenced. As Tierney notes, "When we suggest that the academy absent itself from the political battles of society, we have wrongfully assumed that all individuals are allowed to investigate any issue irrespective of political persuasion" (1993, p. 157). Once again, Bensimon's (1992) portrait of Julia is instructive as she discusses the adoption of a sexual-orientation clause at her institution:

> It would be psychologically very beneficial. Not that I expect to benefit in a legal, practical way. But at a psychological level, it would mean a lot. It would be some peace of mind. It's not that I would do anything so differently, but it would help psychologically. I am who I am. I dress as I dress. I see those I see. I think as I think. Things aren't going to change that way, but I'm going to feel better and I'll transmit that. But with rejection, I give rejection back. Nothing good comes from rejection (p. 108).

The addition of a sexual-orientation clause to an institution's statement of nondiscrimination is only one example of action colleges and universities can take to improve the environment for lesbian, gay, and bisexual faculty and staff. Later in this chapter, I discuss this and other actions institutions might follow in an effort to apply the ideals of affirmative action in a more inclusive manner.

The work setting is not the only place in academe that lesbian, gay, and bisexual faculty and staff face discrimination. Some find gaining employment to be a significant barrier. For example, in their analysis of the job-search experiences of lesbian, gay, and bisexual student affairs professionals, James Croteau and Mark von Destinon (1994) report the following incidents as described by survey respondents: "Our university recently interviewed an openly gay candidate and several members of the staff felt that he wasn't right for the job because he would make people uncomfortable." Another survey respondent remarked, "Our institution was hiring for a resident director position. When one candidate announced she was lesbian and had a committed partner who she would be living with, our director told her that her 'living arrangements' would be permitted. She was not considered for the position." And a third noted, "I was involved in a search committee. One of the candidates discussed his homosexuality during the interview. The director of the department decided not to offer him the position even though he was extremely qualified because he would not 'fit' the institution" (p. 43).

Croteau and von Destinon also note that out of 249 lesbian, gay, or bisexual survey respondents, 26 percent reported that they were discriminated against during the hiring process because of their sexual orientation. There was also a significant difference in reported discrimination during the hiring process between "those who disclosed their sexual orientation" (42 percent reported being discriminated against) and "those who did not disclose" (16 percent reported being discriminated against).

Once on the job, the work settings in which student affairs administrators operate seem just as homophobic and heterosexist as those settings faced by other faculty and staff. For example, Croteau and Julianne Lark (1995) report that 60 percent of lesbian, gay, and bisexual student affairs professionals reported that they had experienced some form of homophobic discrimination ranging from overt expressions of homophobic sentiment to harassment or violence. Thirty-eight percent reported that they had experienced two or more incidents.

## Students

Although my discussion of the experiences of faculty and staff is largely based on literature and research conducted by others, what I present concerning students derives primarily from my own ethnographic study of gay and bisexual college men. The study to which I refer was conducted at a large research university from 1992–1993. As is the case with faculty and staff, issues of coming out and visibility are central to the experiences of gay college students.

Anthony D'Augelli points out, "Although most lesbian and gay adults acknowledge their affectional orientation to themselves during adolescence, most have not come out by the time they enter a college or university" (1991a, p. 140). This means that gay college students will likely be at a point in their lives at which self-disclosure becomes an issue. College is a challenging time for students; for students who also have sexual-identity issues to confront, the college experience may be even more difficult.

For gay as well as straight students, college life represents freedom from parents and high school social networks. "The intense secrecies of high school are dissipated as a result of diminished parental and peer monitoring, as well as the possibility of the creation of new networks. The 'I'll wait until college' syndrome is a powerful one" (D'Augelli, 1991b, p. 3). Seeing other lesbian, gay, or bisexual students out and about on campus is added incentive to self-disclose. Additionally, the parents of today's traditional age college students had children after the gay-liberation movement was well under way and at about the time that the American Psychiatric Association deleted homosexuality as a form of mental illness from the *Diagnostic and Statistical Manual-II* (DSM-II). These historical events have left some middle-aged adults questioning prior definitions of sexuality, possibly making the parents of today's college students more open to and knowledgeable of people who identify with same-sex attraction. Hence, coming out in college has become a significant social, cultural, and political phenomenon.

For many college students, coming out involves a "great awakening." One student described becoming "more confident, less afraid, more open, relieved. I'm about as happy now as I've ever been." A second student discussed his feelings after coming out: "It was a time when everything just hit me and made perfect sense. The whole self-realization was profound." A third student added, "Coming out is achieving a state of honesty with my friends and people in general. It's not hiding anything. It's like achieving a new level of self-confidence." And a fourth talked about coming out as "the greatest thing that ever happened to me. It's given me courage, strength, and a sense of identity to confront all kinds of things in my life."

Some students become involved in gay politics and the struggle to change campus environments. One student discussed how coming out changed his views: "Before I was out and proud and fighting for my rights, I might have gone to a gay-pride rally but only to watch or offer support. But now, instead of merely supporting other advocates, I have become one myself. I have become more of a fighter for my own rights as opposed to a supporter of others fighting for my rights. I do that for myself and for the community." Some students also talked about their sense of obligation to other members of the gay community and their desire to create campus and societal change. One student commented, "It's one thing to think about being gay and how that affects me, but I think I've become much more aware of the impact of anyone being gay.... There are politics behind being gay and I've become much more aware of it and the politics of being a member of any underrepresented group."

But coming out is not all positive. Students who come out in college face significant hostility. Several students discussed being physically and verbally assaulted at college parties and nightspots for appearing too effeminate. One student was harassed by a bouncer for hugging another gay friend whom he had not seen in a long time. He was told to "save it for alternative night," a designated night when the bar acknowledges "alternative lifestyles" and welcomes lesbian, gay, and bisexual students. Another student described a scene in which five men who opened the door to the only gay bar in the town (where my study was conducted) and yelled obscenities at patrons: "I stopped and said, 'Did someone yell "faggot"?' The guy that yelled and the four others got in my face and pushed me to the sidewalk. One was getting ready to punch me in the face, but another one stopped him and said, 'You don't want to get any faggot blood on your hands.'"

A student recalled walking home from a party with his boyfriend when another student punched him in the face without provocation. He had to be taken to the emergency room where he received 18 stitches. Another student also needed hospital treatment after he was assaulted at a party when he commented on the attractiveness of a straight student there. And several students were assaulted at a political rally because they held signs protesting the policies toward gay rights of then-President George Bush.

Out lesbian, gay, and bisexual students who live in residence halls frequently face blatant forms of harassment and discrimination. One student reported that he found the following on the bathroom mirror in his residence hall: "Fag in 408. We don't like cocksuckers on our hall." This student often posted information related to gay issues on his door, which would frequently be torn down, written on, or spit at. "One time I put my clothes in the dryer and this guy got real upset with me because I guess he was next in line or something and so he left a note on the machine, 'Hey fag I was here first.'" Two students involved in my study worked as resident assistants and had to deal with derogatory notes on their doors all the time. For them, harassment was a fact of life. Another student recalled how his residence hall started a petition to get the "fag off the hall." The students were reprimanded by the resident assistant, but in the end, they got what they wanted: The "fag" moved off campus.

The stories of harassment and discrimination seem endless. One student described the feelings of fear he lives with on a daily basis: "I don't feel very safe on campus. I don't really feel comfortable. It's something I put up with, something I tolerate. You just never know when a group of frat boys or jock-types, you know those who are probably most closeted, are going to beat your face in because you remind them of what they can't admit to." Another student refuses to wear T-shirts or buttons with gay symbols or expressions for fear that he might be identified publicly as a gay man: "I don't feel comfortable declaring myself to everyone that walks by because of the possibility of being harassed. If you tell the world you're gay, you have a good chance of getting harassed. I'm not ready yet to be identified to everyone. That would make me nervous."

Most of the discussion of students' experience of harassment and discrimination up to this point primarily have been rooted in homophobia. But other experiences relate more to heterosexism. One student had this to say about heterosexism: "In a way heterosexism hurts more than homophobia. When someone says something or does something homophobic they at least acknowledge you exist. With heterosexism someone is refusing to acknowledge your existence—you remain invisible."

A number of students recalled classroom incidents in which lesbian, gay, and bisexual people were clearly excluded from the class discussion or marginalized by negative comments. In one class, students got to ask each other questions on the first day as an icebreaker. Almost all the questions concerned what students look for in dating the opposite sex. One student remembered a similar incident when the instructor asked the students what they look for in the opposite sex. When the instructor got to this student, he said: "I don't look for anything in women. I date men. I'm gay." A second student's human-development professor talked about behavior modification as a way to treat homosexuals. "I raised my hand to point out that there are some serious issues that we should talk about in relation to whether this kind of strategy is acceptable . . . the idea of 'curing' gays." A fourth student recalled the reactions of his classmates after a professor of Black Studies pointed out three controversies surrounding Bayard Rustin, a key advisor to Martin Luther King, Jr. First, Rustin was a suspected communist. No one in the class said anything. Second, he avoided the draft. Again, no response. Rustin's third political shortcoming was that he was openly gay. Everyone gasped. "That was the one unforgivable thing—that he was gay."

Teachers and students frequently, unwittingly in many cases, discuss the experiences of themselves and peers as if everyone adopts the norm of heterosexuality. This fallacious assumption limits knowledge and awareness of same-sex attraction as a form of expression. Gilda Lopez and Nancy Chism (1993) report similar findings in their study of the classroom concerns of gay and lesbian students: "Assumptions of a traditional heterosexual family, for example, often led instructors to discuss marriage, poverty, power, and other issues in a way that denied the experience of all but heterosexual individuals" (p. 100). To reiterate a point made earlier by a student, heterosexism is in many ways more painful than homophobia, for at least when someone exhibits homophobia they acknowledge a person's existence.

Although heterosexism may in some ways be more damaging psychologically, homophobia takes its toll on students. Many refuse to identify with other out lesbian, gay, and bisexual students for fear they will be harassed or victimized. One student pointed out that he does not get involved in campus pride rallies for fear he will be identified as a gay man. Another student remains closeted for fear his professors will not give him good recommendations. And a third who dreams of becoming a director of athletics at the collegiate level knows that coming out would erase his dream.

## Discussion

The preceding pages highlight some of the experiences of lesbian, gay, and bisexual students, faculty, and staff. As I point out throughout this chapter, much of the discrimination and harassment faced by lesbian, gay, and bisexual people is rooted in heterosexism and homophobia. Indeed, heterosexism and homophobia are defining characteristics of the vast majority of colleges and universities throughout the country. Hostile campus environments lead many lesbian, gay, and bisexual people to remain silent and effectively deny them basic rights and opportunities—as well as human dignity. What we see in academe and across our society is systematic discrimination against an entire category of people. In part, this is what affirmative action is designed to end. Unfortunately, by not including sexual orientation as a protective category of discrimination, affirmative action legislation tacitly suggests that such discrimination is tolerable. This is why affirmative action needs to be more inclusive and also why colleges and universities must adopt their own strategies and policies for confronting heterosexism and homophobia.

The silencing faced by lesbian, gay, and bisexual people revolves around power—who controls discourse, who defines truth, who determines whether forms of knowledge and cultural identities are relevant or irrelevant, legitimate or illegitimate. Power influences who speaks, who listens. Tierney argues that, "Knowledge is socially constructed, and that the act of its construction privileges some and silences others.... Our challenge is to investigate those silences and to develop ways that ensure protection of all individuals and of all groups, so that they are no longer invisible and silent" (1993, p. 159). Thus, improving campus environments involves organizational restructuring in which power is more evenly distributed: where those who have been silenced have opportunities to speak and participate as full members in a truly democratic community, and where those who have been threatened can live and learn in a supportive and protective environment.

The question, then is: How can college and universities be transformed to end the silencing of lesbian, gay, and bisexual people? How can we achieve affirmative action's testament of hope for all people regardless of their sexual orientation? The goal must be to create academic communities in which the lives of lesbian, gay, and bisexual people are a source of strength and understanding and offer sustenance to college and university life.

## Recommendations

I offer nine recommendations for improving campus environments for lesbian, gay, and bisexual students, staff, and faculty. The recommendations build upon previous work I have done (Rhoads, 1995a, 1995c; Tierney & Rhoads, 1993) and certainly are not inclusive of all the complex problems institutions face with regard to lesbian, gay, and bisexual issues. Nonetheless, the recommendations form a starting point from which to create institutional change.

*Recommendation # 1.* Colleges and universities should consider establishing a task force or presidential committee charged with conducting a comprehensive analysis of the campus environment for lesbian, gay, and bisexual students, faculty, and staff. Tierney (1992) discusses such a strategy as a means to "surface the problem." Appointing a committee or task force also sends a message about an institution's commitment to improving the campus environment. The committee or task force should be charged with making specific recommendations to the president, and those recommendations must be seriously considered.

*Recommendation # 2.* Colleges and universities must end discriminatory practices toward lesbian, gay, and bisexual students, faculty, and staff. Sexual-orientation clauses must be added to official statements and policies of nondiscrimination. Additionally, colleges and universities need to rethink all policies and practices that might discriminate against lesbian, gay, and bisexual people. For example, institutions need to rewrite policies concerning domestic-partner benefits to include same-sex couples.

*Recommendation # 3.* Colleges and universities need to encourage faculty to conduct research on lesbian, gay, and bisexual issues, such as the psychological consequences of being forced to hide one's sexual orientation. A small grant program might be established to support this research. Research and teaching are interactive processes: What is researched gets taught and vice versa. By encouraging faculty research on gay issues, such concerns might also become part of classroom discussions which might, in turn, encourage an end to some of the current silencing practices. Also, lesbian, gay, and bisexual studies departments must be created. Such a step offers an arena for the legitimation of knowledge about gay lives and leads to increased understanding and awareness.

*Recommendation # 4.* College and university leaders need to demonstratively and publicly express their condemnation of hate speech and other forms of verbal and physical intimidation directed against lesbian, gay, and bisexual people. It should be made clear that harassment and discrimination directed at these individuals are no more tolerable than racist or sexist behavior and will be subject to the same procedures and penalties.

*Recommendation # 5.* Related to the preceding recommendation is the need for colleges and universities to designate specific offices staffed by appropriately trained personnel to deal with issues of harassment and discrimination. Students and employees who face such behavior must know to whom they should turn. Not only does this action offer greater protection and support, it also conveys an important message to the campus community: Harassment and discrimination directed against lesbian, gay, and bisexual people will not be tolerated. In addition, a gay hot line should be established to receive complaints and provide information.

*Recommendation # 6.* Colleges and universities must develop programs to educate and sensitize members of the campus community to the experiences and concerns of their lesbian, gay, and bisexual colleagues. People need to understand the pain caused by casual remarks and seemingly harmless jokes. To many gay faculty, staff, and students, such remarks or jokes are never painless nor harmless. Educational programs ought to include discussions of the environment that lesbian, gay, and bisexual students face both in and out of class. Moreover, discussions of lesbian, gay, and bisexual issues could be introduced into orientation programs for entering students and into training sessions for resident assistants, student government officials, and other student leaders.

*Recommendation # 7.* Colleges and universities need to provide stable assistance and support for the efforts of lesbian, gay, and bisexual students, faculty, and staff. A good idea is to fund a lecture series pertaining to issues of concern within the gay community (ties). Student groups need to have adequate staff support and staff members need to be rewarded by the institution for their efforts. Student groups offer a vital support network and institutions ought to provide assistance similar to that provided to other student organizations. Creating specific spaces where students can gather, such as a lounge or resource center in the student union, should be considered.

*Recommendation # 8.* College and university leaders need to offer visible support to lesbian, gay, and bisexual students, faculty, and staff by attending their cultural activities. Programs such as lectures on gay or lesbian identity issues are intended not only for members of the gay community, but offer learning opportunities for heterosexuals as well. By offering their visible support, institutional leaders send a significant message to the rest of the campus community.

*Recommendation # 9.* Colleges and universities need to recognize that certain areas of campus life evidence greater degrees of homophobia than others. For example, institutions should ensure that staff members who supervise sports teams and fraternities and sororities develop and implement educational programs about issues of sexual orientation. Research consistently shows high degrees of homophobia in these areas of student life. Other problem areas within the campus community need to be identified and then targeted with specific educational programs.

## Conclusion

When Northeastern University announced its policy to recruit and promote lesbian, gay, and bisexual faculty and staff, it took a courageous step toward ending discrimination and persecution. Oddly enough, one criticism directed at Northeastern was that the new directive violated the spirit of affirmative action (Cage, 1994). I find this logic tainted. It is virtually impossible to determine if lesbian, gay, and bisexual people are underrepresented within academe; because so many are forced to be closeted, ascertaining their numbers is an impractical task. Regardless of whether lesbian, gay, and bisexual people are underrepresented, clearly they are underheard. For years they have been silenced by academic institutions which fail to truly embrace the ideals of affirmative action and instead support homophobia and heterosexism. In the true spirit of affirmative action, the time has come to act. Colleges and universities need to be transformed from exclusionary and denigrating institutions into inclusionary and caring academic communities.

Creating change is difficult. It takes hard work and risk-taking by many people. College and university leaders must continually challenge their institutions, their colleagues, and their students to confront injustice and inequality. The vision of affirmative action as justice for all must never be exclusionary, but rather inclusionary. This means that lesbian, gay, and bisexual people need to have the same opportunities, rights, and protections that are afforded other members of our college and university campuses. We must implement what we have learned about homophobia and heterosexism if we are to create academic communities that truly embrace the underlying philosophical ideals of affirmative action.

## REFERENCES

Badgett, M. V. Lee. (1994). Equal pay for equal families. *Academe, 80*(3), 26–30.

Bensimon, Estela Mara. (1992). Lesbian existence and the challenge to normative constructions of the academy. *Journal of Education, 174*(3), 98–113.

Cage, Mary Crystal. (1994, June 8). Diversity or quotas? *The Chronicle of Higher Education*, A13–14.

Croteau, James M., & Lark, Julianne S. (1995). On being lesbian, gay, or bisexual in student affairs: A national survey of experiences on the job. *NASPA Journal, 32*(3), 189–197.

Croteau, James M., & von Destinon, Mark. (1994). A national survey of job search experiences of lesbian, gay, and bisexual student affairs professionals. *Journal of College Student Development, 35*, 40–45.

Cullen, Maura, & Smart, Jim. (1991). Issues of gay, lesbian, and bisexual student affairs professionals. Alexandria, VA: American College Personnel Association.

D'Augelli, Anthony R. (1988, March). *Anti-lesbian and anti-gay discrimination and violence on university campuses*. Paper presented at the Northeast Regional Conference on Prejudice and Violence, New York, NY.

D'Augelli, Anthony R. (1989a). Lesbians and gay men on campus: Visibility, empowerment, and educational leadership. *Peabody Journal of Education, 66*(3), 124–142.

D'Augelli, Anthony R. (1989b). Lesbians' and gay mens' experiences of discrimination and harassment in a university community. *American Journal of Community Psychology, 17*(3), 317–321.

D'Augelli, Anthony R. (1991a). Gay men in college: Identity adaptations and processes. *Journal of College Student Development, 32,* 140–146.

D'Augelli, Anthony R. (1991b, August). *Out on campus: Dilemmas of identity development for lesbian and gay young adults.* Paper presented at the Annual Meeting of the American Psychological Association, San Francisco, CA.

D'Emilio, John. (1990). The campus environment for gay and lesbian life. *Academe, 76*(1), 16–19.

D'Emilio, John. (1992). *Making trouble: Essays on gay history, politics, and the university.* New York: Routledge.

Friend, Richard A. (1993). Choices, not closets: Heterosexism and homophobia in schools. In L. Weis & M. Fine (Eds.), *Beyond silenced voices: Class, race, and gender in United States schools* (209–235). Albany: State University of New York.

Gentry, Cynthia S. (1987). Social distancing regarding male and female homosexuals. *Journal of Social Psychology, 127,* 199–208.

Glassner, Barry, & Owen, Carol. (1976). Variations in attitudes toward homosexuality. *Cornell Journal of Social Relations, 11,* 161–176.

Greene, Kathanne W. (1989). *Affirmative action and principles of justice.* New York: Greenwood Press.

Grieger, Ingrid, & Ponterotto, Joseph G. (1988). Students' knowledge of AIDS and their attitudes toward gay men and lesbian women. *Journal of College Student Development, 29,* 415–422.

Hansen, Gary L. (1982). Measuring prejudice against homosexuality (homosexism) among college students: A new scale. *The Journal of Social Psychology, 117,* 233–236.

Herdt, Gilbert. (1992). *Gay culture in America: Essays from the field.* Boston: Beacon.

Herek, Gregory M. (1993). Documenting prejudice against lesbians and gay men on campus: The Yale sexual orientation survey. *Journal of Homosexuality, 25*(4), 15–30.

Lopez, Gilda, & Chism, Nancy. (1993). Classroom concerns of gay and lesbian students: The invisible minority. *College Teaching, 41*(3), 97–103.

Lorde, Audre. (1985). *I am your sister: Black women organizing across sexualities.* Latham, NY: Kitchen Table Press: Women of Color Press.

Low, Jane M. (1988). *The Davis social environment: A report of student opinions*. Davis: Student Affairs Research and Information, University of California at Davis.

Nelson, Randy, & Baker, Harley. (1990). *The educational climate for gay, lesbian, and bisexual students*. Santa Cruz: Student Services, University of California at Santa Cruz.

Nelson-Jones, Richard, & Strong, S. R. (1976). Rules, risk and self-disclosure. *British Journal of Guidance and Counselling, 4*(2), 202–211.

Nieberding, Ronald A. (1989). *In every classroom: The report of the President's Select Committee for Lesbian and Gay Concerns*. New Brunswick, NJ: Office of Student Life Policy and Services, Rutgers University.

Quinn, Philip L. (1993). Affirmative action and the multicultural ideal. In S. M. Cahn (Ed.), *Affirmative action and the university: A philosophical inquiry* (197–205). Philadelphia: Temple University Press.

Rawls, John. (1971). *A theory of justice*. Cambridge: Harvard University Press.

Reynolds, Arthur J. (1989). Social environmental conceptions of male homosexual behavior: A university climate analysis. *Journal of College Student Development, 30*, 62–69.

Rhoads, Robert A. (1994). *Coming out in college: The struggle for a queer identity*. Westport, CT: Bergin & Garvey.

Rhoads, Robert A. (1995a). The campus climate for gay students who leave "the closet." *The Chronicle of Higher Education*, January 27, A56.

Rhoads, Robert A. (1995b). The cultural politics of coming out in college: The experiences of male students. *The Review of Higher Education, 19*(1), 3–23.

Rhoads, Robert A. (1995c). Learning from the coming out experiences of college men. *Journal of College Student Development, 36*, 67–74.

Rich, Adrienne. (1986). *Blood, bread, and poetry: Selected prose 1979–1985*. New York: W. W. Norton & Company.

Sedgwick, Eve Kosofsky. (1990). *Epistemology of the closet*. Berkeley: University of California Press.

Signorile, Michelangelo. (1993). *Queer in America: Sex, the media, and the closets of power*. New York: Random House.

Tierney, William G. (1992). Building academic communities of difference: Gays, lesbians, and bisexuals on campus. *Change, 24*(2), 41–46.

Tierney, William G. (1993). Academic freedom and the parameters of knowledge. *Harvard Educational Review, 63*(2), 143–160.

Tierney, William G., & Rhoads, Robert A. (1993). Enhancing academic communities for lesbian, gay, and bisexual faculty. In J. Gainen & R. Boice (Eds), *Building a diverse faculty* (43–49). New Directions for Teaching and Learning, no. 53. San Francisco: Jossey-Bass.

Wells, Joel W., & Franken, Mary L. (1987). University students' knowledge about and attitudes toward homosexuality. *Journal of Humanistic Education and Development, 26*(2), 81–95.

Alfred A. Slocum

# 9

## *Strict Scrutiny: The Law and Its Special Favorites*

This chapter explores the current legal posture of affirmative action in higher education. In doing so, it is necessary to develop some familiarity with the legal standards that apply and the types of programs that have been developed. Additionally, while observing such legal concepts as the appropriate standard of review, it is important to determine the possibilities of legal trends and directions. These trends will be applied to existing affirmative action programs with the hope of predicting the affirmative action program of the future that will pass constitutional muster.

At least one aspect of the review requires consideration of the law's deference to privilege. It is argued by some white males, and quite frankly others, that affirmative action is little more than a euphemism for racial discrimination (Graglia, 1995); while others, including the author, are amazed at such arrogance borne of centuries of white male privilege. The issue of privilege, however, cannot be reviewed in the abstract, devoid of its historical antecedents. Many of the opponents of affirmative action raise the battle cry, "return to a meritocracy" which is tantamount to saying, "return to the void before the beginning of time." The truth, however, is that we have never had a meritocracy. How significant is the law's relationship to privilege? In reviewing the affirmative action landscape one of the questions lurking in the wings will always be, how level is the playing field?

Before turning to the main discussion of affirmative action in graduate and professional schools, a brief comment is necessary to address the status of undergraduate institutions awarding associate and undergraduate degrees. For these institutions, where competition for seats is significantly less intense than for professional schools, the simple solution is some form of open enrollment in the first year followed by a scaling back of enrollment during the second year based upon first-year academic performance. The modified form of open enrollment merely requires the setting of SAT and grade-point-average (GPA) floors, then selecting those candidates who seem to be most attractive for whatever reason.

However, professional schools pose problems of a significantly greater magnitude. Medical schools require significant subsidy; the revenue from even tremendously high tuition stands little chance of financing the enormous costs of providing an education in medicine. Each seat is a coveted commodity, and who gets in is closely monitored by all. Law school seats are watched just as closely but for different reasons. Tuition usually carries a law school without the support of subsidy, but the seats are no less coveted because the rewards are just as great for the successful student. The legal profession is certainly a lucrative profession but more importantly, who gains access to it affects the social fabric of all society. Consequently, no seats will be relinquished without a fight. Similarly, those educators who conduct affirmative action programs because they truly believe in its goals will not dissolve such programs without a fight. As a result, the significant legal challenges thus far have been limited to professional schools.

More litigation can be expected. The Thirteenth, Fourteenth and Fifteenth Amendments, often called the Wartime Amendments, mandated equal and fair play under the law by the states and federal government. The states, under the Black Codes, had virtually run amuck in response to the abolition of slavery and the de jure emancipation of its victims. Yet, the Klan was savage in its insistence upon and devotion to the slave state.

Questions have endured as to what role Congress ought to play in carrying out these mandates of the Wartime Amendments and whether the law plays favorites. Are race-based preferences both necessary and desirable? Just below the surface of all these issues lurks another: How much independence should educational institutions have in compensating for past societal discrimination? This chapter addresses and attempts to answer these questions for the benefit of an improved national higher education program.

## The Standard of Review

An act of Congress declaring it unlawful to discriminate on the basis of race on either public carriers or the accommodations provided by inns was challenged in the United States Supreme Court on the basis that Congress lacked the power to compel the states to recognize such federal authority. The purpose of the statute was without doubt to benefit blacks who had been victimized solely because of their ancestry. The Court, in a stunning decision, held that Congress had no such power. Congressional power under the Fourteenth Amendment, the Court determined, was limited to "corrective" action only. Congress could condemn and correct an errant state with the temerity to discriminate, but it could not fashion laws designed to dictate to the states without a prior showing of wrongful state conduct.

The Court concluded that "there must be some stage in the progress of [the black man's] elevation when he takes the rank of a mere citizen, and ceases to be the special favorite of the laws, and when his rights as a citizen, or a man, are to be protected in the ordinary modes by which other men's rights are protected" (The Civil Rights Cases, 1883). The matter discussed here, called the Civil Rights Cases, involved litigation from several different jurisdictions, all challenging the same act of Congress. These matters were decided in the year 1883—more than 100 years ago, long before women could vote and a mere two decades after slavery's abolishment.

Clearly the case was wrongly decided, for the role carved out for Congress by the Court in the Civil Rights Cases was precisely the role reserved by the Constitution to the judicial branch of government. If the Court is correct in its determination that Congress, the legislative branch, may only react to errant laws enacted by the states, then there is no need for Congress at all in the civil rights context. Under these parameters involving the judicial evisceration of Congress, the Fourteenth Amendment has no policymaking potential, leaving the Court alone to monitor state compliance. Although over a century later the legislative function has been clearly established, a comparison of the 1883 Fourteenth Amendment analysis with recent Supreme Court cases seems strongly to suggest that history does indeed repeat itself.

As recently as June 12, 1995, the United States Supreme Court, in *Adarand v. Pena* revisited the question of the extent to which Congress has the power to impose race-based requirements for any purpose, however well-intended (*Adarand Constructors, Inc. et al. v. Pena*, 1995). The case involved the Small Business Act under which prime contractors doing business with federal agencies were given additional compensation for hiring subcontractors certified as small businesses controlled by "socially and economically disadvantaged individuals" (Small Business Act, 1958). The terms "socially and economically disadvantaged" encompassed certain race-based presumptions, namely that, "[t]he contractor shall presume that socially and economically disadvantaged individuals include Black Americans, Hispanic Americans, Native Americans, and Asian Pacific Americans . . ." (Small Business Act, 1958). The lower courts, relying on prior Supreme Court decisions, applied what is known as an "intermediate standard" of review under the Fourteenth Amendment's equal protection clause and dismissed the challenge.

The Fourteenth Amendment's equal protection clause provides that no state shall deny to any person the equal protection of the laws. However, the equal protection clause is not an absolute bar to a state's power to treat classes of person's differently. Traditionally, acts of Congress are given a presumption of validity and are deemed to pass Constitutional muster, under the equal protection clause of the Fourteenth Amendment, if there is any "rational relationship" between the Act and its stated purpose.

But, if the Act involves a protected class, the test of constitutionality is much higher, and Congressional acts are subjected to "strict scrutiny." Race, as a consequence of the historical discrimination against blacks, is such a class requiring heightened scrutiny. Under this test, the equal protection clause is violated unless the classification is necessarily related to a compelling state interest and sufficiently narrowly tailored to justify the use of race to meet the statute's objectives. "Intermediate scrutiny" lies somewhere between rational relationship and strict scrutiny and requires that the classification be substantially related to an important state interest.

In *Adarand*, the Supreme Court agreed to hear the appeal and raised the issue of whether the federal government ought to be held to a different equal protection standard than the strict scrutiny standard imposed upon the states. The challenge in *Adarand*, here under discussion, was brought under the protection afforded by the Fifth Amendment which, incidently, has no equal protection clause. It is this distinction that caused the Court to provide an historical analysis of equal protection and the federal-state dichotomy. The Court ultimately concluded that its most recent decision on this question, *Metro Broadcasting*, had been decided erroneously. (*Adarand Constructors, Inc. et al. v. Pena*, 1995).

*Metro Broadcasting* held that "benign race-conscious measures mandated by Congress—even if those measures are not 'remedial' in the sense of being designed to compensate victims of past governmental or societal discrimination—are constitutionally permissible to the extent that they serve important governmental objectives within the power of Congress and are substantially related to achievement of those objectives" (*Metro Broadcasting v. FCC*, 1990). Here, the Court determined that "benign" federal racial classifications could pass constitutional muster by meeting an intermediate standard different from that imposed upon the states.

In overruling *Metro Broadcasting* and applying the strict scrutiny standard, the *Adarand* Court questioned Congressional ability to distinguish between benign and invidious legislation while determining "that the Fifth and Fourteenth Amendments to the Constitution protect *persons, not groups*" (emphasis in original text) (*Adarand Constructors, Inc. et al. v. Pena*, 1995). The court went on to conclude that all governmental action based on race constitutes a group classification long recognized as being "in most circumstances irrelevant and therefore prohibited" (*Adarand Constructors, Inc. et al. v. Pena*, 1995, citing *Hirabayashi v. U.S.*, 1943). Such a ruling, which denies the applicability of the Fifth and Fourteenth Amendments to groups, is particularly difficult to digest when one considers that historically the imposition of the most egregious injuries and indignities inflicted by the states and condoned (if not authorized) by the federal government were indeed based on race. And effects of long-term patterns of discrimination are more often than not nearly impossible to pinpoint as such.

The Congressional acts reviewed in both *Metro Broadcasting* and *Adarand* do not represent Congressional efforts intended to remedy past discrimination but, rather, represent attempts by Congress to level the playing field. It seems clear that *Adarand* and *Metro Broadcasting* were carefully considered affirmative efforts to level the playing field for all Americans, simply because of the lingering effects of long-term, race-based national policy in favor of whites, in general, and males in particular.

However, the Supreme Court in *Adarand* has effectively stripped Congress of its major function—to set policy. Judicial overreaching in this instance is particularly disturbing to those who voted for a change in the status quo. A hand-cuffed, color-blind Congress in either 1883 or in 1995 violates the Thirteenth Amendment to the Constitution—as long as the residue of race-based national policy is omnipresent. The authors of the Amendment knew when it was drafted that whites enjoyed preferences in law, equity, and socioeconomic policy. That preference for whites was and continues to be inextricably woven into the fabric of America.

The question then becomes whether Justice Marshall was correct when he stated in his concurring opinion in the Supreme Court's *Fullilove* decision that strict scrutiny may be ". . . strict in theory, but fatal in fact" (*Fullilove et al. v. Klutznick et al.*, 1980). Justice O'Connor denied this conclusion in *Adarand* when she stated that "[t]he unhappy persistence of both the practice and the lingering effects of racial discrimination against minority groups in this country is an unfortunate reality, and government is not disqualified from acting in response to it" (*Adarand Constructors, Inc. et al. v. Pena*, 1995). Examples of the Supreme Court's intervention into state discriminatory practices were then provided. Yet, it is interesting to note that Justice O'Connor offered no examples of Congressional action. Is the judiciary the only branch of government permitted to act in response?

In *Metro Broadcasting*, the "substantial interest" the government identified and the Court accepted was diversity—of ownership, programming, and content. A close reading of Metro Broadcasting's reliance on diversity in the media reveals this fundamental truth—that there is a correlation between minority presence and diversity of thought. (While the analysis in *Metro Broadcasting* focuses on "electromagnetic" communications, it is equally applicable to print and any other medium of broad-based communication). The Court took great pains to establish that Congress, the FCC, the judiciary, and, in more general terms, higher education all agree that information dissemination is widened and significantly enhanced by minority participation.

The exclusion of minorities from the major social and political debates setting both national and local policy is as well-known as the decisions in *Scott v. Sandford* (1857) and *Plessy v. Ferguson* (1896) which placed their imprimatur on such exclusion. Consequently, as recently as World War II, there was little opportunity to dispel the devastating mythology of so-called Negro inferiority which now grasps all people of color in its clutches. For not only was there limited dialogue historically between the races, there was also very little contact. Just as the alleged inferiority of the Negro served the "Peculiar Institution" (slavery) so well, it serves current preferences for whites in the same manner. A judicially imposed colorblind Congress preserves the skewed playing field which both limits the possibilities for diversity in communication, thought and contact, and perpetuates the myths of racial inferiority and superiority.

Indeed, the substance contained in the crucible of ideas that directly control the decisionmaking processes governing our lives is, quite frankly, white, and it is so insulated that affirmative steps must be taken to achieve a melting pot of thought at least somewhat commensurate with population demographics. But will the Court take off the blinders which conceal the historical antecedents of racial discrimination and segregation in America and concede the importance of diversity as a compelling state interest, particularly where the issues relate to information dissemination and policymaking? And, if so, will strict scrutiny strike down these efforts on other grounds? Or, conversely, will it echo the voice of judicial history which declares that too much has been done already? A look at some recent education cases and programs provides some insights.

There were few surprises in the arguments made by the FCC in *Metro Broadcasting*. The diversity argument had been forecast in a prior Supreme Court case, *Regents of the University of California at Davis v. Bakke* (1978). Although the admissions program undertaken at the University of California at Davis was deemed to be impermissible on other grounds, the Court did state that the goal of a diverse student body is conducive to the robust exchange of ideas and is of paramount importance in fulfilling the university's mission and, as such, was a constitutionally permissible goal. The Court, however, in a five-to-four decision, held that the two-track, fixed-number character of the University of California program violated Title VI of the Civil Rights Act of 1964.

It is of significance to note that the University of California program was not created as a remedial measure because of past discrimination. Four members of the Court, led by Justice Brennan, saw the matter in Fourteenth-Amendment terms (*Regents of the University of California at Davis v. Bakke*, 1978). The Brennan group determined that the proper test for the constitutionality of a remedial[1] classification is different from the compelling state-interest test applied to suspect classifications. They argued that the test is whether the program serves an important and articulated purpose, is reasonably related to that purpose, and does not inflict a racial or ethnic stigma on any group. In applying this test at the University of California at Davis, they found the program to meet constitutional muster.

## Diversity and Past Discrimination

As recently as April 19, 1994, a federal district court in *Hopwood v. Texas* (1994), in a memorandum opinion, applied the principles set forth in *Bakke* to a program conducted at The University of Texas Law School. Historically, the University of Texas had overtly and routinely practiced de jure segregation in favor of whites by excluding blacks since its inception. The University is starred on the pages of racial discrimination history as the defendant in *Sweatt v. Painter*, which challenged the creation of a new and all-black law school just for Sweatt as the only student (*Sweatt v. Painter*, 1950). The Court mandated Sweatt's admission into the University of Texas. This victory was the first major chink in the armor of *Plessy v. Ferguson's* (1896) separate but equal mandate. Now there's a euphemism! For, there was nothing equal about it and everyone knew it. Nonetheless, the racially discriminatory ghosts of the University of Texas's past, favoring white males, have yet to dissipate.

Later, in 1983, the District Court for the District of Columbia, speaking in an ongoing Title VI enforcement suit, determined that, "Texas has still not committed itself to the elements of a desegregation plan which . . . complies with Title VI" (*Hopwood v. Texas*, 1994). As recently as January 1994, the Federal Office of Civil Rights (OCR) was continuing to oversee Texas' efforts to eliminate all vestiges of de jure segregation.

The University of Texas had developed a two-track admissions program—regular admissions and a minority subcommittee. After being marked for race and address, all applicants' folders were reviewed to determine presumptive admits. For this purpose, a dual standard was applied to minorities and nonminorities by a single reviewer. The remaining applicants—those who were not selected— were then reexamined with the minority subcommittee reviewing the minority files and the remaining members of the admissions committee reviewing the nonminority files. After the review, the subcommittee made recommendations to the full committee for its decision as to which remaining minority candidates ought to be admitted. The committee as a whole, however, did not review the individual files of these less than presumptive admit minority applicants.

The university defended its admissions program on two grounds: diversity and remediation of past discrimination. The Court, in spite of both the university's blatant history of discrimination and the Title VI consent decree, determined after a review of *Metro Broadcasting* (*Metro Broadcasting v. FCC*, 1990) and *Crosen v. City of Richmond* (*Crosen v. City of Richmond*, 1989) that the appropriate standard of review would be strict scrutiny. The Court, citing *Bakke*, accepted diversity as a compelling state interest along with, yet separate and distinct from, remediation of past discrimination. However, it was a small victory. The district court ultimately determined that because the whole admissions committee did not review all the files of minority applicants, nonminority applicants were not individually compared with all others competing for seats. Consequently, the program was not narrowly tailored enough to meet the strict-scrutiny standard. It is worthy of note that Alan Bakke asserted a claim under Title VI and prevailed against a medical school program of noble purpose and short-term existence. Yet, the black and Mexican American plaintiffs (beneficiaries) of the University of Texas Title VI lawsuit (*Adams v. Richardson*, 1973) were left without an effective remedy after decades of invidious race-based discrimination. The application of the strict-scrutiny standard has caused this anomalous result—the preservation of preferences for whites.

It boggles the mind to consider just how "offensive" designated race-based classifications have suddenly become to the judiciary justifying strict scrutiny as the standard of review for programs virtually handcrafted by a federal court as a remedy for challenged past racial discrimination favoring whites. Serious questions arise about who is the special favorite of Title VI? Is the impact of racial discrimination between the races distinguishable? Is the sting of racial discrimination a function of time and color? It is all too obvious that color does count, and it does come in groups. To deny this obvious truth is to deny this nation's history.

In The Civil Rights Cases (1883), after referring to blacks as the special favorites of the law, racial discrimination was pooh-poohed as little more than a fact of life. The Court used these words: "No one, at that time, thought that it was any invasion of [a black man's] personal status as a freeman because he was not admitted to all the privileges enjoyed by white citizens . . . Mere discriminations on account of race or color were not regarded as badges of slavery" (The Civil Rights Cases, 1883). The trivialization of racial discrimination by the use of the term "mere" hardly suggests the truly denigrating and degrading plight of victims of color. And, neither would the outcome of the *Bakke* and *Hopwood* cases. Yet, the court would suggest blacks as a favorite.

Judicial preemption of Congress on Fourteenth Amendment matters is probably as much a fact of the future as it has been in the past. It does not appear that further Congressional relief through race-based remedies will be permitted by the judiciary. Consequently, it is worthwhile to assess the apparent direction the Court is taking on Fourteenth Amendment standards.

The merits of the *Bakke* and *Hopwood* cases suggest that there may be something about dual-admission programs as opposed to unitary systems that may be particularly offensive. Some suggest that dual admissions too easily raise the specter or presumption of quotas or even "set asides," resulting in "reverse discrimination." Any program that reserves seats for which nonminority applicants cannot compete is suspect.

As to the quota analysis, it is of some consequence that the University of Texas' law school had no fixed goals or targets. Indeed, in the decade from 1983 to 1993, the number and percentage of blacks varied from a low of 3.2 percent in 1987 to a high of 9.3 percent in 1983 and ended in 1993 with a percentage of 5.9 percent. For the same period, Mexican American participation varied from a low of 10.0 percent in both 1983 and 1993 to a high of 14.3 percent in 1984 (*Hopwood v. Texas*, 1994). Clearly, if a dual admissions program creates the presumption of a quota, it was rebutted by the empirical data that was adduced at trial.

But more troubling is the district court's focus on a dual-admission program that was more unitary than not. First, there was no guarantee that any seats would be set aside for less-qualified minority applicants. A review of the admissions processes demonstrates this point. The first step of the admissions review, presumptive admits, was accomplished by a single person based on numerical data which employed a dual standard of point allocations. The next step, discretionary admits, bifurcated the process as to the actual review of the applications, but no final decisions were reached during this bifurcation. The full committee reconvened, and the minority subcommittee reported to the full committee as to the overall quality of the candidates both in terms of points assessed and background information, along with information on the number of quality candidates available. It was the full committee that then decided the ultimate admission question. The Court emphasizes that this was done without having reviewed each individual minority file. Yet, to focus on the temporary bifurcation aspect of a segment of the overall admissions process is to create a distinction without a difference. This was hardly a quota or a "set aside."

But for each seat given to a minority who received a plus on the basis of race, there is the notion that quality is sacrificed and a seat has been set aside or occupied unjustly. As the Court in *Hopwood* determined, "[t]he law school owes a duty to the citizens of Texas to allow access to a legal education to the best qualified applicants" (*Hopwood v. Texas*, 1994). However, no definition of quality is provided, and the use of this term is more than likely rhetorical. Affirmative action has always carried the exhausting baggage of allegedly unqualified beneficiaries to the detriment of more qualified white applicants, but it is an assumption based largely on the assumed inferiority of the minority applicant. Dual-admissions programs do permit allegations of noncompetition with less-than-qualified minority applicants.

At the same time, there are significant arguments justifying dual-admissions programs in professional schools of higher education. In reviewing the *Bakke* decision, the Rutgers School of Law considered the viability of its own dual-admission program.

> Currently, as a consequence of *Bakke*, the whole concept of a quota seems to have been altered. The notion of seats set aside has become the benchmark of a quota system, rather than strict numerical limitations from which no deviation is permissible. The *Bakke* decision focuses upon a two-track versus a unitary system to single out the offensive quota mechanism; for whatever reason, two-track versus unitary has become the real quota issue in our discussions.

> To the extent that history has made the use of quotas based upon race offensive, it does not address in any regard the whole notion of a two-track versus a unitary system because the *offensive* quotas aimed at racial exclusion existed under unitary admissions processes. Educational institutions desiring to exclude or limit participation on the basis of race did not set up collateral admissions criteria. When racial exclusion was the norm in this country, it was done by covert mechanisms and markings married to every step in the unitary selection process. The outcome was nonetheless predictable.

The question of two-track versus unitary, when seen in the historical context of covert discrimination, becomes a false issue, because the current program forthrightly sets out its goals, as well as the mechanism for reaching them, and it is important that these goals exist. Before the advent of the Minority Student Program in 1968, some attempts were made to include blacks and other racial minorities into the law school educational process. These attempts fared poorly because there was no significant minority applicant pool. The history of our country could suggest no other possibility. Racial discrimination in its true sense, not that fashioned for the purpose of remedying an obnoxious condition, operates covertly but is systematized to the point where all are required to "know their place." Prior to the social upheaval of the sixties, blacks and other racial minorities were conditioned to the notion that matriculation in higher education was beyond their "place" in American society. What would be the point in applying when the profession manifested the traditional lily white complexion? It was no accident that the first black member of the American Bar Association did not surface until the late 1950s.

What made the Minority Student Program of Rutgers Law School work was the fact that it publicized the availability of specific seats in the Law School for blacks and later for other racial minorities who were willing to risk seeking a legal education. Because of advertising a firm, recognizable commitment, and because of collateral recruitment, the Law School was able to develop an applicant pool which permitted the attainment of goals initially held to be impossible. Had the Law School employed a unitary system of admission, one that did not announce our commitment to the outlying community from which we draw, the Program would not have approached the levels of success it has achieved. A glance at the pre-1968 entering class shows the results of unitary admissions affirmative action. (Slocum, 1979)

The arguments are certainly persuasive in that they clearly demonstrate that identifiable goals can be reached through dual-admissions programs, but not through unitary programs.

On at least two grounds, *Hopwood* was wrongly decided: First the strict-scrutiny standard of review was wrongly applied; and, second, the alleged dual-track admissions program should have met the standard for a sufficiently narrowly tailored program. With respect to strict scrutiny, how does an institution that has, throughout its history, been deeply immersed in racial discrimination remedy the wrong? If *Hopwood* was not wrongly decided, there is little room for penitent state actors to redeem themselves in the eyes of the *Hopwood* court. If the penitent are to be denied voluntary choices, then only judicially mandated programs stand a chance of survival. In *Hopwood*, the program came into existence as a consequence of a consent decree; yet it was not good enough. Will the court have to assume not only the roles of adjudicator and legislator but the executive as well if an adequate remedy is to be provided?

On the second point, the welcome-mat effect is not to be treated lightly. Centuries of societal racial discrimination had reduced the applicant pools to almost nothing in traditionally white institutions of higher education. Merely deciding to suddenly administer a race-neutral admissions program in a traditionally white institution provides absolutely no remedy whatsoever without serious effective recruitment. Yet, if program recruitment of nonwhites is to be successful, the program parameters must be convincingly marketable. Only dual-track systems meet this burden.

## The Question of Race

So what other obstacles would an acceptable program have to overcome? The FCC program outlined in *Adarand* was described in the litigation as a program based on disadvantage and not race. Indeed, even the Court conceded that, "[T]o the extent that the statutes and regulations involved in this case are race neutral, we agree" (*Adarand Constructors, Inc. et al. v. Pena*, 1995). Yet, the government conceded that the presumptions created by race employed in the statutes and regulations were entitled to "some heightened level of scrutiny" (*Adarand Constructors, Inc. et al. v. Pena*, 1995). It is this concession with which this discussion takes issue. More simply put, does a plus for race constitute the creation of a class?

To say that race is a factor to be considered is not necessarily to create a class. The equal protection clause of the Fourteenth Amendment is concerned with group classifications that result in differential treatment for all members of the group. The disparate treatment applies to all group members simply because of their race. Rebuttable presumptions, such as those set out in *Adarand*, significantly reduce the onus of racial classifications in that all members of the targeted race are not automatically deemed eligible for consideration, and so race alone does not define the class.

The socioeconomic disadvantaged targets of the Small Business Act were the groups subject to review under the Fourteenth Amendment. The use of race-based presumptions merely provided a means of achieving administrative efficiency and, in effect, shifted the burden of administrative costs to those who would challenge the determination of socioeconomic deprivation. Neither benefit nor burden was bestowed as a consequence of race.

The use of race as a presumption of socioeconomic deprivation does no more than take into account the realities of race in America. The overwhelming majority of America's racial minorities are in fact socioeconomically disadvantaged. In this context, race becomes no more than an administrative tool, far removed from the disposition of the matter. This view was expressed by a federal district court when a dual-track minority admissions program was challenged in *Doherty v. Rutgers School of Law—Newark* (1980).

The Minority Student Program at Rutgers-Newark encompasses some 30 percent of each entering class. Eligibility for program review is limited to those who are found to have been disadvantaged (i.e., from low-income families with a history of cyclical poverty or can demonstrate that they have been educationally disadvantaged) or are African American, Hispanic (Latino) American, Asian American, Native American, or socioeconomically disadvantaged and white. In addition, any applicant can elect to have his or her file reviewed by the regular admissions route. The school has unquestionably established a dual-track admissions system. However, both tracks are racially mixed and no particular racial group has a fixed number of seats assigned or even targeted.

The question here, however, is not whether the admissions program is dual or unitary, but rather whether the program is race-based in violation of Fourteenth Amendment standards. In *Doherty*, the Rutgers program was challenged. The plaintiff alleged that the defendants had adopted and maintained an admissions program which violated his rights under the Fourteenth Amendment to the United States Constitution, under Title VI of the Civil Rights Act of 1964 (*Doherty v. Rutgers School of Law—Newark*, 1980).

After an extensive review of the admissions process and Doherty's application, the Court determined that the pro se plaintiff lacked standing to prosecute the claim on two grounds: (1) had there been no Minority Student Program, Doherty would still not have been admitted since his application score total was lower than any applicant in the total regular admit pool; and (2) he was not prohibited from competing for any of the minority program seats simply because of his race.

As to the first basis for the rejection of standing, little more need be said. However, the Court, citing *Bakke*, set the standards for standing in the following language: "The constitutional element of standing is plaintiff's demonstration of any injury to himself that is likely to be redressed by a favorable decision of his claim" (*Doherty v. Rutgers School of Law—Newark*, 1980, citing *Regents of the University of California at Davis v. Bakke*, 1978). The Court went on to say that if Doherty's alleged injury is the denial of his application, to redress the injury plaintiff would have to show that, but for the existence of the Minority Student Program, he would have been admitted. The record revealed otherwise.

But the Court posited an alternative, stating that "if plaintiff's claimed injury is that he was not permitted to compete for all places in the class simply because of his race, then he might have standing regardless of his academic qualifications, for such an injury could be redressed simply by ordering the law school to allow him to compete for all of the seats" (*Doherty v. Rutgers School of Law—Newark*, 1980). In other words, the Court could order the abolishment of the program. As to this issue, the Court held that "no applicant is prohibited from being considered under the minority program on account of his or her race or ethnic background . . . [T]he concept of 'minority' in the challenged program includes economically disadvantaged whites . . . [u]nlike the admissions program in *Bakke* . . . " (*Doherty v. Rutgers School of Law—Newark*, 1978).

The concern with this decision is one of timing. This matter was decided before *Adarand*. *Adarand* was decided on the basis of a stipulation that the presumptions created as a consequence of race created race-based classifications resulting in injury to the plaintiff. Obviously there is a nexus between race-based classification and the possibilities of injury. In applying the principles of both *Adarand* and *Bakke* to the Rutgers program, what would a successful plaintiff look like?

The Minority Student Program (MSP) application review is vastly different from the regular admissions review process in that it is 50 percent subjective. Half of the application review points awarded by the MSP director are based on economics, lifestyle, and background leading toward a determination of disadvantaged status. Anyone can elect review under the aegis of the MSP; however, those with higher scores from advantaged backgrounds would not fare well under the MSP review. The subjective review would probably be fatal under these circumstances. Consequently it does come down to a matter of choice: Each applicant opts for the review he or she feels will most likely be successful.

Does the Fourteenth Amendment bar such a choice? Which unsuccessful candidate could demonstrate injury as a consequence of this dual-track system? Suppose Doherty had been better in the objective criteria and ended up number one on the wait list? Since one of his stated objectives was to have the program ended, he would sue on the ground that, but for the MSP, he would have been admitted, and now he has an injury. But he has a remedy for his injury under the Fourteenth Amendment only if the MSP is race-based and fails to withstand strict scrutiny.

But it is more than obvious that the potential plaintiff had access to either admission process; his race posed no bar. Indeed, at the moment of choice, he was in competition for every seat. Immediately thereafter, regardless of his choice, he could not deny that his race could not exclude him from any seat. Consequently, it would be difficult to make the argument that the choice was skewed as a consequence of race. In this instance, the overwhelming criteria of disadvantaged status within the MSP is truly the focus.

In all probability, a prevailing plaintiff would have to be someone who opted for MSP review and just barely missed the mark. That applicant would assert that the plus given on account of race turned out to be the determining factor, and therefore he or she was rejected on account of his or her race. The upshot of that challenge would be close scrutiny review with all of its pitfalls.

But the analysis does not stop here. Should the plaintiff prevail, wherein lies the remedy? The only remedy would be for the Court to abolish the program and allow the applicant to reapply, perhaps at no cost (*Hopwood v. Texas*, 1994). But what is the likelihood that without the MSP, the applicant would be successful? If the applicant were long on "objectives" and short on "subjectives," he or she would have in all probability opted for regular review—and would not be a likely candidate to challenge the program.

On the other hand, if the applicant had been short on "objectives" and long on "subjectives," to bring suit would be to "shoot oneself in the foot." (Unless the applicant had no true desire to be admitted and was merely playing the role of "stalking horse" for others.) Without MSP, the applicant has little to no chance for admission. Again, this is hardly a likely plaintiff. While there may be someone who just might make it with the right mix—the perfect balance between the objective and subjective criteria—to abolish the program and still make it under regular admissions, but a suit would be highly unlikely.

The potential for this model's survival is good even under close scrutiny, because no one denies the purpose of racial and ethnic diversity in the student body. Still, there are a host of factors pointing in the direction of race that are truly socioeconomic in basis. The utilization of socio-economic criteria along with race may be the best and safest path to achieve a diverse student body, even including the law's true favorites.

This is no new concept in legal education. As early as 1968, the gatekeepers to legal education came together to address the dearth of minorities in the legal profession. The American Bar Association, the Law School Admissions Council, The Association of American

Law Schools, and the National Bar Association came together and created The Council on Legal Education Opportunity (the Council); in 1972, the La Raza National Lawyers' Association joined as well. The Council conducted summer educational institutes for purposes of evaluating law school potential. Although privately funded at the outset, the Council was ultimately funded by the federal government (Higher Education Act, 1965).

The program served students who were "educationally and economically disadvantaged" but nonetheless demonstrated the ability to succeed in law school. In addition to a student's demonstrated academic potential, information about each applicant's background (including parental educational and economic background) was elicited for the purpose of evaluating the quality of life to which each candidate was exposed. Many law schools relied on this accumulated data as a part of their own admissions process. Race was one of many factors taken into account.

It is important to note that in *Adarand*, race was employed to create a presumption of disadvantaged status. But in the examples presented here, it is only one factor and a small one at that, hardly justifying the conclusion that the program is race-based. And, even if they are, the programs outlined are narrowly tailored simply because of their limited use of race as an admission factor. These programs ought to pass constitutional muster regardless of the standard of review.

## Conclusion

For more than one hundred years, Congress has labored over its responsibilities under the Wartime Amendments to eliminate the badges and indicia of slavery. However, the judiciary has, for whatever reason, played a role in opposition, insisting on a kind of racial neutrality that belies the historical antecedents of racial discrimination in America. The judiciary insists that Congress not play favorites. But to blind Congress to color is quite frankly to give every advantage to the dominant culture by preserving the status quo of white male privilege.

Consistent with this tension between the Supreme Court and Congress, efforts to create race-based bonuses in favor of minority contractors were subjected to strict scrutiny, overruling *Metro Broadcasting*, and found to violate the Constitution because the requirements imposed were not sufficiently narrowly tailored. Majority contractors have the benefit of experience and capital which minorities lack as a consequence of past exclusion. Yet the Court was offended by the use of race-based preferences—as if Congressional color-blindness did not maintain existing preferences.

With the Court and Congress in this posture, the possibilities for affirmative action in higher education were explored in some detail. The University of Texas Law School took the spotlight. After a history of de jure racial discrimination excluding nonwhites, a federal district court ruled against a dual-track, race-based admissions program provided to remedy past discrimination by applying strict scrutiny. Although the court approved diversity as a compelling governmental interest, it invalidated the program on the grounds that race-based classifications as employed in the admissions process were not narrowly tailored enough to meet the constitutional standard because plaintiffs were deemed not to be in competition for every seat. The temporary dual-track step in the program proved to be fatal. Nevertheless, there are strong reasons to install a dual-track admissions program as opposed to a unitary one.

Yet, in Texas, the strict-scrutiny standard proved to be too big a hurdle for the program to overcome. The prior years of de jure segregation excluding nonwhites proved to be of little consequence to the Court in determining the constitutionality of the program. The resultant preference for whites is usually blinked at when a determination is made that benign or, as in this case, remedial programs are too discriminatory for the likes of the Fourteenth Amendment. The University of Texas had traditionally been an all-white school. Without an affirmative effort to attract and admit nonwhites, the residue of the past is strong enough to preserve the preference for whites because nonwhites are not likely to apply in any significant numbers.

But the impediments of the Texas program perceived by the district court are not insurmountable. Rutgers School of Law at Newark also has a two-track admission program; its Minority Student Program focuses on disadvantaged status and includes both whites and nonwhites. Although *Adarand* found the language of Congressional edicts focusing on disadvantage status to be facially race neutral, the Court accepted the parties' stipulation that the program was actually race-based. It is doubtful that such a conclusion could be readily obtained in reviewing the Rutgers program. Indeed, the program has been challenged in federal courts and still survives.

In sum, higher education officials can afford to be somewhat optimistic if they choose to be affirmative in their efforts to bring diversity into the educational process. The legal fight has not been at the undergraduate level, because open enrollment or some abbreviated form of open enrollment leaves little room for challenge because there is no injured party. Such mechanisms may be implemented to achieve diversity. But graduate schools must be a bit more sophisticated. There are racial correlations that can be very effective in bringing diversity into the classroom. And although *Adarand* places the individual remedy far above group remedies, there is still room to give race a plus directly to remedy the past rather than by inference, whether or not the law continues to have its favorites.

## REFERENCES

*Adams v. Richardson*, 356 F. Supp. 92 (D. D. C.), modified and aff'd 480 F. 2d 1159 (D.C. Cir. 1973), dismissed sub nom. *Women's Equity Action League v. Cavazos*, 906 F. 2d 742 (D.C. Cir. 1990).
*Adarand Constructors, Inc. et al. v. Pena*, 63 LW 4523, 4530, 4533, 4526.
The Civil Rights Cases of 1883, 109 U.S. 3, 25 (1883).
*Crosen v. City of Richmond*, 488 U.S. 469 (1989).
*Doherty v. Rutgers School of Law—Newark*, 487 F. Supp. 1291, 1292, 1296, 1298 (D. N. J. 1980)
*Fullilove et al. v. Klutznick et al.*, 448 U.S. 448, 519 (1980).
Graglia, L., *Hopwood v. Texas:* Racial Preferences Upheld and Endorsed, 45 AALS *Journal of Legal Education* 79 (March 1995).
Higher Education Act of 1965, as amended, 20 U.S.C. Sec. 1134.
*Hirabayashi v. United States*, 320 U.S. 81, 100 (1943).

*Hopwood v. Texas*, 861 F. Supp. 551, 556, 574, 578 (W.D. Tex. 1994).
*Metro Broadcasting v. FCC*, 497 U.S. 547 (1990).
*Plessy v. Ferguson*, 163 U.S. 537 (1896).
*Regents of University of California v. Bakke*, 438 U.S. 265, 281 n. 14, 324–378, (1978).
*Scott v. Sanford*, 19 How. 393 (1857).
Slocum, A., Report Concurring.

―――――――――――――― NOTE ――――――――――――――

1. Remedial classifications are those classifications which are created with the express purpose of providing a remedy for victims of past discrimination.

# Albert H. Kauffman and Roger Gonzalez

## 10

### *The Hopwood Case: What It Says and What It Doesn't*

In *Hopwood v. State of Texas*, the U.S. Fifth Circuit Court of Appeals[1] held that the University of Texas School of Law discriminated against four white students because of their race in the admissions process at the Law School. The Fifth Circuit based this finding upon a legal holding that an interest in diversity could not support an affirmative action plan and that the Law School could look only to its own history when determining whether there were sufficient present effects of past discrimination at the institution to support affirmative action. The opinion has been strongly criticized and praised, but little understood. This chapter gives a brief summary of Equal Protection law, describes a few relevant cases regarding affirmative action, summarizes the facts and opinions in the *Hopwood* case, lists the issues on appeal to the U.S. Supreme Court, and outlines the implications of the decision.

### Equal Protection Law in a Small Nutshell

We can better understand *Hopwood* and affirmative action cases if we consider them in the general structure of Equal Protection law. Governments constantly classify people into groups. Governments decide to put parks in one part of the city and not in another, give welfare to persons below a certain income and not above that income, admit some persons into college and not others, or hire some persons and not others. Strictly speaking, the governmental entity can deny "equal protection" to persons based on any of these types of classifications, that is, almost everything that the government does benefits or harms some groups of people more than others, and benefits or harms some individuals more than others. In general, the courts have analyzed these classifications and groups three different ways:

1. Most cases are analyzed under a theory called "rational basis," that is, the policy or practice of the government will be upheld as constitutional if the government had a legitimate interest in the area and there is a rational relation between the interest and the practice. For example, the government might say that there was a greater demand for a park in one section of the town or that the land was less expensive, or welfare had to be limited to emergencies and the state's budget, etc. Usually if a court analyzes a case under the rational basis test the policy or practice of the government is upheld. The government has a light burden to show that it had a rational basis for its decision.

2. In some cases the courts have decided that the interests involved are more important ones or that the groups involved deserve more protection. Therefore the government policy or practice will only be upheld if the government has a substantial interest in its policy and there is a significant relationship between that interest and its policy. This "substantial interest" mode of analysis has been applied to cases involving gender discrimination, illegitimacy, and a "complete denial" of education. For example, laws that give males a preference as an executor of a will, or laws that completely deny education to children of undocumented persons, can only be upheld if the state can show a substantial interest and a significant relationship between the law and its interest.

3. The highest level of scrutiny, called "strict scrutiny," applies when a government has a rule, regulation, or law that affects a "suspect" class of persons or "fundamental rights."

For example, laws that classify persons on the basis of race or national origin, or laws that affect the exercise of first amendment rights can only be upheld if the government can show that there is a "compelling interest" in the law or policy, and the policy is narrowly tailored to meet the government's "compelling interest."

For reasons far beyond both the scope of this chapter and the ability of the writers to comprehend, courts have found that cases in which some "plus factor" or "preference" is given to a historically disfavored racial or ethnic group are subjected to strict scrutiny analysis, that is, a policy which gives some preference to African Americans or Latinos can only be upheld if the state can show a compelling interest in the policy and show that the policy is narrowly tailored to meet that interest. Thus, the real issues in these cases become whether the state had a compelling interest and whether the policy was narrowly tailored. The following cases take various stabs at trying to define what are "valid" compelling interests and what types of policies are in fact "narrowly tailored" to meet those interests.

## Summary of Some Relevant Affirmative Action Cases

*Hopwood's* effect on the law of affirmative action and desegregation can best be understood in the context of some of the cases that were either relied upon, ignored, or overruled by the Fifth Circuit in *Hopwood*. The most famous case in the area of affirmative action is *Regents of University of California v. Bakke* (1978). The *Bakke* court reviewed a University of California at Davis Medical School policy that reserved "disadvantaged" minority students 16 of the 100 entering positions. The U.S. Supreme Court held that the policy violated Title VI of the 1964 Civil Rights Act and the U.S. Constitution Equal Protection Clause; *but*, race could be considered as one of the factors in an admissions system. *Bakke* held that, "the interest of diversity is compelling in the context of a university's admissions program"(1978). *Bakke* held that the university had a compelling interest in assuring diversity in its student body, but that the racial classification for a certain number of seats in the entering class was not "necessary" to promote this interest; that is, it was not narrowly tailored.

As an example of an appropriate university admissions program that included race as a factor, but did not "over-do-it," the opinion quoted from and attached a copy of the Harvard undergraduate admissions plan. Both the opinion for the Court by Justice Powell and the separate opinion of four other judges agreed that the Harvard plan was a proper use of "race" in admissions.

*Wygant v. Jackson Board of Education* (1986) provides another insight into the Court's thinking on what constitutes a legitimate state interest. *Wygant* held that a school board could not rely on its interest in overcoming "societal discrimination" to support a plan which would reduce its teaching force by terminating the employment of white teachers with more years of experience than minority teachers, in violation of the agreement between the school and the teacher's union.

Thus, one of the proffered bases for use of race was rejected by the *Wygant* case, but only in the context of the termination of employment of incumbent employees. However, in *Wygant* Justice O'Connor held that "a state interest in the promotion of racial diversity has been found sufficiently compelling, at least in the context of higher education, to support the use of racial considerations in furthering that interest" (1978).

*Richmond v. J.A. Croson Company* (1989) is a leading case considering the scope and breadth of historical discrimination that constitutes a compelling interest. *Croson* held that the City of Richmond could not rely on general discrimination in the construction industry to support a contracting program that gave preferences to minority contracting firms. Nevertheless, the *Croson* court also held that, a state or local subdivision "has the authority to eradicate the effects of private discrimination within its own legislative jurisdiction." *Croson* outlined the type of evidence necessary to support a "compelling interest" as follows:

> Where there is a significant statistical disparity between the number of qualified minority contractors willing and able to perform a particular service and the number of such

contractors actually engaged by the locality or the locality's prime contractors, an inference of discriminatory exclusion could arise (p. 509).

However, all of the cases have not been negative ones. In 1987, the U.S. Supreme Court specifically upheld the use of goals and even racial quotas in cases where there is a clear history of discrimination against persons on the basis of race or national origin, *U.S. v. Paradise* (1987). As in the great majority of affirmative action and desegregation cases, there were several different opinions. However, all of the Justices agreed that the government had a compelling interest in remedying past and present discrimination and that there was a history of discrimination and present effects of that history in the hiring and promotion practices of the Alabama Department of Public Safety. There were differences among the judges whether the remedies ordered by the district court[2] were "narrowly tailored," though there was agreement among the Justices on the following factors to determine whether the remedy was narrowly tailored:

1. the necessity of the relief and the efficacy of alternative remedies,
2. the flexibility and duration of the relief, including the availability of waiver provisions,
3. the relationship of the numerical goals to the relevant labor market, and
4. the impact of the relief on the rights of third parties.

The majority in *Paradise* upheld an order requiring a "50 percent promotional quota in the upper ranks, but only *if* there were qualified black candidates, *if* the rank were less than 25 percent black, and *if* the Department had not developed and implemented a promotion plan without adverse impact for the relevant rank."

## *U.S. v. Fordice*

The State has rightfully taken the position that the *Hopwood* case is a desegregation case, not an affirmative action case. In other words, the actions taken by the State were in response to findings by the U.S. Department of Education Office of Civil Rights that the State had practiced discrimination against African Americans and Mexican Americans. In fact, the Office of Civil Rights has not yet found that Texas has removed the vestiges of discrimination in its higher education system, and has put Texas and other states on notice that their higher education systems are under review to determine compliance with *Fordice*. In *U.S. v. Fordice* (1992), the Supreme Court noted the strong "affirmative duty" of states to remove the vestiges of discrimination against minorities. Under *Fordice*, merely adopting race-neutral policies is not enough. The State must take affirmative steps to ameliorate practices and policies that perpetuate the dual system. The constitutional duty to remove the vestiges of discrimination may require a state either to eliminate or counteract strict reliance on test scores that effectively discriminate against minority students.[3] Although most of the debate in the *Hopwood* case has been around the issue of affirmative action rather than desegregation, this important distinction should have been recognized and acted upon by the Supreme Court. Thus, the *Hopwood* case should have been built on established, but certainly not unambiguous, precedent. Instead, two judges in *Hopwood* in effect overruled *Bakke*, and ignored *Croson, Wygant, Paradise* and *Fordice*.

## The Facts of the Case

### History of the Law School

The University of Texas (UT) Law School was the subject of the most famous law school discrimination case, *Sweatt v. Painter* (1950), a precursor of *Brown v. Board of Education*. By law and Texas Constitutional provision, blacks could not attend school with whites in Texas and at the time no law school in the state accepted blacks. The U.S. Supreme Court unanimously ordered Texas to admit Mr. Sweatt, a black, to the UT Law School. He was admitted after a cynical attempt by the State to create a "separate, but equal" law school was soundly rejected by the Court. After admission, Mr. Sweatt was literally harassed out of the law school. As late as 1971, when one of the authors of this chapter attended the UT Law School, no blacks and only five Mexican Americans out of a class of 500 were admitted to the Law School. Only constant pressure by the Office of Civil Rights and a Washington D. C. federal court caused the Law School and the rest of the Texas Higher Education System to begin to admit and retain some minority enrollment in its graduate, professional, and competitive universities. Finally, by the mid-1980s the Law School had increased its enrollment to about 15 percent minority in a state with a 40 percent minority population, projected to reach 50 percent minority by the year 2010.

## The Admission Program

The admissions program in 1992 at the University of Texas School of Law (Law School) placed heavy emphasis on Grade Point Average (GPA) and Law School Admission Test (LSAT) scores. As primary criteria for admission, the Law School used the Texas Index (TI) Number, a composite of the LSAT and GPA, with approximately 60 percent weight on the LSAT. The Law School used a three-zone system to classify their applicants: (1) a presumptive admit (2) a presumptive deny, and (3) a middle-discretionary zone. The TI score determined the level of scrutiny an applicant would receive. Persons in the presumptive admit zone and the presumptive deny zone received little review; however, persons on the margins of the zones were given some review. Applicants under the middle discretionary zone received the most extensive review. In 1992, the Law School used two different TI scales as a first look to evaluate the Mexican American and black applicants with the white and other minority applicants. The presumptive TI admit score for Mexican Americans and blacks was 189. For whites and other minorities the presumptive admit TI score was 199. The presumptive deny score for blacks and Mexican Americans was 179. For whites and other minorities the presumptive deny score was 192.

The Law School also used special subcommittees to review African American and Mexican American applicants. These two policies—separate zones of scores and separate committees—are the two specific parts of the admissions procedure that have received strong criticism and were the basis for both the District Court and Court of Appeals decision. The Law School vigorously defended the policy arguing that these were just guidelines and that a uniform system was in place, but different committees and zones of scores were in place to issue thorough and consistent considerations of minority applicants.

Cheryl Hopwood, Kenneth Elliot, Douglas Carvell, and David Rogers were denied admission to the University of Texas School of Law. These four white plaintiffs argued they were denied admission to the Law School because they are white and claimed "reverse discrimination" when Hispanics and blacks with lower Texas Index Scores were admitted.

## The Individual Plaintiffs

A consideration of the records of the individual plaintiffs gives an additional structure for consideration of the legal holdings of the courts. Cheryl Hopwood was a certified public accountant in California, had received an associate's degree in accounting from Montgomery County Community College in 1984 and a bachelor's degree in accounting from California State University in Sacramento in 1988. Cheryl Hopwood had the highest TI score among the four plaintiffs at 199 with a GPA of 3.8 and an LSAT score of 39 (83rd percentile).[4] The Law School admissions committee held that Cheryl Hopwood did not attend schools that were academically competitive with those of the majority of the applicants and did a majority of her college work at a junior college. She filed no letters of recommendation, provided no personal statement with the application, and her responses to the questions were brief and did not elaborate on her background and skill.

Kenneth Elliot is a certified public accountant who received a B.B.A. in accounting from the University of Texas in 1984. Elliot had a Texas Index score of 197 with a GPA of 2.98 and LSAT score of 167. Kenneth Elliot was denied admission not only at the University of Texas School of Law but also at the Baylor School of Law.

Douglas Carvell took the LSAT twice receiving a score of 34 on the old scale of LSAT (61st percentile) the first time and a score of 164 (91st percentile) the second time. Carvell's Texas Index Score was 197. Carvell's undergraduate GPA was a 3.28 in political science from Hendrix College in Conway, Arkansas. That GPA only ranked Carvell 98th out of his class of 247 at Hendrix College. Furthermore, one of Carvell's letters of recommendation from a professor at Hendrix College describes Carvell's performance as uneven, disappointing, and mediocre. Carvell was also denied admission to Vanderbilt School of Law and the University of Texas School of Business.

David Rogers had an undergraduate GPA of 3.13 and an LSAT score of 166. Rogers' Texas Index Score was 197. In 1985, Rogers was dismissed from the University of Texas honors program because of poor scholastic performance. Rogers received an undergraduate degree in professional writing from the University of Houston-Downtown. Rogers filed no letters of recommendation.

## General Effects of the Admissions Process

Had the Law School based its 1992 admissions solely on the applicants' TI scores without regard to race or ethnicity, the entering class would have included, at most, nine Blacks and 18 Mexican Americans out of a class of 500. In 1992, only 88 African American applicants to all law schools in the country had scores on the Texas Index equal to or higher than the median for non-Hispanic whites who entered the Law School in the fall of 1992 and only 289 had scores equal to or higher than the Texas Index score marking the bottom of the discretionary zone used for evaluation of non-Hispanic white applicants that year. The comparable numbers for Mexican Americans in the United States were 52 and 96. Furthermore, 109 nonminority residents with numerical scores lower than Cheryl Hopwood were offered admission, and 67 nonminority residents with numerical scores lower than the three other plaintiffs were admitted.

Currently, the Law School does not use a separate minority subcommittee or different presumptive admit or denial scores for minority and nonminority applicants. The Law School still attempts to meet U.S. Department of Education Office of Civil Rights' guidelines by having 10 percent Mexican American students and 5 percent black students in the entering class. These aspirations are not a quota because they are only aspirational according to the quality of the applicants. These aspirations are indeed modest. Texas' population is 25 percent Mexican American and 15 percent African American and even after high school dropouts and college attrition, the college population is 18 percent Mexican American and 11 percent African American.

## The Intervenors

The District Court denied a proposed intervention by black student organizations at the University of Texas at Austin and its Law School. The District Court held that the black student organization could not prove that the state would not aggressively defend its affirmative action program. At the end of the trial, intervenors sought to add evidence regarding the lack of validity of the Texas Index and its inability to predict the actual performance of black law students. The State did not put the evidence into the record and the District Court refused to consider it. Nevertheless the Fifth Circuit affirmed the denial of intervention.[5]

## The District Court Opinion

The District Court (*Hopwood v. Texas*, 1994) held that the Law School had violated the white plaintiffs' Equal Protection rights, but it did not order an injunction because the admission policies had changed and were not before the court. The District Court used a strict scrutiny standard to evaluate the admission program. Only two compelling government interests may support an affirmative action plan at a university: (1) obtaining the educational benefits that flow from a racially and ethnically diverse student body; and (2) the objective of overcoming present effects of historical discrimination.

Relying heavily on *Bakke* the District Court held that the Law School had a compelling governmental interest in having a diverse student body and remedying present effects of past discrimination. On the issue of "present effects of past discrimination," the District Court looked to the history of discrimination by the State in its entire public education system from primary education to professional schools, finding that the "State's institutions of higher education are inextricably linked to the primary and secondary schools in the system" (*Hopwood v. Texas*, 1994). The Court held that the history of discrimination at the University of Texas at Austin would also support affirmative action. Present effects of this discrimination include, (1) the Law School's lingering reputation in the minority community as a "white school," (2) underrepresentation of minorities in the student body, and (3) "some perception that the Law School is a hostile environment for minorities" (*Hopwood v. Texas*, 1994).

The District Court held that the admission program was not narrowly tailored enough because candidates of different races were not compared at some point in the admission process. The District Court granted a declaratory judgment that the plaintiffs had been denied Equal Protection rights, a one dollar nominal damage award and an order allowing plaintiffs to reapply to the Law School without charge. The district court denied plaintiffs' requests for punitive damages, compensatory damages, and an order of admission to law school. The plaintiffs appealed.

## The Fifth Circuit Opinion[6]

Two of the three members of the panel agreed on the opinion of the court. The third judge agreed with the judgment of the panel but strongly disagreed with its reasoning.

The states' racial classification can be supported only if the state has a compelling state interest and the policy is narrowly tailored to meet its obligation. The panel held that the only compelling state interest in affirmative action cases is overcoming present effects of past discrimination and refused to recognize the educational benefits that flow from a racially and ethnically diverse student body as legal. The panel summarized its own opinion as follows:

> In summary, we hold that the University of Texas School of Law may not use race as a factor in deciding which applicants to admit in order to achieve a diverse student body, to combat the perceived effects of a hostile environment at the Law School, to alleviate the Law School's poor reputation in the minority community, or to eliminate any present effects of past discrimination by actors other than the Law School (*Hopwood v. Texas*, 1996).

The Fifth Circuit rejected Justice Powell's Supreme Court opinion in *Bakke*. Justice Powell's decision held that consideration of race or ethnicity for achieving a diverse student body is a compelling interest under the Fourteenth Amendment. The Fifth Circuit argues that the only place in *Bakke* where diversity is mentioned is in Justice Powell's opinion, an opinion that was not supported by the other justices. The panel noted that the purpose of the Fourteenth Amendment is to end all racially motivated state action. "The use of race, in and of itself, to choose students simply achieves a student body that looks different." Such a criterion is no more rational on its own terms than would be choices based upon the physical size or blood type of applicants. Also, a university may properly favor one applicant over another because of his ability to play the cello, make a downfield tackle, or understand chaos theory" (*Hopwood v. Texas*, 1996).

On the issue of "present effects of past discrimination," the Court held that discrimination at UT Law School ended in the late 1960s when the Law School set up its first program designed to recruit minorities; the vast majority of faculty, staff, and students at the Law School had nothing to do with any discrimination that the Law School practiced in the past. Furthermore, the Court held that the Law School has never had an admission policy that excluded Mexican Americans on the basis of race and any racial tension currently occurring at the Law School is created because of the prevalent consideration of race in admissions.

The panel held that the District Court mistakenly expanded the scope of what institutions discriminated to reach all public education within the state. According to the panel, only the Law School itself and not the University of Texas at Austin of which it is one professional school, is best able to measure the harm of its past discrimination. The Fifth Circuit refused to measure the system of education within the State as a whole. It acknowledged the fact that Texas has a history of racial discrimination in its public school systems, but held that the Law School could not effectively measure the present effects of discrimination in primary and secondary schools in Texas.

The Law School operates as a separate functional unit within the system. The Law School had to prove that it adopted the program specifically to remedy the identified present effects of its own past discrimination. Under this holding, only discrimination by the Law School is relevant. Discrimination by the State of Texas and its educational system is not relevant. Because two judges felt diversity can never be a compelling interest and there was insufficient evidence of present effects of past discrimination, they held there was no compelling interest in the use of race or ethnicity as a factor in admissions at the Law School.

## Damages in the Individual Cases

Under the Fifth Circuit opinion, the burden of proof on the damages issues transfers to the defendants; that is, the Law School would have to show that the white applicants would not have been admitted under a "non-discriminatory" admission system. The panel held there was intentional discrimination; that is, that the Law School intended to treat similarly situated persons differently on the basis of race. However, it held that the Law School acted with good intentions, so the Court deemed no punitive damages were necessary but threatened that if the Law School used race again in its admission policies, punitive damages might be appropriate.

## The Concurrence

Although agreeing with the outcome of the case, Circuit Judge Wiener, one of the three judges on the panel, was highly critical of the majority's rationale. Judge Wiener held that this case was not a class action suit and the Court of Appeals should have decided only if the admissions policy used by the Law School in 1992 violated the Equal Protection Clause of the Fourteenth Amendment. Judge Wiener held the Court of Appeals should have remanded to the District Court only to apply the correct burden shifting process and if a remedy is warranted injunctive relief should be given only to these individual plaintiffs.

Judge Wiener refused to find that diversity can never be a compelling governmental interest in a public graduate school. He argued that a three-judge panel of a circuit court does not have the authority to overrule *Bakke*, a Supreme Court decision. Justice Wiener held that a university's attempt to achieve diversity is a compelling governmental interest. Also, Judge Wiener felt that the governmental unit to be considered could have been either the Law School or the entire University of Texas system. Yet, he held that neither the University of Texas system nor the Law School exhibited present effects of past discrimination sufficient to justify the use of a racial classification. Judge Wiener also argued that neither the State of Texas nor its primary and secondary school systems were the relevant governmental units in this case.

Judge Wiener held that the Law School's 1992 admission program focusing on Mexican Americans and blacks was not narrowly tailored enough to achieve diversity. The judge cited that the admissions process ignored non-Mexican Hispanic Americans, Asian Americans, and Native Americans.

Judge Wiener strongly disagreed with the implied injunction leveled by the Court of Appeals. The granting or denial of injunctive relief is in the discretion of the District Court and Judge Wiener argued the Fifth Circuit should not decide the issue, especially because the present policy is not even before the Court.

## Dissent From Failure To Grant Rehearing En Banc

Seven of the 18 members of the Fifth Circuit obviously disagree with the holding of the *Hopwood* decision. Seven is only one short of the number required to set the case again for *en banc* consideration before all the 18 members of the Court. For these seven judges, Chief Judge Politz wrote that the majority opinion of the Fifth Circuit was a textbook example of judicial activism. These seven dissenters argue that until the Supreme Court expressly overrules *Bakke*, student body diversity is a compelling governmental interest for the purposes of strict scrutiny. The Fifth Circuit Court of Appeals, as a constitutionally inferior court, is compelled to follow a directly controlling Supreme Court precedent until the Supreme Court itself decides to overrule it. The dissent was especially concerned with the likely impact of such a radical and unprecedented opinion, strongly criticizing their colleagues on the Court for their failure to take up the issue *en banc*.

## A Separate Dissenting Opinion

Circuit Judge Stewart holds that the majority opinion of the Fifth Circuit Court of Appeals in the *Hopwood* decision maintaining that *Sweatt v. Painter* eliminated de jure segregation was wrong. A year after being admitted, Sweatt left law school without graduating, succumbing to racial slurs from students and professors, cross burnings, and tire slashing. Additionally, there is documentation that during the 1950s and 1960s, the University of Texas continued to carry out discriminatory policies against both black and Mexican American students. As late as 1983, the Department of Education forced the State of Texas to accept a plan to desegregate its higher education system. To this day, Texas's higher education system still has not been declared in compliance with Title VI and the

Fourteenth Amendment. The majority opinion in the *Hopwood* case failed to follow the history of discrimination that occurred after the *Sweatt* decision.

## What the Court Does Say

1. The State's interest in having a diverse student body is not a sufficient "compelling" interest to support the use of race as a factor in admissions. This is not consistent with the *Bakke* case. All other cases on the issue have held that an affirmative action plan can be supported if the state shows an interest in diversity in the student body or wishes to address the present effects of past discrimination. *Hopwood* said that the diversity interest is *never* sufficient to support affirmative action.

2. Redressing the present effects of historical discrimination is a sufficient compelling interest to support an affirmative action plan; that is, *Hopwood* did not say you could never rely on history to support a plan.

3. The particular institution involved can look only to its own history to support affirmative action, not to a larger institution to which it belongs or to a whole state system of education. Specifically, UT Law School could only look to its own history of discrimination and the present effects of discrimination at UT Law School, not at the history or present effects at UT Austin, the UT System, the A&M System, or the Texas Educational System as a whole.

4. There was insufficient evidence of the present effects of discrimination at UT Law School against either Blacks or Mexican Americans. The evidence of discrimination against Mexican Americans itself was very weak.

5. The UT Law School cannot use race or national origin as a factor in admissions.

6. Officials of the UT Law School *could* be liable for actual and *punitive damages* if they use race or national origin as a factor in the future.

## What the Hopwood Case Does Not Say

1. The decision does not say that other parts of the UT system or other public or private institutions of higher education cannot use race or national origin as a factor. The opinion was specifically about the UT Law School, not UT Austin, the UT System, other Texas systems of higher education, or the Texas Higher Education Coordinating Board.

2. The opinion talks about the admission process, *not* about giving out scholarships or loans, recruiting, or other procedures at a university; that is, only about admissions and again only about admissions at the UT Law School. *However*, if other institutions can not use diversity as a "compelling interest," then each of these institutions will have a harder time justifying the use of race or national origin. Each institution will have to look at its own history and its own present effects of past discrimination.

3. The decision did not say that no present effects of history of discrimination at UT Law School *could* be proved only that it was not proved in this case. In other words, the failure to find the present effects of discrimination might be based on the particular judges on the panel or on the failure of the State to put on a sufficient record of history of discrimination.

4. The opinion did not grant any damages to the Anglo plaintiffs but surely would make it much easier for them to get damages on remand.

## What Was Appealed to the U.S. Supreme Court

The State filed a petition for *certiorari,* asking the Supreme Court to hear the case. The brief argued the Supreme Court should reverse the Fifth Circuit opinion because:

a. Diversity *can* be a compelling state interest.

b. The Law School could base its affirmative action plan on the history of discrimination in all Texas education, not just the Law School.

c. Texas' segregation history in higher education and The Office of Civil Rights (OCR) efforts to force Texas to desegregate suggest use of race or national origin as a factor in admission.

d. Texas cannot be sued at all under Title VI of Civil Rights Act.

e. The Fifth Circuit Court should not put the duty on law school to show plaintiffs would *not have been* admitted absent discrimination.

f. The Fifth Circuit Court cannot give injunctive relief in this case because the present admissions policy was not before the Court.

The African American intervenors have also filed a petition for *certiorari,* requesting the Supreme Court to allow them to intervene in the case and to reverse the lower courts for failure to admit evidence on the LSAT test.

## Implications of the Decision

Surprising the State's attorneys and many avid U.S. Supreme Court watchers, the U.S. Supreme Court denied *certiorari,* i.e., decided not to hear the case. Supreme Court Justices Ginsburg and Souter commented that although the case involved issues of paramount public importance, there was no real case to decide. Both white plaintiffs and the State agreed the 1992 admissions procedure was inappropriate and the state had officially abandoned it. Justice Ginsburg noted that the Supreme Court reviewed judgments, not opinions of courts.

Even before the denial of *certiorari* the Texas Attorney General and the general counsels of the Texas university systems had officially abandoned any use of race or national origin in admissions, scholarships, or loans. After the denial of *certiorari*, Texas' public officials—but oddly enough not officials of the other two states in the Fifth Circuit —moved with amazing alacrity to purge any use, and in some instances, even knowledge, of race or national origin in university and college procedures. This incredible rush to judgment leaves universities and others interested in diversity with no plans and little hope in continuing to increase minority enrollment.

However, there are some alternatives that states, universities, and advocates should consider. Each institution with any plan that might be described as "affirmative action" could review all of its admission, hiring, or contracting practices and history, make specific findings regarding its own discriminatory policies, and develop new and more limited policies. Alternatively, state legislatures could make both broad and specific findings on the history of discrimination and its present effects in their states and enable local governments and private entities to make further findings. Given the present political environment at the state legislative and local government levels, these are difficult alternatives.

A more likely alternative would be to devise and implement admission policies using criteria that do not use race, but that strongly promote diversity; for example, family income, first in family to attend college, family responsibilities while attending secondary school or college, bilingual ability, etc. The *Hopwood* panel approved of admission criteria that would correlate with race, possibly inviting the use of such criteria. Unfortunately, some of these would not be as effective as present policies and still would be subject to challenge. However, these factors would have to combine with a deemphasis on the use of standardized test scores.

Lost in much of the debate about the *Hopwood* case is the real core of the problem. The tremendous reliance that the UT Law School, as well as most graduate schools and highly competitive undergraduate schools, place upon standardized test scores creates a need for "affirmative action." As long as these institutions rely so heavily on standardized test scores with their insidious and profound negative effect on minorities, it will be difficult if not impossible to have substantial minority enrollments at these institutions without some sort of "affirmative action." Were these institutions to greatly de-emphasize and remove their reliance on standardized test scores, they would be more likely to devise and implement admissions programs that look at the entire applicants, rather than at just standardized test scores. Unfortunately, the gap between the average test scores of minorities and the average test scores of whites has remained fairly constant over the last 20 or 30 years. We all hope to remove that gap. But as long as that gap remains, and as long as there is so little proof that test scores relate to long-term performance at the institutions and no proof that they relate to long-term performance in professions or after university life, they should either be completely ignored or given only the slightest effect upon the decision whether to admit a person into an educational institution.

## Summary

*Hopwood* is a sad reminder of a court system that has forgotten history and become the sort of activist court that has brought such criticism of the courts in the past. However, the opinion of the two-judge majority and the opinions of the dissenting judges give a good introduction to issues of affirmative action as they evolve in the legal system. As we follow the development of the law of affirmative action, we should keep three venerable rules in mind: (1) bad facts make bad law; (2) eternal vigilance is the price of liberty; and (3) those who are ignorant of history are doomed to repeat it. Hopefully that landmark will be one we can all look to as positive for those in our society who have never had equal opportunity or access.

## REFERENCES

*Hopwood v. Texas*, 861 F. Supp 551 (W.D. Tex. 1994).
*Hopwood v. Texas*, 78 F. 2d 932 (5th Cir. 1996).
*Regents of University of California v. Bakke*, 438 U.S. (1978).
*Richard v. J. A. Croson Company*, 476 U.S. (1986).
*Texas v. Hopwood*, 116 S. Ct. 2580, 2581 (1996).
*U.S. v. Fordice*, 505 U.S. 717 (1992).
*U.S. v. Paradise*, 480 U.S. 149 (1987).
*Wygant v. Jackson Board of Education*, 476 U.S. 267 (1986).

## NOTES

1. Fifth Circuit Court of Appeals is the federal appeals court for Texas, Louisiana, and Mississippi.
2. There are some differences between the powers of a district court to order remedies and the power of a governmental entity to implement remedies voluntarily, but these differences are not crucial to the discussion in this chapter.
3. Brief in support of petition of *certiorari* by State of Texas in *Hopwood v. U.S.* at p. 21.
4. The LSAT scales changed during the litigation from a 10-to-48 scale to a 120-to-180 scale.
5. Black intervenors appealed the denial of intervention before the trial and after the decision of the District Court. Each time the Fifth Circuit denied intervention.
6. *Hopwood v. Texas*, 78 F. 2d 932 (5th Cir. 1996).

# Mildred García

# Conclusions: Strategies for a New Era

> Nearly 400 years ago, the poet John Donne observed that the loss of one person represents more than the loss of one small piece of humanity. If higher education is to meet the needs of all of its constituents, these issues must be confronted—not just because they are important to a special group but because they are vital to all institutions and the nation.
>
> *Daryl Smith, 1989*

At the threshold of the 21st century, affirmative action continues its 30-year battle for survival. The present battlefield has been intense, but, as the authors of this volume have demonstrated, we are convinced that the war has not been lost and cannot be abandoned. At this point in our history, especially in education, we must forcefully and vigorously engage in the battle for the survival of affirmative action policies if we are to be members of a just and democratic society. To us it is clear that until we have reached equality for all of our citizens, affirmative action must be maintained.

## The Case for Affirmative Action

Since the Supreme Court voted not to review *Hopwood* (discussed by Kauffman and Gonzalez in Chapter 10), supporters of affirmative action must seize this opportunity to clearly state the reasons for its existence and to educate and promote public understanding of the essential need to continue this practice. As Michaelson states, "[A]t a time when colleges and universities remain committed to diversity, the obvious task is to explain why" (1996, p. A48).

The changing demographics are clear: More students of color are entering our educational system. There can be no doubt that the health of our nation's economy hinges on graduating women and students of color who will enter into the work force and become productive citizens. If we fail in this effort, we will put the nation at risk economically, socially, and morally.

Diversity in our classrooms introduces differing perspectives, enriching the cultural and intellectual experiences of both students and faculty. Several Harvard University presidents have underscored the necessity of diversity as an educational value. Cornelius C. Felton, who served during the Civil War era, believed that in order to remove prejudices, students needed to be recruited from different parts of the country. Similarly, Charles W. Elliot, president from 1869–1909, wanted Harvard students to represent a variety of "nations, states, schools, families, sects and conditions of life." And current President Neil L. Rudenstine reminds us that the character of American society from the very beginning has been shaped by our collective willingness to carry forward an unprecedented experiment in diversity (Rudenstine, 1996).

Increased diversity in our classrooms brings academic vitality through the presence of different perspectives, different views, different languages, and different cultures. In these venues, questions are appropriately raised by those whose experiences and perspectives might be different from what has been presented in the past. These differing viewpoints can lead to rethinking old knowledge and generating new knowledge. Most important, diversity requires defining and perhaps redefining "truth"—the concept at the core of education and discovery (García and Smith, 1996).

Furthermore, as the enterprise that prepares future leaders, higher education is responsible for educating pioneers who will be successful in a multicultural and global society. Morally, we shoulder the responsibility for providing equal opportunity to all members of our society. Through our efforts to instill in students a commitment to promote racial understanding, we become partners in the process of socially and racially integrating our society (William and Taylor, 1996).

The time is now for proponents of affirmative action to reexamine where our progress has been, justify the reasons why affirmative action policies must remain in place, and explain our goals and practices clearly and convincingly. While *Bakke* remains the law of the land, it is clear that we in higher education are the best judges of what our affirmative action policies should be. As such, we must not—and cannot—wait for the courts to decide the path to take. If we are not prepared, the courts will decide for us (Kauffman and Gonzalez, Chapter 10; Michaelson, 1996; Olivas, 1996).

The strategies and recommendations outlined below form a starting point for discussion and debate. They are strategies for a new era—one that champions the formulation and strengthening of affirmative action policies that will counteract more subtle, covert, and sometimes unconscious practices which systematically exclude qualified individuals from opportunities to enter educational institutions and contribute to the American work force. University communities that fail to engage in the reexamination of what needs to be done to anchor our affirmative action polices are placing our students and nation in jeopardy.

## Strategies for a New Era

### 1. Reestablish the reality that there is continuing and persistent discrimination in this country.

Even if we were to use only quantitative data, the results would clearly indicate that inequities still exist for women and people of color. Both groups still earn less than men in comparable employment, and Caucasian men are still the majority as heads of Fortune 500 companies. Schools that serve our children of color are substandard (Kozol, 1992), dropout rates of students of color throughout K–12 are abysmal (Carter and Wilson, 1996), and students of color still represent only a minute percentage of enrollments at selective colleges and universities. Using New York State as only one example, a Task Force on the Education of Children and Youth at Risk found that the state essentially has two unequal school systems—one in affluent areas and the other in poor areas—and concluded by stating that racism "clearly underlies much of the problem" (Kolbert, 1988). There can be no doubt that favoritism, privilege, and discrimination are alive and well in every aspect of American society.

## 2. Define affirmative action on our own terms.

Institutions of higher education must take a more active role in shaping public policy. Inattention to our opponents, negligence in communicating our position to the public, and a failure to document and convey our results has contributed to the current state of affairs in which our commitment to inclusion and education for all is being forcefully challenged. Only by clearly defining affirmative action—both what it *is* and what it *is not*—will we be able to get the totality of our message across and effectively counter efforts to dismantle affirmative action. To ensure that the rest of the country does not follow California's lead in rendering illegal race- and gender-based preferences at public universities and for state employees and business contracts, we must, with a clear definition in hand, speak out against proposed revisions to other states' affirmative action policies.

Institutions of higher learning must not only define affirmative action, but play an active role in its implementation. At the very core of this definition must be our commitment to the fundamental fact that all children can achieve their potential. We argue that affirmative action policies do not undermine merit, but rather encourage critical inquiry into the definition of quality and qualifications. Our goal is to encourage the talent and excellence of our women, communities of color, and other disenfranchised populations, and to open doors to opportunities for success.

## 3. Review the criteria utilized for admissions into colleges and universities.

It is time that higher education critically review the criteria used for admissions in colleges and universities. The myth of standardized tests needs to be shattered. Despite research demonstrating that standardized tests place women and people of color at a disadvantage when they attempt to enter the colleges and universities of their choice, institutions continue to use them as the yardstick by which they measure and predict academic potential. Olivas (1996) asserts that standardized test scores suggest different things for different populations and cites numerous research studies, one of which documents that the LSAT routinely both underpredicts and overpredicts the performance of first-year Latino law students. Other studies demonstrate how SAT scores have limited utility when gender and race are taken into account (Powell & Steelman, 1984).

If these standardized tests have a disproportionate impact on women and people of color, why have the courts not ruled them illegal? Although the issue in *Griggs* was employment, the court determined that unless the employer could demonstrate a legitimate business purpose or a rational relationship between the employment criterion and the task to be performed, a disproportionate impact on a protected class would render the hiring criteria discriminatory.

If we follow the logic of the court's decision and apply it to college admission, we find ourselves administering standardized exams such as SATs and LSATs which indeed have a disproportionate impact on women and people of color; in effect, these examinations serve to bar women and people of color from the universities of their choice. We can only hope that the courts will use progressive thinking, utilize the full range of available research, and reject theories supporting the correlation of standardized tests with academic success. These steps would provide higher education with the inspiration it so sorely needs to develop and implement less discriminatory practices.

We need to be honest about our admissions criteria. Institutions need to openly convey to potential applicants the realities of weighing various institutional goals in the admissions process. Selective institutions have considered the diversity of the class when choosing from a pool of qualified applicants larger than the number of available seats. They select students not only on the basis of what they have achieved academically—including their performance on the standardized tests—but also on their potential for making significant contributions to the larger society, on their character, curiosity, and determination, on their acknowledgement of tolerance and mutual respect as worthy goals, and on their willingness to engage in decision and debate (Rudenstine, 1996). Institutions also need to examine whether their admissions criteria actually measure the probability of successful retention and graduation of potential students or if they are merely part of a public-relations program aimed at assuring potential donors and students of a "scientific," data-driven means to accurately assess and predict academic performance—despite the fact that none exists. Michaelson (1996) makes a valid point when he states that "just as a half century ago, many institutions needed to stop basing admissions on a tight web of elitist connections and employed standardized test scores as a more democratic approach, a new paradigm seems needed now."

Other strategies for reexamining our admissions standards have been proposed. In Chapter 9, Slocum proposes that some form of open enrollment should be available to every first-year undergraduate. The second year would then be based on the first year's performance and scaling back would occur. By casting a wider net during the first year, open enrollment would attract, develop, and encourage the retention of students whose standardized test scores may have been marginal, but whose first-year performance is bolstered by their motivation and eagerness to succeed.

As Howard states in Chapter 2, it is not immediately obvious why an admissions policy that includes factors such as age and/or geographic diversity is less problematic legally than racial diversity. As has been documented by colleges and universities across the country, race is not the sole criterion for admissions, but is merely one factor among many. The University of California-Los Angeles (UCLA's) undergraduate admissions program, for example, considers applications only from the top 12 percent of a graduating class. To narrow down the number of qualified applicants, not fewer than 17 factors are considered in the admissions process. Race and national origin are only two factors among them. In response to critics, Olivas (1996) argues that selective institutions have thousands of qualified applicants to choose from and that admissions committees are doing what needs to be done to assemble qualified and diverse student bodies. Olivas asserts that *Bakke* sanctions this practice, common sense dictates it, and it underscores that "merit" cannot be measured purely in terms of numbers.

Another example is The University of California system, which mandated the elimination of race, ethnicity, and gender as factors to be considered in admissions, but continued to explore criteria that promote diversity. Factors such as family income, being the first generation in a family to attend college, bilingual ability, and family responsibilities while attending college are some of the factors being proposed.

At the same time, race and ethnicity cannot be dropped from the list of admissions criteria. A series of studies conducted by each University of California campus and the Office of the President concluded that the elimination of the use of race and ethnicity for *qualified* students of color would have an adverse impact on the number of these students admitted to and enrolled in the University. The Office of the President's study also concluded that the consideration of socioeconomic status, which encompasses parents' income and education, results in a decrease in the number of *qualified* students of color entering the University (Yu and Taylor, 1996).

Our concern is that the elimination of race and national origin from the admissions criteria of institutions of higher education will not only threaten the mission of inclusion, but may encourage litigation against institutions of higher learning that challenges such policy shifts as possible violations of current civil rights laws (Edley, 1966).

In summary, since we know that standardized tests have inherent racial biases because they measure how much knowledge an individual has accumulated in their previous academic experiences, we must reconceptualize our admissions criteria. The new paradigm requires a redefinition of the term "merit" which moves away from data to capture the potential of every student to succeed in higher education.

**4. Encourage faculty members to conduct research to substantiate the value and success of diversity and affirmative action policies. The results of these studies need to be published in the popular press and should emphasize the use of strong assessment and evaluation components.**

All too often, discussions of affirmative action in the popular media downplay the facts—both pro and con. Scholars and researchers need to conduct research that solidifies our position. Michaelson (1996) recommends the use of powerful census data and demographic projections. In addition, qualitative studies need to complement quantitative studies since they will contribute the voices and experiences of those who have benefited from affirmative action policies. Studies that track students in higher education from entrance to graduation to post-graduation endeavors would be particularly informative. Still others should document the historical and ongoing barriers encountered by women and people of color in the higher education admissions process. Our scholars must engage in research that definitively demonstrates the benefits of affirmative action polices and the educational value and experiences they promote (Edley, 1996; Michaelson, 1996).

Once these studies are concluded, we must make every effort to communicate our facts and successes clearly to the public through the popular media—magazines, newspapers, television, and radio. For too long, we in higher education have limited ourselves to communicating among ourselves in journals and books which do not reach the public. Thus, our positions have been hidden on library shelves while those of our opponents have gained increasing visibility in the popular press. Research conducted by scholars like Lavin and Hyllegard (1996), Nora and Rendón (1991), Musil (1992), and Rendón (1994) that demonstrates the success of students in institutions that have implemented diversity-promoting policies must become public knowledge. And other studies that document the success of hiring women and people of color and expose the underutilization of these faculty members once they have reached the pinnacles of their educational careers need to be shared with the public at large (Smith, 1995; Myers and Turner, 1994).

Moreover, scholars and policymakers need to collaborate on research that validates our belief that affirmative action benefits our institutions, our communities, and our nation. Through our commitment to assume a proactive stance in communicating our well-documented beliefs, we will gain access to those avenues that lead directly to the general public. It is my strong belief that when the public is made aware of affirmative action's myriad "success stories" and recognizes that students become productive citizens largely as a result of their educational attainment, they will not only come to value affirmative action policies, but will begin to speak out for their survival.

### 5. Encourage open and frank discussion of the problem of discrimination.

We must engage students, faculty, administrators, and staff—in essence, the entire campus community—into dialogues and activities both inside and outside the classroom that address longstanding conflicts, stereotypes, and problems in understanding diversity and combating discrimination.

Boards of Trustees need to reaffirm their commitment to an inclusive educational institution and to affirmative action policies. Presidents and senior administrators need to take a strong and unyielding stand against hate speech and other forms of verbal and physical intimidation, and they must take immediate and decisive action when these incidents occur. Resources must be committed to dealing with issues of harassment and discrimination, and programs need to be implemented to educate and sensitize the college community. Orientation programs for students, faculty, staff, and administrators can be offered which provide an intellectual understanding of the diverse populations that comprise the community we serve. Lecture series can be developed that offer opportunities to both supporters and opponents of affirmative action and provide for thoughtful, informed debate in a risk-free environment.

## 6. Maintain ongoing collaborations with the K-12 system.

Together, the K-12 and higher education communities have recognized that for too long we have been operating independently of each other. In this decade, renewed emphasis on partnership within the entire K-16 system has emerged as a vital and necessary component of an effective education. These partnerships, which include not only the educational system but all of the stakeholders whose contributions are essential to the success of our children (businesses, philanthropic foundations, government, community-based organizations), are cropping up across the country.

Institutions like Kingsborough Community College in New York City, for example, have instituted collaborations with the K-12 system by implementing the Family College, an intergenerational program which opens the door for adults on public assistance to pursue an associate's degree while their children attend an on-campus school. The Family College not only educates and prepares its adult students for the world of work, but offers support services that include workshops on parenting, family literacy, study skills, time management, and career exploration. In California, the K-12 Foshay School entered into a partnership with the University of Southern California to increase the number of at-risk students who receive baccalaureate degrees. Arizona State University has just opened its East Campus on the former Williams Airforce Base; this new East Campus will be building partnerships with educational institutions, the community, and industry and will feature a spectrum of educational enterprises from preschool through graduate school.

Since these efforts have already proven successful, they should be widely used as models for new programs. In fact, all schools should be required to engage in collaborations in their cities and states. With this new engagement of all stakeholders, our educational system will begin to prepare students who can compete for their higher education institutions of choice and become the global leaders our nation so desperately needs.

### 7. Recognize and be sensitive to all sides of the issue.

Affirmative action policies have not only benefited a protected class, but they have had a positive impact on society at large. Recall the discussion by Flores and Slocum in Chapter 4 in which they note that affirmative action policies inspired court decisions allowing men to become flight attendants, short men of all races to become police officers, and individuals who were not of the "union club" to be eligible for apprenticeship professions.

Our policies and positions must be sensitive to all—including the white male—and recognize that the fierce competition for employment and the rise of a global economy has drastically altered our economy, such that there is increased unemployment and underemployment as well as increased competition for seats in our elite institutions. Programs like the one offered at Rutgers Law School should be examined as a model for successful inclusive admissions programs. As described in Chapter 9, allowing economically disadvantaged whites to apply to the Minority Student Program at Rutgers Law School helps to explode the myth that affirmative action programs bar majority males from competing for support programs. Clearly, factoring in both race and socioeconomic criteria in admissions criteria may be one of the best and safest paths to achieving a diverse student body.

Finally, in addition to the our protected groups and the majority male, it is essential that we recognize and be sensitive to the discrimination faced by gays, lesbians, and bisexuals. At the very minimum, institutions of higher education should revise their statements of nondiscrimination to include sexual orientation.

## 8. Allow opponents of affirmative action to defend their actions for change.

By welcoming the voices of our opponents, they will have to answer the "big" questions: What policies and mechanisms do they suggest to replace affirmative action? How will they ensure equal opportunity in the realm of education? How will they ensure that all able citizens contribute to civic life by becoming educated, financially stable participants in their communities? What alternatives will they offer to becoming a nation of "haves" and "have nots"? How will they establish a higher education system that does not continue to confer preference and power to the dominant majority? And will eliminating race and gender as criteria really produce a color-blind admissions process?

We can and must challenge opponents of affirmative action to defend their actions and actively debate their positions. Only by widely airing our dissenting views will the public be made aware that the repeal of affirmative action would, without a doubt, signal a return to a time when access to higher education was limited to individuals born into privilege and opportunity. As a nation, we simply cannot afford to turn back the clock.

## Conclusion

The United States has been recognized throughout the world as a land of opportunity, a place where people are given the chance to succeed. Education has been the key for thousands of individuals to improve their lives, the lives of their families, and the conditions of their community. Until we are at a point in our development as a nation that all children have the same chance to become everything they can be without prejudice, we must continue to find avenues to assist them.

But the question remains: Is a color-blind higher education admissions process even possible? The answer falls in the realm of paradox, for the moment we remove race and gender from the decision-making process is the moment that race and gender become the most influential criteria determining who enters our colleges and universities. Who then is positioned to transform their education into economic, social, psychological, and political success? The paradox is not lost on those of us in higher education. And we must make every effort to see that it is not lost on the millions of Americans whose lives hang in the balance.

## REFERENCES

Carter, Deborah J., and Wilson, Reginald. (1996). *Minorities in Higher Education*, Washington, D.C.: American Council on Education.

Edley, Jr., Christopher. "Contemplating Campus Policy After *Hopwood v. Texas*," *Change*, September/October 1996, 12–15.

García, Mildred, and Smith, Daryl G. "Reflecting Inclusiveness in the College Curriculum," in Laura I. Rendón and Richard O. Hope, *Educating a New Majority*, 1996, San Francisco: Jossey-Bass Publishers.

Kolbert, Elizabeth. "A New York Report Says Racism Creates Two Tiers of Schools," *The New York Times*, October 22, 1988, Pg. 1.

Kozol, Jonathan. (1992). *Savage Inequalities*. New York: Harper Perennial.

Lavin, David E., and Hyllegard, David. (1996). *Changing the Odds— Open Admissions and the Life Chances of the Disadvantaged.* New Haven: Yale University Press.

Michaelson, Michael. "A Time to Increase Public Understanding of Affirmative Action, *The Chronicle of Higher Education*, July 19, 1996, Pg. A48.

Michaelson, Michael. "Academe Must Work Hard to Justify Affirmative Actions Programs," *The Chronicle of Higher Education*, July 28, 1996, Pg. POV.

Musil, Caryn McTighe (ed.) (1992). *The Courage to Question—Women's Studies and Student Learning*. Washington, D.C.: Association of American Colleges and National Women's Studies Association.

Myers, Samuel L., Jr., and Sotello Turner, Caroline. (May 1995). *Midwestern Higher Education Commission Minority Faculty Development Project*. Technical Report. Minneapolis, MN: Midwestern Higher Education Commission.

Nora, Amaury, and Rendon, Laura. (1991). "Determinants of Students' Predisposition to Transfer: A Structural Model," *Research in Higher Education*, 31 (3), 235–255.
Olivas, Michael A. "The Decision is Flatly, Unequivocally Wrong," *The Chronicle of Higher Education*, March 29, 1996, Pg. B3.
Rendon, Laura. (1994). "Validating Culturally Diverse Students: Toward a New Model of Learning and Student Development," *Innovative Higher Education*, 19 (1), 33–51.
Rendon, Laura, and Valadez, James R. (February 1993). "Qualitative Indicators of Hispanic Students Transfer," *Community College Review*, 20, (4), 27–37.
Rudenstine, Neil L. "Why A Diverse Student Body is So Important," *The Chronicle of Higher Education*, April 19, 1996, Pg. B1.
Smith, Daryl G. (1988). *The Challenge of Diversity*, Washington, D.C.: ASHE ERIC Higher Education Report 5.
Smith Daryl G. (1995). The Pipeline for Achieving Faculty Diversity: Debunking the Myths. Unpublished manuscript.
Yu, Corrine M., and Taylor, William L. (Eds.), (1996). *The Resource: An Affirmative Action Guide*, Washington, D.C.: The Citizens' Commission on Civil Rights.

# List of Contributors

**Bonnie Busenberg** is Assistant Dean for Academic Administration at Scripps College, the women's college of the Claremont Colleges. She is also a doctoral student in the higher education program at the Claremont Graduate School. Her research interests focus on academic scientists, particularly women scientists.

**Robert W. Ethridge** is the Associate Vice President for Equal Opportunity Programs and adjunct assistant professor in the Division of Educational Studies at Emory University in Atlanta, Georgia. He is a nationally known and recognized expert in the fields of educational administration, equal opportunity/affirmative action and diversity. He is a speaker and consultant who has served as an officer and board member of numerous academic, professional, service, and nonprofit organizations.

**Linda Flores** received her J. D. from Rutgers University Law School and her Masters of Law from Georgetown University Law Center. She served as both the Executive and Associate Director of the Council on Legal Education Opportunity and as President of the Puerto Rican Legal Defense and Education Fund. She is presently Director of Compliance for The Prudential Insurance

Company of America. The views expressed in this article do not necessarily represent the views of The Prudential.

**Mildred García** is Associate Vice Provost and Associate Professor in the Social and Behavioral Sciences Department at Arizona State University West. In addition, she serves as Associate Director of the Hispanic Research Center at Arizona State University. She received her doctorate in higher education from Teachers College, Columbia University. She is the immediate Past President of the American Association of University Administrators. Her research has concentrated on at-risk students and underrepresented faculty, staff, and administrators, as well as the implications for policy and practice. She received her doctorate in higher education from Teachers College, Columbia University. Her research has concentrated on at-risk students and underrepresented faculty, staff and administrators, as well as the implications for policy and practice.

**Roger Gonzalez** practices law in San Antonio, Texas. He received his B.A. in 1991 from St. Mary's University and received his J.D. in 1995 from St. Mary's University School of Law. Originally from Texas, with immigrant parents, he is the first in his family to obtain a postgraduate degree.

**John Howard** is a Distinguished Service Professor at the State University of New York. He received his Ph.D. in Sociology from Stanford and a J.D. from Pace University. His research concentrates on law and society and on the Supreme Court.

**Sylvia Hurtado** is currently assistant professor of higher education at the Center for the Study of Higher and Postsecondary Education at the University of Michigan. She was an undergraduate admissions officer at Princeton and the Massachusetts Institute of Technology, and coordinated graduate admissions and recruitment at the University of California, Santa Cruz before receiving her Ph.D. at UCLA.

**Albert Kauffman** is a senior litigation attorney at the Mexican American Legal Defense and Educational Fund in San Antonio, Texas. He received his B.S. from the Massachusetts Institute of Technology and his J.D. from the University of Texas Law School. He has been practicing civil rights law for 22 years and has litigated major impact litigation in the area of higher education, school finance, and testing.

**Samuel L. Myers, Jr.** is the Roy Wilkins Professor of Human Relations and Social Justice at the Humphrey Institute of Public Affairs. Dr. Myers earned his Ph.D. from the Massachusetts Institute of Technology. He served as coprincipal investigator with Caroline Turner on the Minority Faculty Development Project for the Midwestern Higher Education Commission, a project designed to provide essential background and planning information on minority faculty representation in Midwestern higher education and to propose regional strategies to advance minority faculty recruitment and retention in Midwestern higher education.

**Christine Navia** is currently a doctoral student at the Center for Study of Higher and Postsecondary Education and conducts research at the Center for the Education of Women at the University of Michigan. She is also a research associate at the Illinois Board of Higher Education.

**Robert Rhoads** is an assistant professor of education in the Department of Education Administration at Michigan State University. He is the author of *Coming Out in College, Democracy, Multiculturalism and the Community College* with James Valadez and *Explorations of the Caring Self* (SUNY Press, Forthcoming). His research interests focus on issues of social justice and equality within college and university settings.

**Alfred Slocum** received his J.D. from Rutgers University School of Law and his Masters of Law from Yale Law School. He is a professor at Rutgers University School of Law and has served as the

Executive Director of the Council on Legal Education Opportunity. He has also served as the Public Advocate and Public Defender for the State of New Jersey as a member of Governor Kean's cabinet.

**Caroline Sotello Viernes Turner** is an associate professor in the Department of Educational Policy and Administration at the University of Minnesota. Her research and teaching interests include access and equity issues in higher education, the use of case study approaches for policy research, and the study of organizational change.

**Daryl G. Smith** is professor of education and psychology at The Claremont Graduate School. In addition, she has served for 25 years as a college administrator. She is the author of numerous publications related to issues of diversity, including *Involvement or Alienation in the Academy* and "Achieving Faculty Diversity: Debunking the Myths."

# Index

academic disciplines: and women, 160, 161
academics, role in debate over affirmative action, 42, 43, 125, 252, 257
access, to colleges and universities: 105–130; goals for, 123–125; strategies for, 125–128
*Adams v. Richardson*, 214
*Adarand Constructors Inc., et al., v. Pena*, 57, 75, 77, 208–210, 218, 223, 225
admissions standards, in higher education: at issue in affirmative action, 5, 6, 68–69, 120–123, 206; criteria for, 42, 106, 110, 111, 119, 126, 222, 253; diversity issues in, 43, 88, 109; preferential bias in criteria, 112–113, 116; misconceptions about, 9–10
adultery, interracial (legal distinction), 22
advertising industry: effect of affirmative action on, 98
affirmative action: abolition of, proposed, 166, 167–169, 245; alleged hindrance to women and minorities, 12–13; and changing circumstances in higher education, 124; and classism, 60, 81, 99, 108, 125; and group rights concept, 27, 209; and seniority, 52, 54, 89; and sexual preference, 181–201, 196–200, 259; and U.S. competitive edge, 3, 8, 12, 44, 62, 98; and women, 149–180, 154–163 (*see also* women); apparent contradiction inherent to, 20, 21, 25, 30, 44, 164–165; assessing, 7; ban, in California, 75, 120, 122, 165; bases for, 12; benefits of, 47, 78–80, 84, 86, 92, 99, 109, 153–154, 157–158, 173, 250; bureaucracy, 168–169; challenges to, 15, 47–72, 75–76; collaboration between K-12 systems and higher education, 258–259; constitutionality of, 32 (*see* individual court cases); continuing need for, 70; current issues, 41; defined, 4, 5, 151–154, 183, 252–253; distin-

267

guished from desegregation, 232; educating the public about, 126, 256, 257; effect on admissions at University of Texas Law School, 235–236; effect on Asian-American students, 116; effect on trade unions, 53; effect on white students, 115–116; effectiveness, evidence of, 49, 60, 63, 64, 65, 70, 76, 94, 97, 99, 117, 120–121; establishment of, 29; evolution of constitutional status, 34–41; failures of proponents, 21, 107, 144–145; fraudulent practices resulting from, 96; goals vs. quotas, 53; guidelines (principles) for financial aid, 58–59; guidelines for faculty hiring, 153-154, 175; history, 2, 19–45, 49–59, 93, 150–151; in graduate and professional schools, 206–225; in higher education, 2–3, 31, 51, 67–68, 80, 87–93, 105–130, 131–148, 151; in hiring, 37, 48, 171–172; interpretations of, 183–184; misconceptions about, 5, 9–13, 70, 76, 92, 105, 106–107, 115–120, 126; multiple aspects of, 31; need for assessment of, 126–127, 251, 256–257; need for inclusiveness, 259; need for media relations efforts, 256; opposition to, 32–41, 60, 66, 75, 93, 95–98, 120–123, 163–164, 166, 175, 260; perceived need for, 30; presidential leadership, 65–66, 105; progress of, 47–72; purpose of, 4, 152, 153; rationale for, 249–251; redress of past discrimination, 38, 53, 77, 82, 88, 94–95, 152, 153, 165, 209, 213; role of academics in, 256; shortcomings and limitations of, 169, 174–175; social stigma (alleged or perceived), 136–137, 173–174; strategies for, 251–260; Supreme Court decisions concerning, 33–41, 51–59; umbrella term, 31; voluntary programs, 36–37, 39, 54, 55, 218
affirmative duty (legal term), 232
*Airline Pilots Association, International, v. United Airlines, Inc.*, 82
airlines: and age discrimination, 86; and gender discrimination, 84, 86
American Association for Affirmative Action, 52
American Association of University Professors (AAUP), 131, 161
American Bar Association, Council for Legal Educational Opportunity, 140–141, 223
American Subcontractors Association, 95
Americans with Disabilities Act, 56
Argonne National Laboratory, 155
Arizona State University, 258
armed services, U.S.: integration of, 87
Association of American Law Schools, 223
attitudinal changes, 175–176
automobile industry, U.S., 78–79, 92
automobiles, American-made, 79
automobiles, Japanese-made, 79

Badgett, Lee, 185
*Bakke v. Regents of the University of California*, 9, 34–37, 36, 37, 50–51, 88–91, 91–92, 93, 95, 214, 220, 238. See also University of California Board of Regents v. Bakke
Bakke, Alan, 36, 88, 214
Banneker Scholarship, 39, 40–41, 57–58, 69

Bensimon, Estela Mara, 188–189
Bergmann, Barbara, 48
Biermann, Leonard, 53
Big Three (U.S. automobile manufacturers), 79
Bingham, John, 23
bisexual. *See* gay, lesbian, and bisexual
Black Codes, 206
Brennan, William J., Jr., 35, 212
Brophy, Roy, 123
*Brotherhood of Railroad Trainmen v. Howard*, 81
*Brown v. Board of Education*, 23, 27, 82, 87–88, 93, 99, 232
Brubacher, John, 106, 124, 128

California Civil Rights Act, 166, 170
California Institute of Technology, 155
Carnegie Institute, 156
Carvell, Douglas, 234, 235
Chandler, Trevor, 37
Chism, Nancy, 196
Citizens' Commission on Civil Rights, 4
civil disobedience, 28
Civil Rights Act of 1866, 22
Civil Rights Act of 1875, 21
Civil Rights Act of 1964, Title VII: as protection from reverse discrimination, 36, 38, 51, 54, 57; described, 28; early exclusion of women as protected class, 150; extended to educational institutions, 151; defines affirmative action, 183; imputed intent of, 38; in Bakke case, 229; inception, 2, 150; limitations of, 29; misconceptions about, 10
*Civil Rights Cases of 1883, The*, 21–22, 23, 77, 207
civil rights movement, U.S.: history of, 19–29; moral issues, 19–20, 23, 24, 25, 26, 90, 93, 99, 151; paradox of affirmative action, 165
Civil Rights Restoration Act, 56
Civil War, U.S., 22
Clark, Joseph, 28
Clark, Kenneth and Mamie, 42
Clinton, William Jefferson (Bill), 4, 75, 152, 166
Cold Spring Harbor, 156
color blind policy, 34
Columbia University, 155
coming out: among undergraduate students, 192; defined, 186; negative effects of, 193; significance of, 186, 193
Community Friendship, Inc. (CFI), 71
compelling interest (legal term), 212, 229, 229–231, 236–237, 241, 242
Confederacy, U.S.: removal of federal troops from former territory (1876), 21
consent decrees, challenged, 54–55
Constitution of the United States: Fifteenth Amendment, 21, 96, 206; Fifth Amendment, 209; Fourteenth Amendment, 21, 22, 23, 34, 77, 78, 96, 206, 207, 208, 209, 212, 214–215, 221, 238; Thirteenth Amendment, 77, 96, 206, 210
Contract with America, 75
Cornell University, 155
Council on Legal Education Opportunity, 88–89, 223
*Crosen v. Richmond*, 34, 39–40, 55, 57, 96, 230
Cullen, Maura, 189
*Cummings v. Richmond County*, 24
Custred, Glynn, 170

D'Augelli, Anthony, 183, 192
*DeFunis v. Odegaard*, 35, 88, 91

DeFunis, Marco, 35, 88
demographics, U.S.: projected changes, 8, 60, 61, 70, 119–120
Detroit (as icon for U.S. automobile manufacturing), 79
*Diagnostic and Statistical Manual-II* (DSM-II), 192
discrimination: as factor in layoffs, 230; based on sexual orientation, 191–192; defined as act against individuals, 30; disparate impact, 30; geographical, 42; historical, as reason for "compelling interest," 230–231, 240; history in U.S., 22–23; in labor movement, 81–82; institutional, 30, 83, 165–166, 173, 176, 184; legal arguments for, 24; need for open discussion on college campuses, 257–258; persistent effects of, 112, 117, 125, 135–138, 251–252; private acts of, 22, 78; proof or disproof of, 55, 56; redress of, 34; scholarships, 68; societal, 88, 97. *See also* redress, affirmative action
disparate impact, 30, 83
diversity: alternative indicators for creating, 255; as an objective, 32; as goal of "substantial interest" or "compelling interest" for government, 211, 229–230, 237, 238, 240, 241; benefits of, 211, 250; effect on corporate success, 12; importance of, in education, 92, 124
*Doherty v. Rutgers School of Law*, 219
Donne, John, 249
Douglas, William O., 35
Douglass, Frederick, 22
Du Bois, W.E.B., 11
dual admission programs, 213, 215–218, 219, 224, 233–234
Duke Power Company, 50, 83
Duke, David, 60–61

earning disparities, racial and gender, 67, 117
economically disadvantaged (as a class), 219–221, 222
Education Amendments of 1972, Title IX: in history of affirmative action, 47, 151
education: discrimination in, 24, 26, 27; failure of public, 99; importance of, in improving race relations, 3; segregation of, 27, 34, 40–41
EEOC. *See* Equal Employment Opportunity Commission
Elliot, Charles W., 250
Elliot, Kenneth, 235
Equal Employment Opportunity Commission (EEOC): effect on minority representation, 64; inception of, 28, 29
equal opportunity, 5
Equal Pay Act (1963), 151
Equal Protection Clause: and racial distinctions, 27; as protection against reverse discrimination, 35; in Bakke case, 229; legal interpretation of, 41. *See also* Constitution of the United States, Fourteenth Amendment
equal protection, 26
equal rights: evolution of legal argument for, 24
equal treatment: 20
equality: defined, 7; history of, 7
*Erie v. Thompkins*, 82
ethnography: as tool in affirmative action research, 187, 192
Ethridge, Robert, 53
Executive Order 11246: 2, 4, 47, 49, 66, 150, 151
Executive Order 11375: 2, 4, 47, 150

Family College (Kingsborough Community College), 258
Felton, Cornelius C., 250

female police officers, performance of, 6
Fiesta Bowl, 57, 58
Fifteenth Amendment. *See* Constitution of the United States, Fifteenth Amendment
Fifth Amendment. *See* Constitution of the United States, Fifth Amendment
financial aid (higher education), 93, 106
*Firefighters Local Union No. 1784 v. Stotts*, 52
Florida State University, 31
Foshay School (California), 258
Fourteenth Amendment. *See* Constitution of the United States, Fourteenth Amendment
freedom riders, 28
Friend, Richard, 184
*Fullilove et al. v. Klutznick et al.*, 210

*Gaines v. Canada*, 26
GATT. *See* General Agreement on Trade and Tariffs
gay politics, 193
gay, lesbian, and bisexual: assault, 194; discrimination against, on college campuses, 182–184, 184–185; faculty and student concerns, 181–182, 187–192; fear among, 189–190, 194; harassment, 193–195, 198–199; hiring practices, 191; identity and professional life, 188–189; incidence of reported discrimination, 191–192; invisibility, 186–187, 188, 197; marginalization, 195–196; need for affirmative action, 259; need for institutional support, 199–200; place of the academy in gay rights issues, 190–191, 198; sensitivity training, 199; strategies for affirmative action, 197–200; students, experiences of, 192–196

gender, alleged irrelevance of, 116–117. *See also* women.
General Agreement on Trade and Tariffs (GATT): assumptions underlying, 76, 78–80
Ginsburg, Ruth Bayder, 244–245
Glass Ceiling Commission, 13, 14, 61
glass ceiling, 11, 13, 48, 70, 160
Goldwater, Barry M., 28
Great Depression, 26
*Gregory v. Litton Systems, Inc.* 86
*Griggs v. Duke Power Company*, 50, 82–83, 86, 99, 253
group classification: analysis of, 228–291; legal distinction of, 33
group protection, 78, 90, 209, 219, 228
group rights, 24, 25
Guinier, Lani, 5–6

Harlan, Marshall, 27
Harvard University, 170, 171, 230, 250
Health, Education, and Welfare, Department of, U.S. (HEW), 151
Helms, Jesse, 169–170
heterosexism: 182; defined, 184–185; effect on students, 195–196; manifestations of, 185
Higher Education Act, 223
hiring criteria: fitness criteria, 85, 86; height, 82; in higher education, 171, 172; unrelated to job requirements, 81–82, 83
hiring goals, 94
hiring patterns: homogeneity of, 10; persistent discrimination in, 11; and unqualified applicants, 12
homophobia: 182; defined, 185; effect of, on students, 196; manifestations of, 185; on college campuses, 200; source of harassment and assault, 193–195

homosexual. *See* gay, lesbian, and bisexual
*Hopwood v. Texas:* background, 233–236; District Court opinion, 236–237; effect on Texas university systems, 245; Fifth Circuit Court of Appeals opinion, 237–242; grounds for appeal to U.S. Supreme Court, 244; implications for affirmative action plans, 245–246; injunctive relief, 240; interpreted, 242–243; limited to University of Texas Law School, 243; potential damages, 239–240, 243; preemption of Congressional power, 212–218; proposed intervention, 236; summarized, 227; Supreme Court denies *certiorari*, 244–245
Hopwood, Cheryl, 234
Houston, Charles, 26
Hughes, Charles Evans, 25, 26
Humphrey, Hubert, 28

incomes: median family, compared, 7; of blacks, per-capita, 97
Institute for Nuclear Studies (University of Chicago), 155
institutional racism, 30, 132. *See also* discrimination, institutional
intermediate scrutiny (legal term), 209

J.B. Bonn Company, 40
Jackson, Jesse, 4
Jim Crow Laws, 23
Johns Hopkins University, 155
*Johnson v. Pike Corporation of America*, 86
*Johnson v. Transportation Agency of Santa Clara County, California*, 54
Johnson, Lyndon B., 2, 4, 42, 131

Kaiser Aluminum and Chemical Corporation, 37–38, 51–52
Kaiser Wilhelm Institute (Berlin), 155–156
Kennedy, Anthony, 39
Kennedy, John F., 1, 2, 4, 28
King, Martin Luther, 27, 29
Kingsborough Community College (New York), 258
*Korematsu v. United States*, 33
Kozol, Jonathan, 7

La Raza National Lawyers' Association, 223
labor movement: history of, 80–82; racial and gender discrimination in, 81–82
Labor, Department of, U.S., 150
*Laffey v. Northwest Airlines, Inc.*, 81
Landrum-Griffin Act, 80, 81
last hired, first fired, 52, 54
Law School Admissions Council, 222
Law School Admissions Test (LSAT): 6, 233, 234, 235. *See also* standardized tests
legacy students, 170–171
Leonard, Jonathan, 49
lesbian. *See* gay, lesbian, and bisexual
*Local 28, Sheet Metal Workers v. EEOC*, 53
Lopez, Gilda, 196
Lorde, Audre, 184, 185
Los Angeles, California, 29

*Maldonado v. Yellow Freight Systems, Inc.*, 86
manifest imbalance, 54
Marshall, Thurgood: dissents in *Crosen v. City of Richmond*, 97; dissents in *DeFunis v. Odegaard*, 35; opinion in

*Fullilove et al. v. Klutznick et al.*, 210; supports Supreme Court majority in *Gaines v. Canada*, 26
Martin Luther King Scholarship, 57
*Martin v. Wilkes*, 54–55, 56
Mary Washington College, 31
Mayer, Maria Goeppert, 155, 156
*McCabe v. Atcheson*, 24, 25, 26
McClintock, Barbara, 155–156
mentoring, need for, 132, 140–142
merit, as employment and admission standard, 11, 86, 107–108, 119, 169–173
meritocracy: fallacies of, 169–173; proponents of, 205
*Metro Broadcasting v. FCC*, 209–212, 213, 224
Midwestern Higher Education Commission (MHEC): described, 48, 132–147; study of minority faculty, 132-147
Million Man March, 11
minority faculty (higher education): African-American, 134, 139, 140, 141; barriers to recruitment and retention, 132, 143–145; demands on, 137–138; hiring guidelines, 152; hiring issues, 131–132; Native American, 134, 139–140, 140–141, 142; Latino, 134, 140, 141, 142; perceptions among, 135–138; strategies for improving conditions of, 138–142, 145–147; underemployment of, 144; underrepresentation, 123–147, 134–135, 144
Minority Student Program. *See* Rutgers Law School Minority Student Program
minority students (higher education): college acceptance rates, 116; effect of affirmative action on, 116; participation rates, 117–118
minority students, performance at Ivy League schools, 43
minority-owned business, 95
Montgomery, Ala., 28
Motz, Frederick, 41

NAACP. *See* National Association for the Advancement of Colored People
NAFTA. *See* North American Free Trade Agreement
narrowly tailored (legal term), 223, 224, 229, 231, 237, 240
National Association for the Advancement of Colored People (NAACP), 26
National Bar Association, 223
National Labor Relations Act, 80
National Labor Relations Board, 80
Nazism: influence on American thinking about race relations, 26
Negro "inferiority," 78, 211
networks, 71–72, 139–140
New Deal, 26
New York Board of Education, 31
New York City Police Department, 6, 82
Newcomb, Betty, 53
*NLRB v. Local 106, Glass Bottle Blowers*, 81
*NLRB v. Mansion House Center Management Corp.*, 81
normative criteria, 172–173
North American Free Trade Agreement (NAFTA): assumptions underlying, 76, 78–80
*North Carolina State Board of Education v. Swann*, 34, 35
Northeastern University, 200

O'Connor, Sandra Day: Supreme Court Justice, 39; opinion in

*Adarand Constructors, Inc., v. Pena*, 210; opinion in *Crosen v. Richmond*, 96–97, 101, 213–200, 225
occupational stress, among minorities, 132
Office of Federal Contract Compliance Programs, 61, 96–97, 150
open enrollment, 88, 206, 254
Order No. 4 (U.S. Labor Department): effect of, 49; issuance of, 49, 66

*Pace v. Alabama*, 22
Panetta, Leon, 120
Pearlstein, Mitch, 48
Pendleton, Clarence, 53
Pennsylvania State University, 183
*Peterson v. Rath Packing Co.*, 81
Phillips, Wendall, 23
*Plessy v. Ferguson*, 8, 22, 99; and group rights concept, 25; repudiated, 26, 77, 82, 87, 211, 213; significance of, 23
*Podberesky v. Kirwin*, 34, 57
Podberesky, Daniel, 40–41
police departments: and gender discrimination, 84; and racial discrimination, 84; positive effects of affirmative action on, 84
political correctness, 60
Politz, Henry A., 241
Powell, Adam Clayton, 90, 230, 238
preferences, 152, 170, 229
preferential treatment: for African-Americans, 19; for certain classes, 77, 152; no legal requirement for, 164
prior discrimination. *See* redress
privilege, 205
protected class: and "strict scrutiny," 208, 228–229; defined, 55; improved participation of, 60, 83; race as a factor, 219, 220; women as, 140, 150
psychometrics, 83, 84–85
public accommodations, 21, 25, 55
Public Use Micro Sample Census data, 133–134
public works, 93–94, 96

qualifications, comparative, 5, 168, 216
Quinn, Philip, 183
quotas, and dual-admission programs, 215, 216–217
quotas, hiring: defined, 53; device for attacking civil rights advocates, 28, 88; misconceptions, 9

race-based remedies: constitutionality of, 78, 218–220, 229–230, 242–243
race: legal distinction of, 33, 34, 37, 41; alleged irrelevance of, 116, and economic disadvantage (as a class), 219–221; alternative indicators of, 255; as admission criterion, 254–255
racial classification, purposes and legitimacy of, 34
rational basis (legal term), 228
Rawls, John, 183
Reagan, Ronald, 39
redress (for past discrimination): 38, 53, 77, 82, 88, 94–95, 152; as "compelling interest," 230, 231, 237, 238, 239, 242; in higher education, 153, 212, 213
Rehabilitation Act of 1973, 55
Rehnquist, William: chief justice of U.S. Supreme Court, 39; dissents to *United Steelworkers v. Weber*, 38
Reich, Robert, 14
remedial classifications, defined, 226

remedy (for past discrimination). *See* redress; affirmative action; discrimination
research and publication, support for minority faculty: 141–142
reverse discrimination, 10, 20, 38, 42, 51, 76–77, 114–116, 167–168, 239
Revised Order No. 4 (U.S. Labor Department), issuance of, 49
Reynolds, Arthur, 182
Reynolds, William Bradford, 53
Rich, Adrienne, 187–188
riots, in U.S., 29
Rogers, David, 234, 235
Roosevelt, Franklin D., 4, 26
Rudenstine, Neil L., 250
Rutgers Law School Minority Student Program, 69, 216–217, 221, 224–225

sanctions, 66
Sarah Lawrence College, 155
Scalia, Antonin, 39
scholarships: and diversity, 68; and redress of discrimination, 68; effectiveness of, 69; need-based, 69
Scholastic Assessment Test (SAT): 6. *See also* standardized tests
schools, urban: conditions in, 7; segregation in, 7, 8
*Scott v. Sanford*, 77, 211
segregation: moral issues of, 27; persistence of, 8, 99, 132; postbellum alternative to slavery, 23; zenith of, 26
senior–management positions, lack of diversity in, 8
separate but equal, 24, 87
set aside: frauds, 96; inception of federal, state, and municipal programs, 31, 94; must correct identifiable prior discrimination, 55; subject of Supreme Court litigation, 33, 39–40, 95–96
sexual orientation. *See* gay, lesbian, and bisexual
sexual-orientation clauses, 190, 191, 198, 259
Shaiken, Harley, 170
Simpson, O.J., 11
sit-in demonstrations, 28
slavery: abolition of, 22; based on race in U.S., 78; consequences of, 77
Small Business Act, 208, 219
Smart, Jim, 189
Smith, Daryl, 249
socially and economically disadvantaged (legal term), 208
socio-economic criteria (as cue to diversity), 222
Souter, David H., 244–245
Spencer Grants, 142
*Sprogis v. United Air Lines, Inc.*, 81
standardized tests: and merit, 11, 92; as predictors of success, 6, 43; as sole college admission criterion, 75, 102-103, 110, 119; at University of Texas School of Law (Hopwood case), 233, 235–236; effect on minorities and women, 253; failings of, 6–7, 246, 253; in hiring, 50, 84–85; range of error, 6; unequal preparation for, in public schools, 7
Stanford University, 170
state interests, 90, 91
*Steele v. Louisville and Nashville Railroad*, 81
Steelworkers Union, 37–38
stereotypes, racial and gender, 13, 114, 138
Stevens, Thaddeus, 23
Stewart, Carl E., 241–242

strict scrutiny (legal term), 33, 57, 97, 205–225, 208, 213, 214, 224, 225, 241
substantial interest (legal term), 211, 228
success: correlated to SAT scores and socioeconomic background, 6; defined, 6
Summitt, Gazella, 53
Supreme Court, United States: 20–21, 23; moral force of decisions, 32, 50–59; ; decisions concerning affirmative action, 33–41, role of, in affirmative action, 224. *See also* individual case titles and names of individual Supreme Court justices
*Sweatt v. Painter*, 27, 87, 212, 232, 241
*Swift v. Tyson*, 82

Taft-Hartley Act, 80–81
Texas Index Number, 233, 234, 235
The Citadel of South Carolina, 92
*Thirteenth Annual Status Report of Minorities in Higher Education*, 67
Tierney, William, 190
Title IX. *See* Education Amendments of 1972
Title VII. *See* Civil Rights Act of 1964
tokenism, 136–137
Truman, Harry S., 87
Turner, Caroline Sotello Viernes, 48

U.S. Congress: effect of *Adarand Constructors, Inc., et al., v. Pena*, 210; judicial preemption of, 214–215; power to compel nondiscrimination, 207, 210
underrepresentation: patterns of, 134–135; remedies for, 54, 237
underserved communities, 91

United States Court of Appeals, Fourth Circuit, 41
*United States v. Fordice*, 231–232
*United States v. Paradise*, 231
University of California at Davis: Medical School, 36; intolerance of homosexuality at, 182. *See also Bakke v. University of California Board of Regents* and *University of California Board of Regents v. Bakke*
*University of California Board of Regents v. Bakke*, 165, 212, 229
University of California Board of Regents, 120–123, 165. *See also Bakke v. University of California Board of Regents* and *University of California Board of Regents v. Bakke*
University of Chicago, 156
University of Maryland, 40
University of Missouri, 156
University of Southern California, 258
University of Texas Law School, 87, 212, 224; history of discrimination, 232–233, 241–242. *See also Hopwood v. Texas*
University of Virginia, 170, 182
University of Washington Law School, 35, 88, 91
upward mobility, 118–119
utilization analyses, 153

Veysey, Laurence, 107–108

Wagner Act, 80
Ward, Connerly, 5, 118
*Wards Cove Packing Company v. Antonio*, 55, 56
Wartime Amendments, 206, 223
Washington Legal Foundation, 32
Watts (Los Angeles, California), 29
*Weber v. United Steelworkers of America*, 34, 37–39, 51–52, 95

Weber, Brian, 38, 51
West, Cornel, 109
White, Byron R., 35
Wiener, Jacques Jr., 240
William, Michael, 57
Wilson, Beth, 53
Wilson, Pete, 61, 75, 121–122
Winters, Everett, 53
women, as minority: and tenure, 160–161; as protected class, 150; as targets of discrimination, 154–155; compared to racial minorities, 159; current status of, in academia, 157–162; effects of affirmative action on, 157–158; experiences differing from ethnic minorities, 150, 162; factors in advancement of, 159–160; female-dominated academic disciplines, 160, 161; historic underrepresentation on college faculties, 156–157, 158, 159; in academic administration, 161–162; in higher education, 155; need for affirmative action, 177; Nobel laureates, 155; opposition to affirmative action for, 154; "social stigma" of affirmative action, 173–174; resistance to affirmative action among, 174, 176; uncertain future of gains for, 176–177
Work Force 2000 (U.S. Department of Labor report), 62
Work Opportunity Program, 71
*Wygant v. Jackson Board of Education*, 52, 230

zero-sum game, and academic access: 120–123, 124